WHAT HAPPENED ON THE BOUNTY

BENGT DANIELSSON

WHAT HAPPENED ON THE BOUNTY

*Translated from the Swedish
by Alan Tapsell*

London
GEORGE ALLEN & UNWIN LTD
RUSKIN HOUSE MUSEUM STREET

Translated from
Med Bounty til Soderhavet
(Saxon & Lindstrom)
© Bengt Danielsson 1962

PRINTED IN GREAT BRITAIN
in 11 point Pilgrim type
BY EAST MIDLAND PRINTING CO. LTD.
BURY ST. EDMUNDS, SUFFOLK

FOREWORD

The wealth of literature on the mutiny on the *Bounty* and on the thrilling events which ensued consists mainly of dry accounts in diary form, wildly partisan argumentation, and romanticised novels full of grotesque mistakes and flights of imagination. This is the more remarkable because in various archives and libraries throughout the world there are quantities of log books, reports, letters and other documents, with the help of which it is possible to reconstruct in detail the whole course of events. This book is based on an exhaustive study of this mass of original material, and should really be called *The True and Complete Story of All that Happened on Board the Bounty on her Voyage to the South Seas 1787-1789 with an Account of What Happened after the Mutiny to the Protagonists in the Drama*. My otherwise kind and accommodating publisher has, however, remorselessly insisted on a somewhat shorter title.

I would emphasise that all the remarks and dialogue which occur in the text have been taken from original accounts and letters written by individuals who took part in the historic voyage, so that the value due to them and to the fabrications so often found in literature is of a completely different order. Another serious failing in most of the books on the *Bounty* hitherto published has been that the erroneous ideas and prejudices typical of the time, which the mutineers held concerning the different South Seas peoples with whom they came into contact, have been uncritically accepted and presented as historic and ethnological facts. Here too I have tried to give a true picture, based mainly on the studies and observations I have myself made during a fifteen-year sojourn in the South Seas.

Papehue, Tahiti, May 1962

BENGT DANIELSSON

CONTENTS

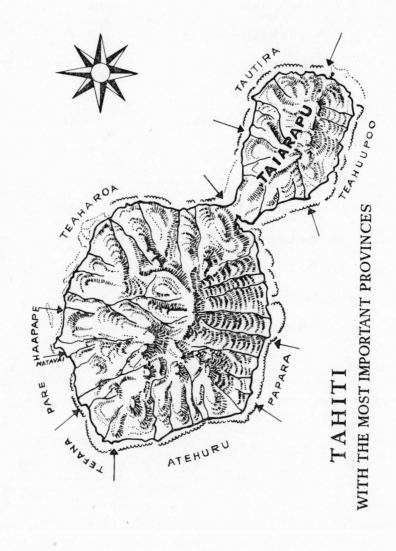

TAHITI

WITH THE MOST IMPORTANT PROVINCES

CHAPTER I

ROYAL MUNIFICENCE

IN 1768, when Captain Cook began his systematic explorations of the region, the Pacific bounded what was still a relatively unknown world. By the time of his death, a mere eleven years later, through his consummate skill and the remarkable methods he used to keep his crews in good health he had succeeded in mapping the larger part of the world's greatest ocean.

Cook's bold voyages of discovery revealed a completely new world, a world where everything was fantastic and different, as sensational perhaps, as the first description of a journey to another planet would be today. And yet it is more than likely that the descriptions of space travel which may appear within the foreseeable future will be less entertaining to read than Cook's logbooks, since it is improbable that space captains landing elsewhere in the universe will be met by such remarkable and charming creatures as Cook found on the South Sea islands.

Reading Cook's descriptions of his Pacific travels, one is particularly impressed how easily mankind's two most essential needs were provided for in those islands. Wherever the sailors went ashore they were invariably met and made thoroughly welcome by beautiful, well-endowed, warm-blooded young women, while, in the second place, bread was to be found everywhere growing on the trees.

We now know perfectly well that the sexual habits of the South Seas natives were not so completely uninhibited and libidinous as the earliest European visitors there liked to think, but on the other hand it is quite literally true that daily bread grew on the trees. The tree in question belongs to the Morindae species, which also includes the fig and the mulberry tree, and looks with its large, well-foliaged crown and serrated leaves more like an elm or a maple. The round or oval fruit is about the size of a head of cabbage but, on account of its green, rough skinned peel, looks more like an overgrown lemon.

Long before Cook's time various intrepid travellers had discovered breadfruit in Melanesia, Micronesia and Indonesia. But in these parts the fruit was anything but plentiful, and was not appreciated to the same degree as in the Polynesian islands of the eastern Pacific. Thus the tree is only briefly mentioned in the few early descriptions of the former island groups. Cook, who devoted the greater part of his time to Polynesia, not only carefully described and sketched the tree but also gave a detailed description of its cultivation and of the harvesting and preparing of the fruit.

According to Captain Cook, Tahiti was the foremost island of the breadfruit, and the Swedish botanist, Daniel Solander, who accompanied Cook on his first South Seas voyage, described some ten different types. (In point of fact there are nearly forty different types of breadfruit, though it is often difficult even for a trained botanist to distinguish between these types, since the principal criteria are the form of the leaves and the shape of the fruit.) The two German naturalists, J. R. and Georg Forster, who accompanied Cook on his second South Seas voyage, confirmed their predecessor's observations and further pointed out that two or three breadfruit trees were enough to provide a Tahitian with food for a whole year; nine months in the form of fresh fruit and the remaining three months as a sort of sharp paste which was easily conservable in leaf-lined holes in the ground.

Regarding the cultivation of the trees, Cook himself claimed that once they were properly planted they needed no further attention. The Scottish doctor, Anderson, who took part in the third South Sea voyage, found it necessary, meanwhile, to correct his captain on this point. Anderson found to his amazement that the Tahitians did not even have to plant their breadfruit trees. He concludes:

'This indeed must be evident to everyone who will examine the places where the young trees come up. It will be always observed that they spring from the roots of the older ones; which run along near the surface of the ground. So that the bread-fruit trees may be reckoned those that would naturally cover the plains, even supposing that the islands were not inhabited . . . . And from this we may observe that the inhabitants of Otaheite, instead of being obliged to plant his bread, will rather be under a necessity to prevent its progress; which I suppose is sometimes done, to give him room for trees of another sort, to afford him some variety in his food.'

In one respect, however, the Tahitian is required to make a certain amount of effort since the breadfruit cannot be eaten raw. It has to be cooked, either by toasting it over a fire or by roasting it in a ground oven. By the first method the fruit is simply laid on top of a fire of twigs, after which the burnt skin is scraped off before serving. The second method is to skin the fruit, cut it into slices and spread it out on the hot stones inside the ground oven. Whichever way it is prepared, the breadfruit has about the same consistency as a rye-meal loaf and tastes something like a cross between white bread and potatoes. Visitors to the South Seas have often claimed that breadfruit tastes disappointingly flat, but this is chiefly due to the fact that the natives, eager to please, have cooked the slices of fruit in a casserole in the European manner, apparently a very unsatisfactory method of preparation.

Boswell, with his unswerving instinct for any subject which might give rise to a controversy, approached Dr Johnson on the subject of breadfruit as soon as he had finished reading Cook's description of his first voyage. At the same time, in order to add fuel to the fire, he commented:

'I am well assured that the people of Otaheite who have the bread tree, the fruit of which serves them for bread, laughed heartily when they were informed of the tedious process necessary with us to have bread; plowing, sowing, harrowing, reaping, threshing, grinding, baking.'

One can well imagine the great Johnson, the champion of British progress and order, booming his rejoinder in a mixture of indignation and self-righteousness:

'Why sir, all ignorant savages will laugh when they are told of the advantages of civilized life. Were you to tell men who

PLAN OF 'THE BOUNTY'

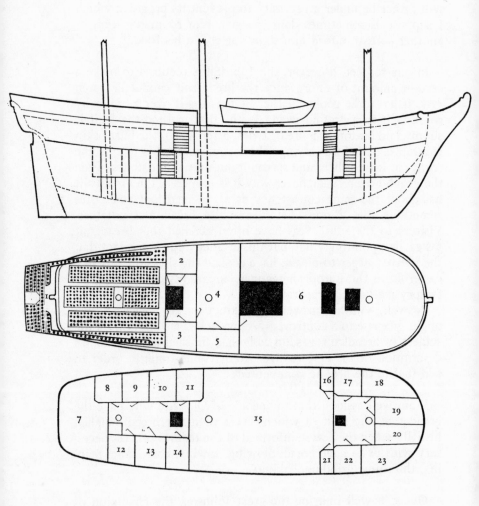

KEY

1. *Main cabin with bread-fruit plants*
2. *Fryer's cabin*
3. *Bligh's cabin*
4. *Officers' mess*
5. *Galley*
6. *Fore-castle*
7. *Galley stores*
8. *Steward's room*
9. *Surgeon's cabin*
10. *Writer Samuel's cabin*
11. *Botanist Nelson's cabin*
12. *Gunner Peckover's cabin*
13. *Captain's store-room*
14. *Store-room*
15. *Main hold*
16. *Store-room*
17. *Boatswain's cabin*
18. *Sail-room*
19. *Boatswain's store-room*
20. *Gunner's store-room*
21. *Pitch-room*
22. *Chief Carpenter Purcell's cabin*
23. *Carpenters' store-room*

live without houses how we pile brick upon brick and rafter upon rafter, and that after a house is raised to a certain height a man tumbles off a scaffold and breaks his neck, they would laugh heartily at your folly in building; but it does not follow that men are better off without houses. No sir, (holding up a slice of a good loaf) this is better than the bread tree.'

But with the exception of Dr Johnson all who read Cook's descriptions of his voyages were filled with admiration and praise for the remarkable tree, the existence of which was generally regarded as further evidence of the Almighty's limitless goodness and international planning skill. In contrast to the hardy potato, however, which at this time was just becoming the most important utility plant in Europe, there was no question of cultivating the breadfruit tree in such northerly latitudes, and thus in England the interest in the discovery was principally academic.

On the other side of the Atlantic, in the West Indies, there was a warm damp climate which was very similar to that in Tahiti, and several of the planters in Jamaica and Dominica had quickly realized how valuable the newly-discovered tree could be to them. Naturally they had no particular desire to adopt a breadfruit diet themselves, but their innumerable slaves were another matter. The majority of these were negroes—the natives themselves having long since been exterminated by the process of civilization—employed in the sugar plantations, and although these slaves were not paid anything they still cost their masters a great deal of money on account of their enormous appetites. Thus the prospect of cutting running costs by the introduction of a breadfruit diet was an attractive one.

For the most part the West Indian slaves subsisted on bananas, which were also very easy to produce. But unfortunately the trunk of the banana tree is so fragile and the roots so weak that the trees can be destroyed by a gale. And this in itself was a considerable problem on account of the storms and cyclones which so often hit the West Indies. Every time this happened the unfortunate plantation owners had to sustain their employees on bread, maize or other expensive foodstuffs imported from England or North America. Apart from all its other admirable qualities it seemed that the breadfruit was also structurally hardy and resistant and ought therefore to be well suited to conditions in the West Indies.

But to their chagrin the planters discovered that there were a great many difficulties attached to transferring the trees from Tahiti to the West Indies. The main obstacle was that the plant itself (or at least the one which Cook described) could only be reared from shoot cuttings. Even with the fastest of sailing vessels the journey would take at least six months, and it was extremely improbable that it would be possible to keep alive a collection of breadfruit shoots for such a long time under such artificial conditions. In 1775 at a meeting of the Standing Committee of West Indian Planters and Merchants the plantation owners issued a formal statement, wherein they indicated that they were prepared to meet 'all reasonable costs' if anyone would undertake to provide them with a number of breadfruit plants. The planters placed most of their hopes in the captains of the numerous ships which plied the East Indies trade routes, and they even went so far as to produce a short guide on the art of transporting plant shoots halfway round the world. This was prepared by the English botanist, John Ellis, Fellow of the Royal Societies of London and Uppsala and Agent for Dominica. It concluded a detailed description of the breadfruit tree, and a complete sketch of a transportable growing case with a singularly ingenious watering and ventilation system. As a further spur the Society of Arts and Manufacture and Commerce shortly afterwards promised a gold medal 'to the first person who conveyed from the Islands in the South Sea to the Islands in the West Indies, six plants of one or both species of the bread-fruit tree, in a growing state'.

But sea captains and gardeners are far removed from each other, and to the great disappointment of the West Indian plantation owners the mariners showed but little enthusiasm for the project. Shortly afterwards England became involved in a life and death struggle to stifle the restless spirit of the settlers in America, and it is thus not surprising that the plan, and its exceedingly modest rewards for success, was forgotten.

But the plantation owners were not prepared to give up the project entirely, and in the middle of the 1780's, when things had more or less returned to normal again, they began fresh negotiations. Since they were still unwilling to involve themselves in any major expense in order to acquire the plant, they adopted a policy which has been used many times both before and since to achieve a particular end. They contrived to convince both themselves and others that their problem was of major national importance, and that it was thus only right that the government should help them. A great deal of the ultimate authority was at this time in the hands of George III and his principal scientific adviser Sir Joseph Banks. With his diplomatic talents and his bountiful nature the scholarly Sir Joseph held a key position in English science. By a stroke of good fortune he was well versed in this very matter since he had accompanied Cook on his first South Seas voyage, and in company with his colleague, Daniel Solander, had many times eaten and enjoyed breadfruit during his three months stay on Tahiti in 1769. Thus, naturally enough, the planters turned to Sir Joseph, and after considerable negotiations the latter personally submitted a petition to George III. The adventurous spirit and the novelty of the project appealed to the king immediately and without more ado he instructed the Admiralty to despatch a ship to Tahiti to collect breadfruit cuttings and convey them to the West Indies. At the same time—the royal order was dated May 5, 1787—the first members of the expedition were selected, and these included a botanist, David Nelson, who at Sir Joseph Banks's expense had accompanied Cook on his last South Seas voyage, and one William Brown, gardener at Kew Gardens.

The first and most important move was to find a suitable ship with space not only for a large crew and extensive provisions, but also for several hundred flowerpots. There was not one ship in the English fleet which fulfilled these requirements, even though the navy at that time consisted of more than 600 units of every shape and size from humble barges up to vast, unwieldy 100-gun ships of the line. To build a ship of the type required would take too long, and the only alternative therefore was to buy one which, without too much difficulty, could be converted into a sort of floating greenhouse. With unusual alacrity (chiefly because the king was personally interested in the project) the Admiralty made it known that they were looking for a second-hand merchant vessel in good shape and of a maximum 250 tons. Six different ships were offered and only one of these, an ex-coastal trading fullrigger, the *Bethia*, was found to meet the actual demands. Once Sir Joseph Banks had inspected and approved the vessel and the owner had cut the price from £2,600 to £1,950, the deal was closed. This was the 23rd May, less than three weeks after the Admiralty had received the royal command. A few days later *Bethia* was taken into the naval dockyard at Deptford for conversion and special equipping for the estimated two year voyage ahead of her. The first thing the Admiralty did was to re-christen her *Bounty*, on account of the munificent nature of the enterprise. In recognition of her sudden rise in status it was also decided that the *Bounty* should be equipped with four 4-pounder carriage guns and ten half-pounder swivel guns.

His Majesty's Armed Merchant Vessel Bounty, as she was subsequently designated, weighed only 215 tons according to the naval register, and was thus no larger than a normal sized coastal ferry boat of today. Her overall length was a mere 91 feet and her maximum beam 23 feet 3 inches. As in most ocean-going vessels at this time there was no superstructure whatsoever and all the cabins were situated below decks. Compared with her length and beam the *Bounty* was a high ship, and the distance from keel to navigation deck was no less than 10 feet 3 inches. In two other aspects her design was typical of the time since the bow was flat and bulky while the stern rose straight and abrupt. As became a true fullrigger she had three masts, and these varied in height between 48 and 59 feet. The number of yards were in correct proportion to her size: three on the fore and mainmast and two on the mizzen mast. Finally, as was to be expected, the 30 foot bowsprit was supported by the figure of a woman, in riding habit for some bizarre reason.

By today's standards the *Bounty* was, in fact, an unbelievably small vessel and even compared with the ships which Captain Cook used for his South Seas voyages, the *Endeavour* 368 tons, the *Resolution* 462 tons and the *Adventure* 336 tons, the *Bounty* would seem to have been of the minimum possible tonnage for such an undertaking. On the other hand, however, she was only two and a half years old and in first-class condition, besides which the Admiralty had taken the added precaution of having her sheathed with copper-plating below the waterline. At this time this was the only effective means of protecting a ship's timbers against shipworm—which despite gales, pirates and cannibals, was still the principal menace to a vessel spending a long time in tropical waters. In the matter of rigging improvements, too, their otherwise parsimonious lordships did not hesitate to go to a great deal of extra expense, which clearly indicates the vast importance attached to the enterprise.

But irrespective of how well the ship might be prepared and equipped, the success of the expedition, nevertheless, depended entirely upon whether or not it would be possible to keep the breadfruit shoots alive during the extremely long journey. At a very early stage of the proceedings, however, the meticulously thorough Sir Joseph had given much thought to this matter, and thus, when the Admiralty once more turned to him for advice, he was able to give them sensible, and as it subsequently emerged, perfectly correct instructions. To begin with he insisted that it would be necessary to collect at least five hundred breadfruit shoots from Tahiti in order to ensure that a sufficiently large number would survive, and also pointed out that the results would undoubtedly be better if each shoot were planted in a separate pot. Finally each and every one of these plants would have to be watered regularly with fresh water during a homeward journey which might easily take upwards of six months.

The only place on board the *Bounty* where room could be found for five hundred flowerpots was the main cabin in the stern. Sir Joseph proposed that this cabin should be converted into a greenhouse and the Admiralty obediently followed his suggestions. First, the cabin floor was covered entirely in lead sheeting, cross beams were nailed into position over this at regular intervals, and planks were then nailed over these so as to form a sort of second deck. The planks had already been furnished with holes large enough to accommodate a flowerpot, and when the work was finished the egg-box-like construction, together with similarly holed shelves around the walls, provided secure accommodation for no less than six hundred and twenty-six pots. Finally two holes were bored in the under decking, so that any of the precious water which might drain off the flowerpots would run across the lead sheeting and down through these holes into a couple of barrels which had been put into position on the deck below. For the purpose of improving ventilation three additional air holes were bored in the ship's side just below the cabin roof. At the same time, however, in order to ensure that the tropical shoots were not killed by the chill of a more temperate atmosphere as the *Bounty* went south around the Cape, a large copper stove was installed in the improvised greenhouse.

This work was all carefully superintended by Sir Joseph's assistants, Nelson the botanist and Brown the Kew gardener— so far the only established members of the crew. Towards the end of July, however, so much progress had been made that the admiralty decided that it was time to put an officer on board and get the ship fully crewed and equipped. Posterity has tended to regard Bligh and the *Bounty* as synonymous, like Columbus and the *Santa Maria* or Nelson and the *Victory*, and hitherto it has certainly seemed as if the ill-fated breadfruit cruise was from the very outset of the plan dominated by the notorious Captain Bligh. In point of fact, however, Bligh's entry on to the scene of the drama was both modest and unremarkable. At the time of his appointment as captain of the *Bounty* Bligh was still an anonymous junior officer in the Navy, holding the rank of a mere lieutenant and not even on active service.

His command was really the result of the influence of his wife's uncle Duncan Campbell, a ship-owner who had made a fortune slave-running and who also owned several sugar plantations and a mercantile house in the West Indies. From the beginning Campbell had been one of the keenest advocates of the introduction of the breadfruit tree to the West Indies, and it was he who had been chiefly instrumental in securing the support of Sir Joseph Banks for the scheme. (Various historians claim that the *Bounty* was originally owned by Campbell, but this is quite wrong. The mistake probably derives from the fact that Campbell had at the time offered the Admiralty a vessel of his own, the *Lynx*, which was subsequently turned down in favour of the *Bethia*.) Fully aware of the great influence of Sir Joseph, Campbell set out to convince him that Bligh was the right man to command the expedition, and needless to say the appointment was duly made.

The fact that Bligh was able to thank one of his relations for his command is unfortunate evidence of the uninhibited favouritism which was rife in the English fleet at this time. This does not imply, however, that Bligh was necessarily incapable or undeserving of the honour which had been bestowed upon him. As a matter of fact he was a singularly capable officer, and would undoubtedly have qualified before many others if the Admiralty had made the selection on the basis of merit. He had just that training and specific experience which was required to lead an expedition of this type. In the first place he had a long and creditable career as a naval officer behind him. Secondly, he had already made one journey to the South Seas and actually landed on Tahiti, and thirdly, he knew the West Indies well and was held in considerable esteem by the planters there.

It has often been claimed that Bligh was an uneducated upstart who had begun his career as an ordinary seaman. Several of his critics have more or less implied that his misfortunes and difficulties are really attributable to the fact that neither by birth nor upbringing was he a gentleman. The truth of the matter, however, is quite the opposite, since for several generations the male side of the Bligh line had been men of substance: country gentlemen, officers, physicians, lawyers and government officials. William Bligh's father had been an Inspector of Customs, and the boy himself was born in the venerable city of Plymouth in Devonshire on September 9, 1754. Another completely erroneous claim is that Bligh was sent to sea when only seven years old. There is no doubt whatsoever that while he was still very young his parents had decided that he should become a naval officer, and it must be admitted that even as late as the nineteenth century minors and immature youngsters were enrolled as ship's boys in the English fleet. In Bligh's case, however, the boy was simply entered on the books of a naval vessel shortly before his eighth birthday. This unsound and very unfair practice was fairly common in the English fleet at this time, the shrewd intention being that in due course it gave the aspiring officer more years of seniority and better claims to promotion.

William Bligh started his school career, not his naval career, at the age of seven. Not much is known about this period of his life, but he must have had good teachers and been both talented and industrious, since it emerged in later years that his knowledge of such subjects as Latin, mathematics and English was considerably superior to that of most naval officers of his day. It was not until 1770, when he was 16 years old, that young Bligh first embarked upon his naval career and then continued to be mustered as a seaman, even though he had the same position and duties as a midshipman. He must have made a good impression upon his superiors because a mere six months later he was made a midshipman proper. It should perhaps be pointed out here that the title midshipman at this time implied a post rather than a rank, and consequently some hapless mariners remained midshipmen all their lives.

During the next five years Bligh served on three different ships, including three years on the 26-gun frigate *HMS Crescent*, and was given a sound, fundamental training in seamanship. This was a peaceful period in English history, and consequently the young sailor's life was never endangered by action. But at the same time the general trend of life on board was hard, raw and dangerous, and for its successful pursuit required just that degree of patience and stubbornness of which Bligh was possessed. The soundest way of ensuring promotion was, of course, to acquire some sort of influential support in the fleet itself or at the Admiralty, but this means was not open to Bligh—which explains possibly why he was still a midshipman five years later.

In the long run, however, William Bligh was not to be overlooked, particularly when at the beginning of 1776, at the age of twenty-two, he passed with distinction the theoretical part of his officer's examinations. This did not result, however, in his being immediately commissioned since according to fleet regulations all officer candidates, at least in peacetime, were required to do long and thorough service as warrant officers before they were finally commissioned. In view of this, and also on account of his tender age, it must have been a great triumph for him and a clear demonstration of the confidence he had won when he was given the highly sought-after position of master* on *HMS Resolution* which in company with *HMS Discovery*, the latter under the command of the by now world-famous Captain Cook, was about to leave for the South Seas in order to find out whether there was access this way to the legendary Northwest Passage.

In view of the special nature of the expedition, Bligh was given a number of unusual duties, such as sounding unknown waters, making complicated computations, drawing charts, negotiating with suspicious natives and keeping an accurate logbook. He quickly adapted himself to his new duties, however, and carried them out energetically, effectively and with a

---

*Formerly an officer ranking next below a lieutenant, and performing duties of the navigation officer of today.

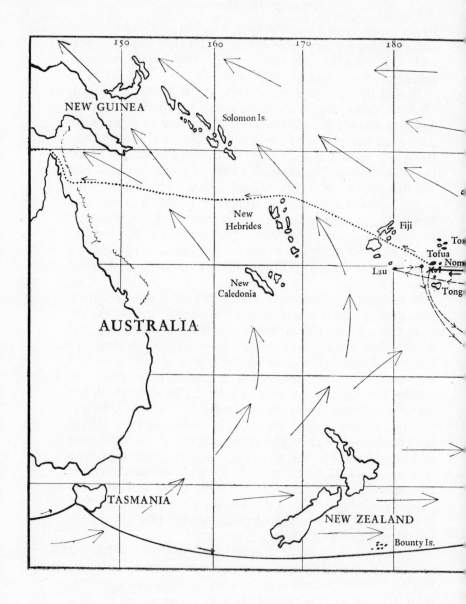

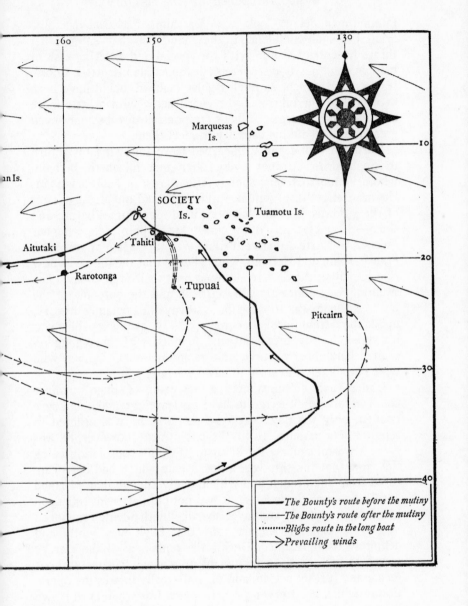

minimum of delay. Cook, who was himself a strict disciplin-
arian, had such confidence in the young man that among other
things he entrusted him with the special and exacting task of
mapping the newly-discovered Hawaiian islands. After Cook's
tragic death which, as Bligh rightly claimed, could have been
avoided had the officer of the guard acted with a little more
alacrity and courage, Bligh's responsibilities became even
greater, and so did his capacity to meet them.

During his long and well-earned leave following his return
to England in October 1780, Bligh met Elizabeth Betham,
whom he married very shortly afterwards, in February 1781.
His most effective argument in his swift and impatient pursuit
of the girl was one that has been used many times before and
since—the uncertainty of the times. At this point, following her
reverses in North America, Britain was once again at war with
France, Spain and Holland, who believed that the time was now
ripe to deliver the decisive blow against their arch enemy. The
situation was unquestionably critical, and the outcome of the
bitter struggle was to depend, as always in England's history,
upon the strength of her navy. Every available ship was
mustered, hastily fitted out and manned with press-gang recruited landlubbers, retired officers and merchant seamen who
were completely unversed in naval warfare.

Under such circumstances a navigator of Bligh's calibre
could hardly be expected to have his leave extended, and sure
enough, only ten days after the wedding, he was ordered to
report to Portsmouth. To his disappointment, however, he was
given a warrant officer's post again, the only consolation being
this time that the ship was a fine frigate which had been captured from the French and which, oddly enough, had retained
her Gallic name, *Belle Poule*. It was not until after his squadron
had fought a bloody and indecisive duel with a Dutch squadron
at Dogger Bank in August 1781 that Bligh was finally and
definitely commissioned. During the remainder of the war he
served as fifth or sixth lieutenant on various frigates without
seeing any further action, and the only really interesting operation in which he afterwards participated was when Lord Howe
went to the assistance of beleaguered Gibraltar at the close of
1782.

In gratitude for having saved their country in a critical
situation, numerous naval officers were dismissed from active

service as soon as peace was concluded at the beginning of 1783; a peace, incidentally, which was greatly to the advantage of England. Bligh was among the first to be retired for an indefinite period, and like the remainder of his colleagues he was then put on half pay. In his case this amounted to two shillings a day which, even for a man as careful as Bligh, was by no means sufficient to support a family, particularly since this now included a daughter and another child on the way. It was at this point that Elizabeth Bligh's uncle, Duncan Campbell, came to the family's aid for the first time by giving his niece's husband, whom he scarcely knew, command of one of his merchantmen. For the next four years Bligh traded between England and the West Indies for Campbell, and often enough also served as Campbell's agent in business transactions with the Jamaica planters. He must have conducted these affairs well and won the confidence of Campbell, otherwise it is hardly likely that Campbell would have gone to so much trouble to get Bligh appointed as captain of *His Majesty's Armed Vessel Bounty* as soon as he got word of the pending breadfruit expedition in the spring of 1787.

Bligh was in the West Indies when the conversion work on the *Bounty* began, and not until he arrived back in England at the end of July did he realize how much trouble Campbell had gone to to secure his appointment. Meanwhile it had been Bligh's dream to re-enter active service for the Crown, and he was quick to realize now what an excellent opportunity this was for him. Thus, without fully appreciating what he was letting himself in for or what was expected of him, he immediately accepted the offer. Two weeks later, on the 16th August, he received his appointment officially from the Admiralty—although he was not, as he hoped, promoted to the rank of full captain—and immediately assumed responsibility for the crewing and equipping of his new ship. At this turning point in his career William Bligh was only thirty-three years old. We know little about his appearance except that he was somewhat below average height, robust and with a tendency towards corpulence, also that he was possessed of the curious combination of dark hair and brilliant blue eyes. His complexion has been described as 'pale or even pallid'.

Concerning his character we know only from the few contemporary documents available that he was regarded by his

superiors as being singularly intelligent, energetic and conscientious.

Bligh was quite satisfied with his ship and demanded only
two major modifications: first that her masts should be somewhat shortened, and second that he must quite definitely have
new and larger ship's boats. The Admiralty acceded to his
wishes, although the matter of the masts subsequently proved
quite unnecessary, since during the course of the voyage he
found it necessary to heighten the yards in order to raise the
truck centre of the sails. On the other hand he was quite right
in claiming that Bounty's three original ship's boats were
altogether too small, and the day was to come when he was to
think himself lucky that he had gone to the trouble of having
these boats replaced. The new boats consisted of a 23 foot
launch, a 20 foot cutter and a 16 foot jolly-boat.

According to Admiralty instructions the crew, with the exception of the botanist and the gardener, was to comprise forty-
five men, which was fairly normal for a ship of this size. As
was often the case when ships were being sent out on long
voyages, the captain was given a great deal of liberty in the
matter of selecting the crew. Bligh did not pay much attention
to this prerogative, however, and the few choices that he did
make personally were to prove to be anything but happy ones.
Among those whom he selected because he knew them and had
confidence in them—a fact which has often been overlooked
in previous accounts of the *Bounty* mutiny—was one Fletcher
Christian.

Fletcher Christian had as much claim to being a gentleman as
Bligh himself. He was a member of a landed family which had
estates both on the Isle of Man and in Cumberland. Like Bligh,
Christian had had a comparatively sound education before he
went (or possibly ran away) to sea. As early as 1782 he was in
HMS Cambridge with Bligh during the Gibraltar mission, but
then the twenty-eight-year-old Bligh was already a lieutenant
while the eighteen-year-old Christian, because of lack of
seniority, was still only a ship's boy. It is thus hardly likely that
they knew each other particularly well at this time. Three years
later, however, when Christian, by this time a midshipman,
was released from active service it was probably one of his
relations who forwarded his request to be allowed to accompany Bligh on the latter's next West Indies voyage. Bligh, con-

scious of a certain degree of obligation to this young man on account of the friendship between Christian's and his wife's families, replied that there was unfortunately no post available as master, which was what Christian had asked for, but that he would be prepared to treat him as a gentleman and permit him to eat at his table if Christian cared to enlist as an ordinary seaman. For want of a better opportunity Christian accepted this offer.

Unfortunately there exists no proper description of Fletcher Christian, but he is reputed to have been of a 'bright, pleasing countenance' and well built, though 'rather bow-legged'. His manner was described as direct, amiable and charming. With these qualities it is only natural that he should have been attractive to women, and he in his turn was very fond of the opposite sex. It may well have been the direct contrast between the two of them that drew Bligh to Christian, and apparently throughout the entire West Indies voyage Bligh looked after the welfare of his protégé and coached him in both astronomy and navigation. Their friendship continued in subsequent voyages, and was further strengthened when Bligh managed to get Christian promoted gunner while the latter awaited an opening for an officer's post. It was therefore a natural thing that Bligh should take Christian with him when he was given command of the *Bounty* in the August of 1787. Two other men who had also served with Bligh on the West Indies run, a sailmaker, Liboque, and a quartermaster, Norton, also transferred to the *Bounty* in their same capacities. Finally there were two more of Bligh's companions from Cook's third South Seas voyage, the versatile gunner, Peckover, and the good-natured botanist, Nelson. Of these two Bligh had selected Peckover himself, while Nelson had Sir Joseph Banks to thank for his appointment.

Even though, from the captain's point of view, there were undoubtedly certain advantages in being able to choose his own crew, Bligh soon realized that there were also a number of drawbacks. The belief that every island in the South Seas was a paradise in itself—particularly for men—was by this time well established, and from the very outset Bligh was overwhelmed by applications from officers, seamen and even civilians to be allowed to accompany him on the voyage. As usual the most formidable and persistent requests came from the mothers of ambitious midshipmen, who were convinced that the quickest route to advancement for their sons lay in just such an expedition as the *Bounty* was about to embark upon. The ship's list provided for two midshipmen's posts, but Bligh's wife, Duncan Campbell and various other relations and friends argued so strongly on behalf of their different protégés that in the end Bligh found himself with no less than five midshipmen on board. Altogether, as a result of the great attraction of an expedition of this type, it turned out that when the crew was finally mustered there was not one shanghaied or pressed man on board, a singularly unusual state of affairs in the British fleet in those days. Two-thirds of the crew were less than thirty years of age, and the oldest man on board seems to have been the forty-year-old sailmaker, Liboque. Twenty-seven men were so young and inexperienced in fact that they had never yet been south of the equator.

The Admiralty were equally forthcoming in the matter of the provisioning of the *Bounty*. One of the lessons which Bligh had learned during his voyages to the South Seas with Cook was that the notorious scurvy was nothing more than a deficiency disease, which could easily be combated by the proper consumption of certain nutritious foods (i.e. those which we now know to contain vitamin-C). Thus, besides the usual rations of ship's biscuits, flour, salt beef, pork, dried peas, butter and cheese, Bligh also had stored on board supplies of lemon juice, malt essence, dried malt, sauerkraut and 'portable soup' or 'solid broth', this being the latest thing in preserving techniques. Finally, as an extra security, a whole selection of livestock was taken aboard, including chickens, pigs and sheep, so that the crew would be able to have fresh meat at least once a week during the first few months of the voyage. Convinced as he was that regular exercise would help to keep the men in good shape Bligh also tried, unsuccessfully at first, to find a musician to join the crew: he apparently believed that dancing was the most suitable form of exercise on board!

Sir Joseph Banks came down to the shipyard at the beginning of September to make Bligh's acquaintance and to see how he was carrying out his duties. He was immediately impressed by the *Bounty's* young captain and declared his extreme satisfaction with all that he saw. As usual Sir Joseph was filled with ideas, and he now set about composing a list of the bartering goods which would be needed during the actual visit to Tahiti.

This list was long and diverse, and included such items as six dozen shirts, one thousand pounds of nails, forty-eight dozen knives, a large selection of saws, files and drills, and no less than two hundred and thirty-four dozen specially manufactured adzes of the same design as the Tahitians' own stone axes. For the equally important bargaining with the island womenfolk the list also included fourteen dozen mirrors and one hundred pounds of glass pearls. The Admiralty again promptly saw to it that the contents of this list were quickly made up and delivered to the ship.

On the 9th October all the supplies were on board, and the *Bounty* sailed down the Thames to the armoury at Longbeach for the loading of her guns and ammunition. Once this final business had been settled she continued as far as the Thames estuary to await a suitable moment for the trip to Portsmouth, from whence the official departure was to take place. But the typically fitful and stormy weather of the English Channel forced Bligh to abandon his first attempt to get out to sea, and it was not until his second attempt in the beginning of November that he managed to enter the Channel. Even so, hard winds drove him almost over to the French coast, and it was not without a great deal of difficulty that the ship finally reached the shelter of Spithead.

During the following two weeks the weather was exceptionally favourable with steady land breezes. And yet to Bligh's intense annoyance and impatience their lordships in London seemed in no hurry whatsoever to issue the promised detailed instructions, without which the ship could not leave.

Even though she was now once more with child, Mrs Bligh came down from London together with her four daughters to bid her husband a final goodbye, a clear indication of how fond they were of each other. For once, now, Bligh really had a little time to spare for his family, since the only outstanding business on hand was that of replacing one ordinary seaman who had deserted while the ship was lying in the Thames estuary. He was still after a musician and now he actually acquired one, though there must have been a great dearth of musical talent in the fleet at this time since the character whom he finally found was a half-blind fiddler called Michael Byrne. On account of his affliction Byrne was, needless to say, totally useless for all normal ship's duties, but Bligh's mind was made up, and before

Byrne really knew what was happening he was signed up for the voyage. At the same time, apparently, Bligh did his utmost to have the ship's surgeon replaced, the existing one, Huggan, being a hopeless drunkard. But his efforts were fruitless, Admiralty bureaucracy prevailed and no new surgeon was forthcoming.

Finally on the 24th November the Admiralty's instructions and sailing orders arrived. According to these the captain was to weigh anchor 'at the first favourable opportunity of wind and weather', and was to proceed around Cape Horn to the Society Islands without stopping en route. As soon as a sufficient number of breadfruit shoots had been taken on board from one of several of these islands—in other words it was not specifically stated that Bligh should make directly for Tahiti—the home voyage should commence via the treacherous Torres Straits and the Cape of Good Hope. On this home journey Bligh was to put into Java and replace any dead breadfruit shoots with other valuable tropical plants. Having completed the circumnavigation half of the surviving breadfruit shoots were to be delivered to the Botanical Gardens at Kingstown, St Vincent, while the remainder would go to the Botanical Gardens at Kingston, Jamaica.

False rumours must have been circulated among the crew (who in accordance with the prevailing regulations were not permitted to know anything about the route or the purpose of the voyage until the ship had definitely left England) since two seamen deserted shortly afterwards. These two were duly replaced by a couple of pressed men, there being no time for any other form of enlistment.

On the 28th November the entire crew were given two months' pay in advance, which enabled them to spend a final and undoubtedly very wet evening ashore. Early the following morning the *Bounty* set sail.

On the 3rd December the weary crew were back in Spithead again after having fought against heavy seas and strong head winds for three full days. The two pressed men immediately took the opportunity to desert, and Bligh in his turn, having finally lost all confidence in the drunken ship's surgeon, cunningly took advantage of the situation and engaged as a replacement for one of the deserters Thomas Ledward, a young ship's surgeon who was prepared to sign on as a temporary able seaman.

On the 6th December a favourable northerly land breeze began to blow and Bligh made another attempt to get away. But once more he had scarcely got out into the Channel before the wind changed direction, and in a full southwesterly gale the *Bounty* was again forced to retreat to Spithead. Delays of this sort were a regular occurrence for sailing ships, and the average captain was prepared to accept it with equanimity. But Bligh felt that he had every right to be impatient, knowing as he did that if the departure were delayed for another week or two he would run the risk of reaching Cape Horn so late in the season that the winter storms would prevent him from rounding it. The whole business was particularly frustrating, since he was well aware that had it not been for the slackness on the part of the Admiralty he could have left in excellent weather at the beginning of the month.

Meanwhile the bad weather seemed to be generally worsening rather than abating, and after a few more days of impatient hanging about Bligh very wisely wrote to the Admiralty and requested permission, should the necessity arise, to take the outward route as well via the Cape of Good Hope. The Admiralty could hardly refuse the *Bounty's* captain this request, but due to the poor postal service between Portsmouth and London yet another week was lost in between. Christmas celebrations were just about to begin at the naval port when the wind suddenly turned again and began to ease off. With grim determination Bligh immediately gave orders for the sails to be set, and in no time at all the *Bounty* was out in the Channel and hull down in the tail end of the bad weather. Come what may this time Bligh was absolutely resolved not to turn back again.

Apart from the laxity on the Admiralty's part over the final sailing orders, there can be no denying that the expedition was most carefully prepared. A great deal of money and hard work had gone into improving and fitting out the ship, but one very significant consideration had been overlooked, the actual manning of the *Bounty*, which in the event had much to do with the subsequent tragedy, and is a point which should not be forgotten.

According to Admiralty orders the *Bounty's* crew was to comprise forty-five men plus the botanist and the gardener, who were regarded more or less as passengers. It is quite true that forty-five men were enlisted in London, but for some unknown reason the two deserters from Portsmouth were not replaced, except by the young ship's surgeon whom Bligh himself had found. The crew of forty-four were thus made up as follows:

Seamen personnel :

1 captain
1 master
2 master's mates
2 midshipmen
2 quartermasters
1 quartermaster's mate
1 boatswain
1 boatswain's mate
23 able seamen.

Other personnel :

3 carpenters
1 sailmaker
1 gunner
1 gunner's mate
1 armourer
1 corporal
1 surgeon
1 clerk

Thus it would seem that the seamen personnel consisted of thirty-four men, including twenty-three able seamen and eleven others—a fairly well-proportioned selection on the face of it. Closer examination of existing documents, however, makes it quite evident that many of the personnel who were supposed to be able seamen were in fact anything but that. To begin with, as has already been mentioned, three of them were extra midshipmen who in their capacity as gentlemen could hardly be expected to be apt with sail or rope. Other so-called able seamen included two ship's cooks, Bligh's steward and the master's brother-in-law, Tinkler, a young gentleman who could only be classed as a sort of reserve midshipman. If one finally excludes the young ship's surgeon Ledward and the half-blind fiddler Byrne, there remains but fourteen able seamen. Thus all in all the *Bounty* was definitely undermanned, and the crew members who did actually keep watch had far too much to do all round.

Another serious drawback was that Bligh had no commissioned officers to assist him. This greatly increased his own work and responsibilities, and must also have heightened the feeling of isolation and loneliness which is the lot of every ship's captain, even under the most favourable conditions. Another singularly unsatisfactory arrangement was that Bligh, as was often the case on smaller vessels, also had to act as ship's purser, which in turn gave the crew further opportunity for complaints.

Bligh's lack of commissioned-officer assistance, likewise his assumption of the purser's duties, was chiefly the result of shortage of space on board. For this same reason he was not permitted to have a contingent of marines with him, which in itself was the gravest mistake of all in the planning of the expedition. Practically all British naval vessels at this time carried a marine detachment who not only served as supporting troops during naval actions but were also there to help the captain maintain discipline and to protect him against mutiny. Sending the *Bounty* out on a long and arduous voyage with nothing more than one hapless corporal on board was a very dangerous risk to take. All these shortcomings in fact could have been avoided by the simple expedient of having originally selected a larger vessel for the project.

Bligh was only too well aware of this, but he was far too confident a man to have allowed it to worry him unduly. The only thing which really irked him was the fact that, despite the pleas on his behalf by Sir Joseph Banks, their lordships at the Admiralty had refused to promote him captain, so that he still retained the rank of a mere lieutenant. His one real consolation was the knowledge that, if he fulfilled his duties properly on this voyage, he would be bound to enjoy swifter promotion upon his return. And he never doubted for one moment that the difficult task ahead of him would be carried out with anything short of the greatest success.

CHAPTER II

STORMY PASSAGE

AFTER a further two days of heavy weather the gale abated sufficiently to allow the crew to relax for a while and enjoy a Christmas dinner of roast beef and Christmas pudding. But they were to need the extra strength and fortitude built up by this hearty fare, because by Boxing Day the wind was back to full strength again and the sea was so rough that Bligh did not dare heave to, choosing instead to run before the wind with nothing more than a few square yards of sail on the foremast. To Bligh's great relief the *Bounty* now showed herself to be remarkably steady in heavy weather, although careful as the helmsman might be it was impossible to prevent the larger waves from sweeping the decks. By nightfall the situation had worsened and the crew were in constant danger of being swept overboard or blown out of the rigging. One giant wave landed full on the three ship's boats, which were stowed amidships above the main hold, and it was only with the utmost effort that the numbed and saturated seamen were able to save them from being torn loose and dashed to pieces. Another heavy sea carried away several barrels of ale and reserve spars before anyone could intervene. A few hours later another wave shattered the stern superstructure, with the result that the provisions stowed in a small hold below the main cabin were completely soaked in salt water.

Despite the fact that the manoeuvre still entailed great risk, on the afternoon of the 27th Bligh brought his ship about and hove to until the next morning, when he had the rigging checked and all the salt water pumped out of the bilges. Slowly but surely now the weather began to improve, giving the crew a chance to rest a little and dry out their clothing and belongings. In view of the fact that it was difficult to make any proper repairs at sea, and since a large part of the provisions seemed to have been more or less spoiled by water, Bligh decided to put into the Canary Islands for proper repairs and trimming before embarking on the passage around Cape Horn, a run which would certainly prove much rougher than anything they had met so far.

As soon as he had anchored in Santa Cruz on Tenerife on the morning of the 6th January, Bligh sent Fletcher Christian off on a courtesy visit to the governor. Despite the latent hostilities between Spain and England at this time, the governor nevertheless invited Bligh to dinner, and offered him any assistance that he might need. Characteristic of his almost pedantic diligence, Bligh utilized the five days at Santa Cruz not only for superintending the repairing and reprovisioning of the ship, but also for taking a series of accurate position fixes, noting the prices of the most usual ship's victuals, checking compass variation and acquainting himself with local economic conditions. He also sent Nelson and Brown out on a number of botanical excursions, and finally made a detailed description of the local orphanage. This somewhat bizarre detail in the breadfruit expedition chronicle is concluded in a manner which is typical of Bligh:

'By this humane institution a number of people are rendered useful and industrious, in a country where the poor, from the indulgence of the climate, are too apt to prefer a life of inactivity, though attended with wretchedness, to obtaining the comforts of life by industry and labour.'

A further example of Bligh's excessive zeal was the trouble to which he went to purchase two barrels of local wine, with the intention of conveying them around the world for his patron Sir Joseph Banks.

At the same time some 4,000 litres of wine were brought on board to eke out the supplies of sour and yeasty beer. On the other hand it was impossible to get hold of anything like enough vegetables and fresh meat in these islands, and the only addition on board in the form of food, when the *Bounty* sailed again on the 10th January, was a few casks of poor quality salted meat, two live goats and a small supply of pumpkins. Once again the crew could be glad that while in England the captain had been far-sighted enough to take on additional quantities of specially nutritious foodstuffs.

Shortly after leaving Tenerife, Bligh put his crew into three watches instead of the usual two. This unusual and considerate measure meant that in future every man would be able to rest a full eight hours between his watches instead of the severe routine of being on watch every other four hours all round the clock. On account of this new routine an extra master's mate was needed, and Bligh immediately gave the post to Fletcher Christian. Another well-meant, though less popular, innovation was an inspection system to maintain a reasonable standard of personal cleanliness among the men. During these inspections any man who was found to be unwashed or in possession of dirty clothes immediately had his rum ration withdrawn as a punishment. Another measure in the interests of hygiene, which Bligh had learned from Captain Cook, was ensuring that the forecastle and cabins were regularly washed through with acetic solution, in order to exterminate cockroaches and other insects. One of the chief discomforts, as on all wooden ships, was the penetrating stench of bilge water which leaked in around the keel during the course of a voyage. This, too, Bligh did his best to overcome by having the bilges pumped out and the timbers subsequently flushed down with clean seawater regularly every day. In the captain's opinion the pumping work had the advantage of giving the crew much-needed exercise. With the same object in view he also had the half-blind fiddler play a few merry tunes several evenings a week, and in order to ensure that no one played truant from these extraordinary gatherings Bligh was always present himself to superintend them. Many of Bligh's critics have since interpreted these compulsory dancing exercises as an expression of sadism on his part, which of course is just as unreasonable as to go to the other extreme and claim that his scrupulous concern for the welfare of his men was born of his sheer love of mankind. The truth of the matter undoubtedly is that his actions were motivated by his perfectly understandable eagerness to carry out his mission with the utmost success, an ambition which would be more likely to succeed if he could maintain a satisfied and healthy crew.

Apart from the regular inspections and enforced exercises, life on board throughout the whole of January was fairly agreeable. The weather was mainly fine and sunny with day temperatures around 70° and night temperatures of not much less than 50°. What little rainfall there was offered a welcome shower bath to everybody on board, and also supplemented the ship's fresh water supplies. Thanks to a canvas awning that the captain had been thoughtful enough to have erected, the crew were able to spend their leisure hours above decks in the fresh air, where cards and shark fishing seem to have been the most popular pastimes. The only serious problem at this time was the wind, since on the days when there was not a complete calm the breeze was so slight that the *Bounty* made no more than four knots at the most, which explains why she did not cross the equator before the 4th February. Crossing the line was celebrated in the traditional manner with Father Neptune and all the regular trappings, and was apparently an unusually enjoyable affair since Bligh had strictly forbidden any unnecessary coarseness or brutality. This small instance once again tends to suggest that the *Bounty's* commander was not the heartless villain that he is reputed to have been, and that he could, in fact, without any ulterior motives, be as human and considerate as the next man.

Just south of the equator the *Bounty* entered the trade wind belt, and was soon covering between 100 and 150 nautical miles a day. As a result of this vastly improved progress, by the 17th February she had passed the Tropic of Capricorn and was down off the coast of Brazil, roughly on a level with Rio de Janeiro. On the same day she overtook an English whaling vessel, the *British Queen*, which was bound for the Cape of Good Hope. The two ships made contact, and Bligh learned that the *British Queen* had left England eighteen days before the *Bounty* and had not put in anywhere en route, which indicates that for her size the *Bounty* must have been a fast ship in those days. Before their ways parted, Bligh took the opportunity to forward via the *British Queen* the following somewhat over-optimistic report to his patron Duncan Campbell:

'We are all in good spirits and my little ship fit to go round a half-score of worlds. My men all active good fellows, and what has given me much pleasure is that I have not yet been obliged to punish any one. My officers and young gentlemen are all tractable and well disposed, and we now understand each other so well that we shall remain so the whole voyage, unless I fall out with the doctor, who I have trouble from preventing being in bed fifteen hours out of the twenty-four. I am at present determined to push round the Cape Horn without touching anywhere as I have plenty of water, but that must depend on the winds. We have laid in a good stock of wines at Teneriffe and our allowance among four is a bottle every day and one bottle of porter, this with fine sour krout, pumpkins and dried greens and a fresh meal five times a week, I think is not bad living. My men are not badly off either, as they share in all but the poultry, and with much content and cheerfulness, dancing always from four to eight at night. I am happy to hope I shall bring them all home well.'

Conditions on board, however, were not quite so harmonious as Bligh claimed in his report, as can be seen from subsequent comments and descriptions. Above all, the crew seems to have complained about the food, and in view of the wealth of accusations which have been levelled at Bligh ever since, it is only fair here to examine a little more closely the victualling arrangements on board. Apart from the additional rations mentioned in Bligh's report to Duncan Campbell, each seaman received the following rations:

Biscuits: 1 lb. daily
Salt Beef: 2 lbs. twice weekly
Salt Pork: 1 lb. twice weekly
Dried Fish: 2 ozs thrice weekly
Butter: 2 ozs. thrice weekly
Cheese: 4 ozs. thrice weekly
Peas: 8 ozs. every four days
Beer: 1 gallon daily

As was always the case on long voyages, the food was not particularly appetizing, which is hardly surprising in view of the primitive methods of preservation which were in use at the time. The greater part of the provisions was stowed in wooden barrels, stacked one on top of the other in the holds, and before any ship had been long at sea—especially if she were in tropical waters—the contents of the barrels invariably began to ferment, rot or turn rancid. It was likewise equally difficult to keep the foodstuffs free from weevils and other grubs, which were even capable of boring their way into the iron-hard ship's biscuits. It was the custom in those days for the seamen before they bit into their biscuits, to rap them soundly on the edge of the table in order to shake out the occupants; this steady rapping is said to have been one of the most typical sounds on board during mealtimes. The only biscuits which the sailors refused to eat in fact were those which did not contain any worms, their point being, quite logically, that if the worms refused them then they could scarcely be fit for human consumption.

In order to overcome the rotten or rancid taste of the food the ship's cooks were very liberal in their use of salt, pepper, mustard and vinegar, and this in its turn led to the question of water supplies on board. Fresh water was a major problem since, apart from the putrescent state of the stagnant water, it was also liable to contain both typhus and diphtheria germs. This problem was solved to a large extent, once the sharp-witted West Indies planters had persuaded the Admiralty to purchase their rum in large quantities and issue it to the sailors daily, well mixed with water. Thus good strong spirit did for the dubious water on board what the good strong spices did for the dubious food. Oddly enough this important advance in the realm of medicine reached the British fleet comparatively late, since the medicinal value of 'grog', called after a British admiral, Vernon, nicknamed 'Old Grog', had been discovered as early as 1740.

To return to conditions on board the *Bounty* at this time, it should be pointed out that the grumbling of the sailors over the food was not because it was bad or uneatable. They were accustomed to half-rotten food and hardly expected anything else. But on the other hand they considered themselves grievously wronged if they thought they were being given short rations. On one occasion at least Bligh deliberately cut the crew's rations, as on the day after they left Tenerife when he withdrew one third of the biscuit ration. At the same time, however, he ordered the increased distribution of pumpkin, pointing out to everybody on board that the passage around Cape Horn might easily be a bad one, and it was thus in everyone's interest to conserve their food supplies as far as possible. This seemed to be a perfectly justifiable precaution and was apparently accepted as such by all on board. Shortly after passing the equator, however, the biscuit ration was for a short time entirely replaced by a lesser quantity of pumpkin, since the pumpkins were beginning to be affected by the heat and had to be eaten up as quickly as possible. This news was not accepted with the same equanimity with which the previous changes in rations had been met, and the sailors proceeded to give full vent to their dissatisfaction. Upon hearing this Bligh immediately confronted his crew and upbraided them in the most violent terms. His furious final comment is reputed to have been as follows:

'You damned infernal scoundrels, I'll make you eat grass or anything you can snatch before I've done with you!'

It has many times been claimed that in his capacity as purser Bligh lined his own pocket by giving his crew short rations. There is absolutely no evidence whatsoever to support this. On the contrary, he did everything he could to ensure fair shares and fair distribution. There can be no denying, at the same time, that cheating and conniving were practised on a large scale in the British fleet at this time, and it was generally accepted that the suppliers made a great deal of profit not only through selling second-rate goods but also by delivering in short measure. Because of this there was a general rule on board ships that all food barrels should be opened in the presence of the entire crew, and this rule was properly observed on the *Bounty* at all times.

It was, however, during the course of a public opening of one of these barrels that Bligh seriously compromised himself in the eyes of everybody on board. It was found that two whole cheeses were missing, and Bligh, instead of simply noting this down, immediately declared that someone must have been at the keg and stolen them. Thereupon, to the complete astonishment of everybody present, a cooper by the name of Hillbrant spoke up and pointed out that the keg had been opened back at Longreach on the order of a clerk, and the two cheeses in question sent up to Bligh's residence. Bligh turned white with rage, threatened to have the cooper flogged unless he kept his mouth shut, and immediately announced the withdrawal of everybody's cheese ration for a period sufficient to make the loss good. Since Hillbrant's claim was subsequently confirmed in the forecastle, where several sailors remembered having carried cheeses up to the Bligh residence, the rations cut was generally condemned as grossly unfair.

Once again it should be remembered on the other hand that the majority of naval officers at that time profited from their opportunities much more blatantly than Bligh, and also with the full knowledge and approval of the Admiralty. In Bligh's particular case their lordships had apparently made it quite clear that he was authorized to make as much out of his purser's office as he could—and with this in view they cut his pay by two shillings a day! It is difficult to say to what extent Bligh took advantage of this shady arrangement, although in a number of private letters he complained bitterly over the poor state of his finances, which seems to indicate that he had not been clever enough initially to cheat the suppliers who were the arch swindlers. One thing, however, is quite certain, and can be confirmed both by figures and reports from the times; Bligh was as a rule extremely generous when it came to the feeding of his crew. General grumbling over poor food always has been and always will be an accepted thing in all naval ships and military establishments, and it is therefore understandable that Bligh did not bother to mention the sporadic complaints which had reached him when he submitted his report to Duncan Campbell.

Scarcely two weeks after the *Bounty* had passed the *British Queen* another unfortunate episode occurred. This time it was the petty officers on board who felt themselves wronged. As has already been pointed out, the Admiralty made a serious mistake in not giving Bligh additional commissioned officers to assist him. As the voyage progressed and Bligh found himself increasingly inconvenienced by the existing circumstances, he resolved to take the matter into his own hands and appoint from among the warrant and petty officers an acting lieutenant and second-in-command. According to the regulations he had the right to do this if he felt it necessary. The oldest and most senior warrant officer on board was the thirty-six-year-old master, John Fryer, and he should thus have been appointed. But Bligh found Fryer altogether too tiresome, slow and irresolute, and the only individual on board in whom he had any real confidence was Fletcher Christian. There is no doubt at all that Christian was the most able and competent man on board, besides which he was generally liked and admired, and was consequently readily obeyed by all and sundry. Thus Bligh ignored the fact that Fryer was theoretically more qualified, and directly after morning service on the 2nd March, in the presence of the entire ship's company, he handed Fletcher Christian written confirmation of his appointment as lieutenant and second-in-command on board. Fryer, previously Christian's senior, was now subordinate to the twelve years younger man. This was a bitter fact which he never learned fully to accept, and for the rest of the voyage he was to do everything in his power to make life as difficult as possible for Captain Bligh.

Fryer's difficulty, shortly afterwards, in getting one of the seamen to obey him showed that he lacked those qualities of authority necessary in an officer. Fryer decided that there was nothing for it but to report the recalcitrant sailor, one Matthew Quintal, to the captain for 'insolence and contempt'. The offence was a serious one, and Bligh had no choice but to order flogging. The number of lashes, however, was remarkably low; a mere two dozen.

On the date this episode occurred, the 9th March, the *Bounty* was in the same latitude as Buenos Aires, and the temperature had sunk to about 40°. Each day that passed it became increasingly cold, with heavy cloud and mist, making the problem of navigation more and more complicated. Unable to take a bearing on the sun for days at a time, Bligh was forced to make regular soundings in case unknown currents might be driving the ship in towards the shallow and poorly charted coast of Patagonia.

On the 22nd March really bad weather set in and at a particularly unsuitable time, since at this point the *Bounty* was running dangerously close to the treacherous Tierra del Fuego where the least mistake in navigation could be fatal. But Bligh was so sure of himself that he continued to drive south with only slightly reefed sails. During the night the moon broke through the clouds and revealed a long chain of snow-capped mountains, and when day broke the *Bounty* was exactly where she should be—opposite the Lemaire Straits between the most southeasterly point of Tierra del Fuego and Staten Island. Unfortunately the head wind was so strong that it was impossible to take the ship through the straits, and instead Bligh was forced to go round Staten Island. But this only involved a delay of about twenty-four hours, and on the 24th March Bligh made the following satisfied entry in his logbook: 'Fresh gales with very heavy snow squalls. We are now entered into the South Sea under tripled-reefed topsails and reefed courses.'

During the eighty-seven days which had passed since the ship left England she had maintained an average speed of four knots and had covered eight thousand five hundred nautical miles. Thus the well-trimmed little vessel had already covered more than half the distance to her destination, and there remained 'a mere' seven thousand miles.

In order to clear Cape Horn Bligh had to continue a little farther south, and he therefore set a southwesterly course as soon as he had rounded Staten Island. Thanks to a predominantly northwesterly wind, he was able to hold this course fairly steadily, and only five days later he crossed the Cape Horn latitude, though without actually sighting the Cape itself. A still present danger, however, was the steep and rocky coast of Tierra del Fuego, which continued northwesterly in a great curve right up as far as 77° west, and Bligh knew perfectly well that he would have to hold his present course for at least another three hundred and fifty miles before he dared swing north again to leave the dangerous area astern. Everything now depended upon how quickly the *Bounty* could cover those three hundred and fifty miles, because the Antarctic winter was close at hand, and the boat had not yet been built which could stand up to the fury of the winds that blew down there at that time of year.

The *Bounty* had passed Cape Horn on the 29th March, and by the 1st April the strong head wind had increased to full gale force. Bligh, who was a man not easily alarmed, wrote in his logbook: 'The wind exceeded anything I had ever met with and a sea higher than I had ever seen before. The sea, from the frequent shifting of the wind, broke very high, and by running in contrary directions became highly dangerous. By this time all the sails had been reefed except a miniature storm foresail and we now hove to.'

For four days and nights the *Bounty* lurched and pitched in the same spot, her bows held defiantly up into the wind. On the 4th April, however, the captain's stubborn tactics were crowned with success, the wind eased and they were able to resume their interrupted westerly tack. But there was still no cause for jubilation, since for several more days the stiff wind was so capricious that the sails had to be watched continuously. The safest measure would have been to continue to heave to for a few more days, but Bligh was in a hurry and was determined to push on at all costs. It was a risky policy that he was pursuing, and his judgment was constantly being tried. On the one hand it was necessary to carry sufficient sail to give the ship fair speed, but on the other hand too much sail could easily lead to the loss of a mast.

Because the *Bounty* was so deplorably undermanned it was often necessary under such conditions for the off-duty watches to turn to as well, and as a result nobody on board got the real rest and sleep that they needed. On top of everything it was all the time bitterly cold and either snowing or raining heavily, making watch keeping and going aloft both miserable and dangerous. Neither was life below decks much better. The few stoves on board were completely inadequate to keep the ship warm or dry in conditions like these. All the hatches, except the sternmost one, had been battened down for weeks now, and since there was no other means of ventilation the air in the forecastle and the cabins was appallingly bad. Added to this was not only the stench from forty-six unwashed bodies, but also that of the pigs, goats, sheep and hens which were still alive. Last but not least there was the suffocating fumes from the galley stoves. As usual Bligh did his utmost during these trying days to keep up the spirits of his men and to make life as tolerable as possible for them. Thus, for example, he detailed two men at a time from whichever watch was off duty to dry clothes and to serve hot gruel for breakfast every morning. But what undoubtedly did most to maintain the crew's morale and keep them warm was the extra ration of undiluted rum that the captain ordered daily.

Thanks to Bligh's decision to press on in the face of everything, the *Bounty* passed the enchanted 77th parallel of longitude on the 9th April, and there before them on a compass sweep of 180° north to south stretched the mighty Pacific. The delight of everyone on board was unbounded. The great moment had arrived when they should turn north again. Soon the ship would be back in the course of the trade winds and on her way to the Eden of Tahiti. . . .

But their delight was short-lived. Scarcely had the captain given orders to change course when a violent squall came beating down on them. Before the hapless deck hands had time to do anything about the sails, the ship had become the plaything of the wind, a wind which made the gales that they had been through so far seem like a spring breeze. All Bligh could do was heave to again and hope for the best. But this time the seas were so mountainous that the *Bounty's* decks were constantly flooded, and no one could do anything but hang on for dear life. From the moment the first squall hit her, the *Bounty* was being driven backwards again in the direction from which she had come, and then, as if this were not enough, she sprung a leak. Had this leak been a straightforward hole there is little doubt that it could have been remedied, but the fact that the planking was sprung made it virtually impossible for anyone to do anything about it. Somehow or other the crew managed to get a safety line fastened across the deck so that the pumps could be manned. But despite the line several men including, inevitably, the drunken ship's surgeon, were swept from their positions and almost lost. Another discomfort which was even worse than the waves was the biting cold. Several seamen who were sent aloft were so affected by this that they were unable to speak when they managed to struggle down to the deck again. Others suffered so badly from acute attacks of rheumatism that they were incapable of coming up from below decks. Bligh now opened the main aft cabin to house the men who were most badly swamped in the forecastle.

For an entire week the *Bounty* continued to be driven back eastwards at a rate of some fifteen to twenty miles a day. Meanwhile the sick list on board grew longer and longer. The leak was now so serious that the pumps had to be manned once an hour, twenty-four hours a day. On the 17th April the miserable ship had been buffeted and blown so far eastwards that she was once again on the same parallel of longitude as she had been on the 1st April! Five men were altogether too ill or hurt to be of any use whatsoever, and the remainder were practically exhausted. Reluctantly Bligh decided to give up the one-sided struggle and instead to sail halfway around the world in the opposite direction. Months previously, it will be remembered, he had asked for and been granted permission to take this course of action should the necessity arise. Finally, before putting about, Bligh called the entire ship's company together and thanked them warmly for their skill and endurance during the extreme trials of the past few weeks.

Blight had been aware from the outset that his chances of taking the ship around Cape Horn so late in the year were minimal. A less conscientious officer would undoubtedly have made no more than a half-hearted attempt to carry out the Admiralty's unreasonable order to try the Cape Horn route, and then hurriedly set course for Good Hope. But as far as William Bligh was concerned an Admiralty order was more sacred than the Bible itself. Thus, although he had pushed himself and his crew almost to breaking point for a full three weeks, the decision to turn round was still a difficult one for him. Consequently, when on the same evening the wind changed again to south the *Bounty* once more swung round to resume her westerly course. But, needless to say, the southerly wind lasted only a few hours before it swung back to the west and increased steadily in force. Unbelievable though it may sound Bligh stuck to his latest decision for another four days, despite the fact that his ship was continually being driven backwards. It is likely enough that he would have gone on defying the weather even longer had not his supply of able crew continued to dwindle steadily. By the 21st April eight men were completely incapacitated, and the remainder of the crew were lacking in both spirit and strength. Finally the ship itself was leaking worse than ever.

All in all the conditions were such that even Bligh had to resign himself to them. The helmsman was given the long-awaited order to turn about, every possible bit of sail was set and the *Bounty* surged away at a full eight knots. Still unable to swallow the bitter pill of defeat Bligh now spent many hours writing a long and detailed defence of his capitulation in the logbook. His main argument here of course was that it was up to him not to hazard the success of the expedition by taking unnecessary risks at this relatively early stage. Two days later, on April 23rd, the *Bounty* stormed past Staten Island, which they had first sighted a month previously, and now the ship turned north once more towards warmer latitudes. Meanwhile the final haven, Tahiti, was just as far off as it had been when they first sailed from England.

Even though the position was by no means hapless, the ship

was nevertheless badly in need of repairs and fresh stores. The
nearest port on this route where an English ship could reckon
on a friendly reception was Cape Town in Dutch South Africa,
and Bligh decided to make for there as swiftly as possible. Borne
onwards by the steady following wind the *Bounty* soon passed
the Falkland Islands, and continued diagonally up towards
Tristan da Cunha. In contrast to the Falklands this desolate
island was so seldom visited by anyone that its exact position
had never been properly fixed. This was the sort of opportunity
that was irresistible to a man like Bligh, and thus, even though
he did not really have time, he spent three entire days and
nights looking for the island so that he could fix its position
once and for all. Much to his chagrin, however, his efforts were
to no avail, and he had to continue the voyage without having
found the island. By this time—it was now the middle of May
—the weather had grown much milder and the temperature
continued to rise steadily. The ship, too, was now clean and
in order, and the sailors were once more able to spend their
leisure hours under the deck awning. Bligh, anxious lest his
men slacken off as a result of this comparatively easy existence,
reintroduced the dancing regularly every evening. Furthermore
the ship still had to be pumped out once every hour, so that it
is not unreasonable to assume that the crew had plenty of all-
round exercise to keep them fit.

After another uneventful week Table Mountain appeared
over the horizon. Bligh knew that the main harbour was risky
at this time of year, and he decided therefore to drop anchor
in a bay some twenty-five miles farther south. The first thing
he now did was to fill several pages of the log with details
concerning victualling and watchkeeping during the voyage so
far. His general summing up is worth quoting here:

'Seamen will seldom attend to themselves in any particular
and simply to give directions that they are to keep themselves
clean and dry as circumstances will allow, is of little avail, they
must be watched like Children as the most recent danger has
little effect to prevent them from the same fate.'

The mere expression 'watched like children' is particularly
indicative, one feels, of Bligh's whole attitude to his crew.

Completely in keeping with this patriarchal attitude, as soon as they reached Cape Colony Bligh ordered on board large quantities of foodstuffs, and during the entire stay here he ensured that his men were given the most generous possible daily rations. These included two pounds of fresh meat, a pint of wine and a regular variety of cabbage, celery, onions and daily new-baked bread. A check on the remaining stores on board revealed that a large quantity of meat, fish and ship's biscuits were either rotten or mouldy, and these were promptly replaced by fresh provisions. Finally the fresh water and wood supplies were also replenished. The main problem, however, was the repairing of the sails and rigging and the stopping of the sprung planking. To expedite this work Bligh hired the additional assistance of a number of Dutch shipwrights, and at last on the 1st July the *Bounty* set sail again. Once more she was in good shape, well loaded with supplies, which included over seven thousand pounds of flour, nine thousand pounds of bread, seven hundred gallons of wine and five live sheep; she also carried a supply of special seeds and shoots for possible transplanting on Tahiti itself.

The only land of any size between the Cape of Good Hope and Tahiti is Australia and the islands of New Zealand, and with the exception of the newly-founded penal colony on the east coast of Australia (no news of which had yet been received in England when the *Bounty* sailed), the entire area was at this time lacking in any sort of inhabitants except 'savages'. In view of this Bligh resolved to make the briefest possible halt in Australia, and in order to make the crossing as quickly as possible he chose to sail along the 40th parallel where the fierce westerly gales, which had pounded him so savagely off Cape Horn when sailing in the opposite direction, would now blow him on his way at full speed. It was an audacious decision, and one which no other ship had ever been known to try during the wild winter months of July and August.

This time, however, everybody on board was better prepared, and since the course did not go so far south into the Antarctic as during the passage round Cape Horn, the weather remained altogether warmer and more temperate. From time to time, of course, the ship ran into spells of bad weather and had to hove to and ride it out, but by now the crew were hardened to the routine and thought nothing of it. About halfway over on the singularly uneventful passage to Australia, Bligh was once again given the opportunity to indulge his favourite occupation of position fixing. This time he came straight upon the stark rocks of St Paul's Island for which he had been keeping a look out—remarkably enough the island proved to be in the actual position shown on the charts.

After fifty-one days at sea, on the 19th August, the lookout sighted Brunio Island, which lies directly south of the entrance to the present capital of Tasmania, Hobart. According to the charts the island was then part of the mainland, and when Bligh dropped anchor in Adventure Bay, which he had visited previously with Cook, he was unaware that this was an island which was next to another island, which in its turn lay off the Australian mainland. No other ship appeared to have visited this bay since Bligh had last been there eleven years before, and its desolation was further enhanced by the complete absence of any sort of life. (It was not until several days later that a group of stark naked Tasmanian natives—'the most wretched and stupid people existing', according to Bligh—appeared at a respectful distance on the edge of the forest.) As soon as they had dropped anchor, Bligh sent a patrol ashore under Fletcher Christian and Peckover to look for fresh water and collect wood. But in the final issue Bligh only really trusted himself, and time and time again he went ashore to superintend the work going on there. As usual he did not mince his words when he found that things were not being done properly, but most of what he said had little effect, and this made him more furious than ever. Among the crew there was a ship's carpenter called Purcell, who was known to be just as hot-tempered and sharp-tongued as the captain himself. Up until now these two kindred spirits had had but little contact with each other, but on the second day ashore on Tasmania a dispute arose when Bligh accused Purcell of slacking by cutting his logs too long. Purcell immediately lost his temper and replied: 'It strikes me you only come ashore for the sake of criticizing people.'

Bligh showed great restraint on this occasion, and simply sent the man back on board and gave him something else to do. But his reasonableness was of no avail, for a few days later Purcell refused to carry out an order to help lift aboard a number of water casks, arguing that as a ship's carpenter he was not required to carry out an ordinary seaman's duties. The irresolute Fryer, who was in charge of the operation, knew of no alternative but to report Purcell to the captain. Despite violent threats from Bligh, Purcell maintained his argument, and his refusal to co-operate resulted in a most compromising situation. Had it been an ordinary sailor the captain could have had him flogged, but a ship's carpenter held the rank of warrant officer and as such, according to the statutes, he could not be flogged. The proper procedure would have been to put him in irons and keep him there until he could be brought to trial in England. But Bligh had no desire whatsoever to continue on a voyage of undeterminate length with a man in irons, any more than he could forego, as the cunning Purcell doubtless realized, the services of his most skilful ship's carpenter. In the end he got over the problem simply by withdrawing the man's rations and forbidding the remainder of the crew, on pain of flogging, from giving him anything either to eat or drink. Purcell, who was by no means a popular figure on board, realized that he was bested and relented.

At one time or another the petty officers on board all felt the lash of Bligh's tongue, since he never hesitated to upbraid any one of them for incompetence or slackness. But there is no record at this juncture of further open disobedience, and to what extent Bligh's general criticism of his crew was justified it is impossible to judge without the support of proper evidence.

By the end of the second week in Tasmania the water supplies were fully topped up, and the galley wood stocks had been replenished by a further thirty tons of logs, plenty for the remaining journey to Tahiti. Contrary to common expectation, there was such a dearth of wild life and fish on and around Tasmania that only a few fresh food meals could be produced during the stay there. On the morning of the 4th September, after Bligh had completed a whole series of position fixes and compass checks, the *Bounty* weighed anchor and continued on her way south east.

Shortly afterwards she was back again on the windy 40th parallel, which is so aptly named 'the roaring forties'. The only significant event during September which is described in any detail was the sudden appearance on the 19th of a group of rocky and uninhabited islands just south of New Zealand. Bligh immediately christened these the Bounty Islands, a name which they have retained ever since. Now, as then, the only living creatures to be seen are the thousands of penguins which by their pungent smell and clamorous squawking effectively warn approaching ships in good time of dangerous navigational obstacles. More important than all this, however, though unfortunately less carefully recorded, was the series of psychological complications developing on board at this time. The basis of the trouble seems to have been that the disciplinary breach back in Adventure Bay was still rankling in Bligh's mind and such was his ill-humour that he could not help badgering his subordinates, particularly at dinner time when, according to custom, the acting officers and petty officers dined by rota at the captain's table. The most unfortunate victim of all, or possibly the most touchy, was the miserable Fryer, who by the end of the month had flatly refused to take his turn at dining with Bligh.

The next victim of Bligh's ill-will was the ship's surgeon, Huggan, who since he ranked as a warrant officer dined regularly at the captain's table. Thanks to Bligh's great concern for the welfare of his crew the doctor had had very little to do so far. But during the Tasmanian halt one of the seamen had been forced to consult Huggan for a 'mild complaint' which was in fact asthma. Huggan immediately bled him, the only result being that shortly afterwards the arm which had been bled became inflamed. By the end of September the unfortunate man, Valentine, was suffering from a high fever and congestion of the lungs. Huggan now adopted popular treatment number two, and applied canthazidal plaster to the chest. What finally caused Bligh to explode was not the amateurishness of the treatment but Huggan's persistence in daily assuring the captain that Valentine's condition was improving. It was not until 6th October, when Valentine was already dying, that one of the petty officers told Bligh the truth. It was too late now to do anything for the unfortunate sailor, who died shortly afterwards, but Bligh considered, quite rightly, that Huggan had been grossly negligent, and he proceeded to tell him so in no uncertain terms. Filled with indignation Huggan now likewise refused to sit at the captain's table or to show himself on deck again. The latter feat would probably have been impossible for him to perform anyway, since following the episode he started drinking more steadily and heavily than ever.

It was inevitable that the tension between Bligh and Fryer, too, should sooner or later develop into a full-scale clash, and sure enough this came shortly afterwards. According to routine Bligh had sent his clerk, Samuel, to Fryer with the ship's account books for the latter's signature. Instead of signing for the months of August and September, however, Fryer coolly sent the clerk back to the captain with a sort of testimonial which he had prepared for himself, requesting first the captain's signature. The testimonial was exceedingly commendatory and emphasized the fact that Fryer 'had done nothing amiss during his time on board'. Many of Bligh's maligners have claimed that Fryer's peculiar course of action arose from his suspicion that the captain had been falsifying the books. It would seem rather, that his excessive eagerness to keep himself in the clear had more to do with his own bad conscience. Bligh was not to be put out by this, however, and sent for Fryer and delivered yet another broadside, accusing him point blank of attempted blackmail. Once again Fryer refused to sign the account books, turned his back on the captain and left.

Bligh did not hesitate for one moment. He immediately called the whole crew up on deck, produced the Naval Articles and read aloud those sections which gave in detail the frightening punishments which could be inflicted for disobedience of orders. Having done this he again confronted Fryer with the account books, and ordered him to sign them or else to present in writing his reasons for refusing. Had Fryer really desired to accuse the captain of breach of duty, here in front of the entire ship's company would have been the best occasion to do so. But he did not; instead he signed the books with alacrity, and without further protest. Bligh stated in the ship's log book that he immediately forgave Fryer once the incident was over, but unfortunately it looks as if Fryer never forgave Bligh, because from that day onwards he scarcely ever addressed his captain again, except in the course of duty, and even then only when it was absolutely necessary.

At this point the *Bounty* was already well south of Tahiti, and ready to swing northwards again towards the island—the broad belt of easterly trade winds, which runs between the equator and the Tropic of Capricorn, making it impossible to come straight in under sail from the west. By this time, despite the fact that the air was becoming daily warmer, the crew were beginning to complain of lethargy, muscular pain and rashes. Huggan staggered up on deck once more, diagnosed scurvy and then proceeded to put himself on the sicklist. But Bligh took this diagnosis as a personal insult. So far as he was concerned scurvy was an anachronism, a disease of the past, the outbreak of which represented criminal negligence on the part of the captain. The idea that it could exist on board his ship was unthinkable. It was quite evident, he argued, that the men were suffering from rheumatism and nettle-rash, and there was an end of it! Nevertheless, to be on the safe side, he prescribed large doses of malt extract, and shortly afterwards he ordered that everyone on board should daily take elixir vitriol, another much commended but highly suspect patent medicine. Two men immediately demurred, Huggan and, inevitably, Purcell. Purcell flatly refused to have anything to do with elixir vitriol, but rapidly changed his mind when Bligh threatened to withdraw his rum ration. Huggan on the other hand preferred to try to cure himself with rum and gin, and passed out shortly afterwards from an overdose of medicine. This was the last straw as far as Bligh was concerned; he lost his patience with Huggan and ordered the confiscation of the still plentiful remains of the surgeon's private cellar. At the same time he gave orders for a general cleaning of Huggan's cabin, an operation which proved to be 'not only troublesome but offensive in the highest degree'.

It was a fairly common occurrence at this time for sickness, indiscipline and general confusion to predominate in the final stages of a long sea voyage, and in the *Bounty's* case there was every good reason for it. She was a small ship, and even though she was undermanned it was still disagreeably cramped on board. Many of the crew were perverse. Bligh's temper was not always of the best, and the outward voyage had already taken far longer than it should have done. Finally, the appalling weather which persisted for practically the whole time had made watch keeping and general duties infinitely more trying than they should have been. So far the iron will of the captain had triumphed in all situations, nor is there any indication that he doubted his capacity to continue in this way. But Bligh, like everyone else on board, must have been feeling the strain of the tension, and it was high time the *Bounty* reached her destination.

CHAPTER III

TAHITI

THE limitations of methods of observation at this time made it difficult to establish a longitudinal position with any degree of accuracy. Bligh was fully aware of this, and now that he was nearing Tahiti he decided to use the natives' own means of approach. He would make a wide swing round to the windward side of the island until the ship was on the proper latitude, which could be fixed more accurately, and then bear straight down on his objective. A convenient landmark to help this operation was the rocky island of Meetu, 1,200 feet high and sixty miles due east of Tahiti.

The *Bounty* reached the required latitude at ten o'clock in the evening on the 25th October, and the helmsman was now given the order to set a due westerly course. If Bligh's calculations were correct then Meetu should be sighted at sunrise the following morning. Needless to say his calculations were correct, and sure enough the jutting rocks appeared as required at the proper time and place in the morning.

Meetu (now known as Meetia or Menetia) had been discovered at the same time as Tahiti 21 years previously by another English naval officer, Samuel Wallis, and Cook, too, had sailed along Meetu's southern side on several occasions. On the other hand, no one had ever bothered to investigate the northern shore, and this alone was sufficient reason for Bligh to do so. It was hardly worth the trouble, however, since this proved to be even steeper and barer than the south side.

The crew, who had very definite ideas about what life on a South Sea island should be like, glowered resentfully at the few natives who were to be glimpsed among the craggy rocks, and then cast longing looks towards the Tahitian horizon in the west. Thanks to Bligh's foresight in confiscating Huggan's private supplies of alcohol two days earlier, the ship's surgeon was now sufficiently sober to appear on deck and carry out, to a certain degree, his duties. Bligh, who was fully aware of what was in the minds of his seamen, and who did not expect that 'the intercourse of my people with the natives should be of a reserved nature', immediately ordered his 'sawbones', as he called Huggan, to examine everybody on board. Huggan carried out his examination suspiciously quickly, and reported that every man, including the scurvy cases, was in the best of health and that it would be impossible for any of them to infect the Tahitians in any way. Whether Huggan's optimism was born of sheer nonchalance or of a complete ignorance of venereal disease it is impossible to say.

Bligh's next step was to post an official notice on the mizzen-mast. This ran as follows:

Rules to be observed by every person on board, or belonging to the *Bounty*, for the better establishing a trade for supplies of provisions, and good intercourse with the natives of the South Seas, wherever the ship may be at.

1. At the Society, or Friendly Islands, no person whatever is to intimate that Captain Cook was killed by Indians, or that he is dead.

2. No person is ever to speak, or give the least hint, that we have come on purpose to get the bread-fruit plant, until I have made my plan known to the chiefs.

3. Every person is to study to gain the goodwill and esteem of the natives; to treat them with all kindness; and not to take from them by violent means anything that they have stolen; and no one is ever to fire but in defence of his life.

4. Every person employed on service is to take care that no arms or implements of any kind under their charges are stolen; the value of such things being lost shall be charged against their wages.

5. No man is to embezzle, or offer to sale, directly or indirectly any part of the king's stores of what nature soever.

6. A proper person or persons will be appointed to regulate trade and barter with the natives, and no officer or other person belonging to the ship, is to trade for any kind of provisions or

curiosities; but if such officer or seaman wishes to purchase any particular thing he is to apply to the provider to do it for him. By this means a regular market will be carried on, and all disputes which otherwise may happen with the natives will be avoided. All boats are to have everything handed out of them at sunset.

Given under my hand on board the *Bounty*
Otaheite, 25th October 1788.
Wm. Bligh.

There is no denying that these regulations were not only sensible but also humanitarian, particularly if they are compared with the attitudes of other explorers in the Americas and Africa at that time.

It was only some thirty miles to Tahiti now, and just before sunset the crew had the satisfaction of seeing the line of the horizon broken by the peaks of the mountains on the Taiar peninsula. Cook, who had visited Tahiti four times in all, had always used Matavai Bay on the north side, regarding this as the best and safest anchorage. Bligh, too, who had anchored in Matavai Bay with Cook in 1771, shared the latter's opinion and it was this bay that he now aimed for.

Early the following morning the *Bounty* entered Matavai Bay and dropped anchor there. It was now more than a year since she had left the naval dockyard in London, and altogether, according to Bligh's scrupulously kept log, she had covered a distance of 27,086 nautical miles. Her average speed had thus been 108 miles in 24 hours, or four and a half knots, a remarkably good speed in view of the impossible weather which they had had to contend with during the greater part of the voyage.

The sight which met the *Bounty's* crew at sunrise that morning must in itself have been ample reward for the past twelve months of toil and discomfort. Of all the beautiful bays in the world there is scarcely one to surpass the little harbour of Matavai. It begins in the west with a great bare rocky rise, which Wallis prosaically christened One Tree Hill, for the simple reason that when Tahiti was discovered in 1767 there was but one solitary tree on the hill. From this point the shore curves round to the northeast for a full three miles, right out to the end of Venus Point. The origin of this name, too, is much more prosaic than one would imagine. Cook named it thus, not on account of the amorous goings-on which took place there, but rather because it was from this point that he had observed the course of the planet Venus in 1769. As is often the case on Tahiti, the shore was covered in rich, coal-black lava sand, over which the white foam of the surf formed ever shifting patterns. Behind the sandy shore was a broad belt of succulent, dark-green breadfruit and coconut palms. But what really gives Matavai Bay its fantastic beauty is not so much the perfectly formed shoreline and unique colour harmonies as the grandiose background of ravines, plateaus and waterfalls which are set off by two mighty peaks rising 7,000 feet against the tropical sky.

But the crew's attention was quickly drawn to something else. At the same moment as the ship swung round Venus Point into the calm water of the bay a whole fleet of outrigger canoes bore down upon her from the shore. The canoes were paddled by muscular, well-built natives who, in the best traditions of Tahitian hospitality, had with them a plentiful supply of the sort of presents which they knew from experience were most appreciated by mariners at the end of a long voyage; fresh coconuts, fresh fruit, plump suckling pigs—and comely young women.

'Peretane? Rima?' shouted the men in the canoe as soon as they were near enough to make themselves heard.

Peretane was the Tahitian's way of pronouncing Britain, while by Rima they meant Spaniards, since the Spanish ship which had visited the island some ten years previously had hailed from Lima. This was all the islanders knew of foreign languages, but it was sufficient at the time.

'Taio peretane' (English friends) shouted Bligh and one or two of the others on board who knew a little Tahitian.

'To amtou taio Parai' (our friend Bligh) cried the natives in delight, and moments later they were swarming aboard. Within ten minutes the main deck was so crowded with laughing, chattering men, women and children that Bligh was unable to make himself heard and the seamen unable to carry out their duties. This invasion came at rather an inopportune moment, however, because no sooner were the Tahitians all on board than the breeze died away entirely, and for a while the *Bounty* drifted helplessly in towards the shore of One Tree Hill. But with his usual resource and determination Bligh succeeded in getting some sort of order aboard and had the anchor dropped and the sails lowered. There is little doubt that in the same firm manner he could have cleared the decks and got the natives back into their canoes again. But he was not anxious to go this far, partly since he did not want to hurt their feelings and partly because he undoubtedly felt that his crew had earned the right to a little relaxation in pleasant company. It was not before sunset that he interrupted them again, and then only to order all the male natives ashore, those of the women who wished, being permitted to spend the night on board.

The next morning Bligh moved the ship a little farther up into the bay to a better anchorage, and no sooner had he done this than the native invasion began again. But even more important than making friends with the crowd was the business of establishing good relations with the influential chieftains in order to ensure their friendship and assistance. Thus, as soon as Chief Poino of Haapape, the small kingdom adjoining Matavai Bay, came aboard Bligh promptly offered him a choice of his selection of adzes and nails. Poino in his turn courteously invited Bligh to attend a banquet of welcome ashore, and in due course, in his full dress uniform with knee breeches, skirted coat and lace ruffles, Bligh landed at Venus Point in a temperature of over ninety in the shade, and was led off to Poino's residence. This simple yet graceful creation consisted of nothing more than a broad leaf-woven roof supported by four corner poles. With all the simplicity and politeness which is characteristic of the Polynesians, Poino rolled out a palmleaf mat on the floor of crushed coral and offered his guest refreshment in the form of cool coconut milk.

Two of Poino's wives who were engaged in dyeing a length of bark cloth immediately stopped what they were doing, produced a mantle of the same material and ceremoniously draped it about the shoulders of the already perspiring English naval officer. The same ladies—Bligh himself assures us that 'they deserve to be called such from their natural and unaffected manners and elegance'—later afforded him the delightful honour of each taking one of his hands and leading him back to the ship's boat.

Despite the fact that Poino had treated him so well Bligh was anxious not to reveal the true purpose of his journey until he had met his old friend Chief Tu and secured his permission.

Bligh, like Cook, believed Tu to be the most powerful and influential chieftain on the island. In point of fact Tu was only
chief of Pare-Arue, an insignificant kingdom on the other side
of One Tree Hill; furthermore he was regarded by the other
island chieftains as an upstart of dubious origins. Through his
importunity, slyness and calculating willingness, however, Tu
had long since won the confidence of visiting English officers
and become their particular favourite. He ought really to have
been the first to have welcomed Bligh back to Tahiti, but unfortunately, had Bligh but known it, he was quite unable to do
so. His little kingdom behind the hill had recently been sacked
by other, more powerful, chieftains, and he was now living as a
fugitive with a relative on the Taiarupu peninsula. Thus it was
not until the third day after the arrival of the *Bounty* that he
showed up at Matavai Bay. Full of hope and thoroughly determined to resume his previous role of senior chieftain, he
ostentatiously sent a messenger to the ship requesting to be
collected in the launch rather than paddling himself out as
Poino had been content to do. Bligh felt in all good faith that
it was of the utmost importance to keep on the right side of
Tu, and he despatched the launch forthwith. Tu, who at this
point was only thirty-five years old was, like most of the Tahitian chieftains, an extremely big man. Bligh, who needless to
say had him measured and duly recorded the results, stated in
the ship's log that he was six feet three inches tall. Apart from
his size, however, it would seem that he was completely lacking
in the masculine qualities of authority, courage, generosity,
good-breeding, quick-wittedness and humour, all of which were
both appreciated and required by the Tahitian hierarchy as a
whole. As recompense, however, Tu's favourite wife, Itia, was
extremely masculine in her manner, and there is little doubt
that the real political ambition rested with her. Bligh himself
admitted that, 'Tu's talents are only fit for a quiet life. I think
that he is one of the most timorous men existing.'

Bligh welcomed 'King' Tu aboard with the traditional Tahitian gesture of nose rubbing, and was subsequently informed, to
his surprise, that Tu had changed his name and was now known
as Teina (name changing was, and still is, a very common
practice in Tahiti, and Tu-Teina has gone down in history under
his third and better known name of Pomare). Bligh now went
through the customary routine of producing his gifts of friend-

ship: a good assortment of iron tools for Teina, and earrings, necklaces and glass pearls for his wife Itia. Itia showed her true character at this juncture by contemptuously dismissing the feminine adornments and demanding equally as many adzes, knives and saws as her husband.

No sooner had these gifts been received than they asked to be allowed to look at Bligh's cabin. Somewhat against his will Bligh complied, and, just as he feared, they at once began to cadge every object they could see that was not a fixture. Still believing that Teina was the most powerful man on the island Bligh felt it best to give them whatever they asked for. Finally the royal couple went up on deck again, begged of everyone in sight everything they liked the look of, and rounded it all off by demanding that the captain fire a salute in their honour. Once again Bligh complied, though the subsequent thunder of the cannons apparently frightened the timid Teina out of his life. The visit was concluded by an elaborate meal at the captain's table, whereupon the greedy chieftain is reputed to have eaten unprecedented quantities of food before he and Itia left with full pomp and ceremony. The last request of this impudent couple was that all the presents that they had acquired during the visit should be stowed in safety on board in case their subjects ashore should try to steal them.

After a few more formal dinners for visiting chieftains from the other side of the island Bligh decided that it would now be politic to pay a return visit to Teina—or rather to his six-year-old son who, according to Teina, was the real sovereign of Tahiti. Nor is this as odd as it might sound. In the reigning Tahitian families the succession takes place nominally upon the birth of the first son, and not, as in the case of European royalty, upon the death of the father or mother. But the fact remained, however, that it was a deliberate lie on Teina's part to claim that his son was the true sovereign of Tahiti.

The return visit began badly, since at the time fixed for Bligh's collection by Teina's men there was no sign of a canoe, and when a messenger did finally show up it was only to report that His Majesty King Teina was frightened and had gone away and hidden himself. It appears that on the previous day a number of iron objects had been purloined from the *Bounty*, and Teina was frightened that Bligh would seize him and hold him as a hostage until the goods were returned. When Bligh finally succeeded in assuring him through the messenger that he would do him no harm, he turned up on board, together with Itia and Poino as moral support. Bligh had the launch manned and got his tricky host off the ship again as quickly as possible. During the subsequent trip in the launch Teina recovered himself and went on to assure Bligh how much he appreciated the English king, the English people and everything else English, especially English adzes, English knives and English nails. Bligh now seized his chance and asked Teina if he had thought perhaps of sending King George some gifts from his own kingdom. Indeed he had; and Teina immediately began to reckon up everything that was made or grew on Tahiti, including breadfruit. Bligh, who had obviously expected this sort of reply, mentioned casually that he felt sure breadfruit shoots would be a greatly appreciated gift. Delighted at the chance of being able to get away with it so cheaply, Teina pointed out enthusiastically that his entire kingdom was full of breadfruit trees—and for once he was not lying.

Teina's reception by his people was somewhat cool, but the tremendous respect that they showed for his six-year-old son tended to confirm Bligh's confidence in the dynasty. He was even more pleased when Teina's frank and good-natured brother Ariipaea succeeded in recovering the stolen equipment from the ship. The visit was concluded with a court concert where three musicians performed on nose flutes, while a fourth accompanied them on a sharkskin drum. Teina was not slow now in taking advantage of his increased prestige to make further demands upon Bligh's generosity. Not satisfied with more tools he now wanted armchairs and a bed, and Bligh noted sarcastically in his log that no better gift than the latter was conceivable for a man of Teina's disposition.

When this visit had been completed Bligh decided that he had established sufficient goodwill and that it was time to begin the business of collecting the shoots. Since there were just as many breadfruit trees in Haapape as there were in Pare, however, he decided, to the vast disappointment of Teina, to remain where he was.

On Sunday the 2nd November—only a week after his arrival—Bligh had a tent erected on Venus Point and detailed off four seamen to help Nelson and Brown with the building of a greenhouse and collecting of breadfruit shoots. He put Fletcher

Christian in charge of the breadfruit patrol, which from now onwards would stay ashore, and sent the young midshipman Peter Heywood to assist him. Gunner Peckover, who spoke better Tahitian than anybody else on board, was given the privilege of opening a store ashore.

Meanwhile Teina had the unhappy feeling that he was beginning to lose some of his status, and early the next morning he set out to remedy this. Part of the *Bounty's* rudder equipment had recently been stolen, and one of the seamen, Alec Smith, had been given twelve lashes for slackness on guard duty. Teina now took advantage of what had happened and appointed himself as tent watchman, a step which he had no right to take since he had no authority whatsoever in Chief Poino's kingdom. At the same time another volunteer appeared. The new Anglophile was a simple fellow of low birth by the name of Hitihiti, who had accompanied Cook on his famous voyage into Antarctic waters fifteen years earlier, and who enjoyed the honour of actually being mentioned by name in Cook's account of the voyage. Hitihiti, who was about thirty years of age, was really a native of Borabora, and it was only by chance that he was in Tahiti at this time. He still remembered various English words and expressions, and this ability alone made him a great success on board. It might be of interest to point out that the humble Hitihiti, who served as a sort of errand boy for Bligh, was for some inexplicable reason elevated to the rank of chief of Haapape in Nordhoff and Hall's well-known novel on the *Bounty* mutiny, and has been permitted to retain the rank in the latest Hollywood film production where Mr. Marlon Brando plays the role of a somewhat ennobled Fletcher Christian.

It can be fairly safely claimed that never in the history of the British fleet has a body of men been given a more delightful duty to perform than that of the *Bounty* breadfruit patrol. Every day they set out on extended tours of the surroundings, and everywhere they went they were met with the same genuine hospitality and friendliness. If they were hot and tired they were welcome to rest in a cool hut where plentiful supplies of fresh fruits and coconut milk awaited them. Charming girls were on hand to give them Tahitian massage whenever they required it. Bright-eyed youngsters vied with each other to carry the shoots, and if they came to a river there was invariably someone big enough and powerful enough to carry them across to the other side. As if all this were not enough there were also their taio friends, or namesakes. One of the principal obligations of a taio friend was to offer his namesake his wife, or wives if he happened to be a chieftain. To refuse such an offer was a serious affront, and here at any rate the *Bounty* men did their utmost to show their appreciation of their taio friends' hospitable custom. Furthermore, in contrast to their married taio friends, the sailors also enjoyed the right to indulge in sexual intercourse with any unmarried girl they chose. Boatswain Morrison observed with satisfaction that:

'Every officer and man in the ship were provided with new friends who none understood the language, yet we found it very easy to converse by signs at which these people are adepts, and some of the women . . . became very intelligent in a short time and soon brought their quondum husbands into a method of discourse by which everything was transacted.'

Every evening when work was over all the inhabitants from around Matavai Bay assembled at Venus Point to divert themselves in company with the crew of the *Bounty*. Bligh has described a typical game on such an occasion in the following manner:

'The women divide into parties of about 30 or 50 Yards apart and perform a kind of recitative accompanied with a stamping of the feet and clapping the hands with many wanton odd motions. A breadfruit is then taken by a person of one party, and being placed on the foot is thrown over to the others. If it is caught that party performs the dance and the others look on, but if it is not caught the party who threw it has the dance in token of the victory, and the ball is thrown by turns from side to side.'

The men apparently wrestled instead of danced and Bligh continues:

'There are only two combatants at a time, and as soon as these have tried their skill two others take the ground. A fair fall like as it is in England is to be thrown on the back, but if

E 65

they fall to the ground anyway the trial for that time is over. They grapple by the hair, legs or any part they can lay hold of, however they have the art of the cross buttock as in Cornwall, but the man who takes the method is generally thrown or obliged to quit it, if the opponent is stronger than himself. The greatest good humour is carried through the whole, and the man that is thrown laughs at his overthrow as much as the other does at his success.

'Another amusement of the men and boys is throwing a light lance at a stump of a plaintain tree about 30 yards distant, and this time they do it with so much skill as generally to strike it. Yet this does not as one would imagine lead to any martial exploit, for we know of no such mode of fighting, any more than with bows and arrows, although they have the use of them likewise for their diversion. The bow is strong and would answer for war, but the arrows are only reeds pointed with wood and not winged.'

Admittedly parts of the crew had to spend the nights on board but no one complained about this. In the first case many of the sailors were ashore during the daytime, drying and patching sails and fetching wood and water, besides which Bligh permitted the Tahitian girls to come aboard at night and stay if they felt so inclined. Another important factor was that, thanks to Peckover's aptitude as a storekeeper-bargainer, the crew enjoyed the advantage of vast daily rations of pork, yams and breadfruit. It should be pointed out here that, in accordance with the regulations which had been issued, the captain con-fiscated all pigs which were privately purchased by members of the crew. He has since been sharply and quite unjustifiably criticized for this, since his sole object in doing so was to con-fine trade to Peckover's store, and thus keep prices down to a reasonable level.

The one person who probably least enjoyed the day-to-day routine was Bligh himself, who in Christian's absence had to keep an eye on everything that went on aboard, and who was also caught up in an unending series of official banquets for the constant stream of visiting chieftains. The fact that these elaborate meals were served in the tiny wardroom on board, which was like a hothouse, must have made them a consider-able strain. The most regular diner of course, was Teina, who never hesitated to leave his self-appointed guard post if there was a meal in the offing. Fully clad in his lieutenant's dress uniform Bligh was equally polite to each and every one of his guests, questioning them carefully at the same time on matters pertaining to harbour conditions, wind, weather, customs and habits.

Bligh, who like the Tahitians, was always in the best of tempers when with them, and revealed from time to time some semblance of humour respecting them. He describes one amusing incident as follows:

'The barber I have with me brought with him from town a tete such as the hair dressers have in their shops to show the different fashions of dressing hair, and it fortunately was formed with regular good features and well coloured, he also dressed the hair with much taste and neatness, and fixing it on a stick he formed a kind of body with cloth, as soon as this was done I ordered it to be brought out, when there was a general shout of "Huheino no Pretanee myty". One half of them really believed it was an English lady and asked if it was my wife, and one woman ran with a basket of breadfruit and a piece of cloth and presented as a present; but they were all delighted with it even when they knew it was not real. Tynah and other chiefs were mad after it, and I was enjoined to bring some English women when I came out again. Some joined noses with it and others kissed it. Tynah said it was, "Myty de timorodee huheine no Pretanee" and asked me, if he went to see them in England, if I would bring him back, in short all the mens ideas about the English women were on that head, and if they were to come they would have the question put to them before they were twelve hours in the country. They have nevertheless a high opinion of England.'

Occasionally Bligh would even become sentimental about the islanders, writing in the log for example:

'On many occasions they show themselves possessed of great sensibility, and if I may judge of their regard from their conduct and expressions they are certainly very much tyed to us. They say frequently to me, "Oee worrow worrow eoah no t'inharro Otaheite", which is, "You have many sincere friends here whose love and regard for you is not from the tongue but from the heart". What people can have language of this kind without having that goodness about them, which one might have conceived could only have been acquired through the means of civilization and society?'

Although it is not known whether the captain himself actually indulged in any amorous pastimes during the stay at Tahiti, it is nevertheless quite certain that he was by no means indifferent to the charms of the local girls. Thus he writes elsewhere in the log that they are: 'handsome, mild in their manners and conversations, possessed of great sensibility, and have sufficient delicacy to make themselves admired and loved.'

Altogether the *Bounty* remained in Tahiti for five months, that is from November 1788 until April 1789. There is no denying that this was a considerable stay, and many people have since wondered why the captain chose to remain there so long. The most common explanation is that the ship arrived at the wrong time of year, so that the crew were obliged to wait several months before they could begin collecting the shoots. This theory, however, is completely false. Breadfruit shoots can be cut on Tahiti at practically any time of the year. Moreover conditions are particularly favourable during the rainy period, which is around the beginning of November and just when the *Bounty* arrived. One or two historians have gone to the trouble of checking this point, but otherwise it has been generally claimed that the delay must have been on account of the time involved in cutting and transplanting the shoots. This claim, too, is just as false. To cut six hundred breadfruit shoots and plant them in tubs is a very simple matter which half a dozen men could manage easily within a week. Another erroneous idea is that the sailors deliberately sabotaged the growth of the shoots in order to remain on Tahiti as long as possible. There is no evidence for this whatever.

A closer examination of the logbook reveals that the shoot collecting began on the 4th November. Two days later Christian and Nelson and their assistants had planted sixty-two shoots in the new greenhouse, and the number of shoots then continued to increase as follows:

7 November		110 shoots collected	
8	,,	168	,,	,,
9	,,	252	,,	,,
10	,,	340	,,	,,
11	,,	401	,,	,,
12	,,	487	,,	,,
13	,,	609	,,	,,
14	,,	719	,,	,,
15	,,	774	,,	,,

In other words Bligh had completed his mission within three weeks of his arrival in Tahiti. Although it is understandable, considering the state of the ship's stores and so forth, that he did not weigh anchor and sail for home immediately, it is nevertheless difficult to understand why he should have remained there almost another twenty weeks. It might be claimed that he was not prepared to set sail until he was quite sure that all the shoots had taken properly, but a month ought to have been sufficient for this, which would have meant that by Christmas the *Bounty* could have been homeward bound again.

What then was the real explanation for this long delay? The answer can be found by taking a closer look into the captain's instructions from the Admiralty. Here Bligh was ordered to return via the Torres Straits and Java, and he was fully aware that between February and March, with the wind blowing steadily from the west, it was virtually impossible to sail a ship through the Torres Straits. When their lordships issued their instructions they assumed that Bligh would reach Tahiti via Cape Horn, and thus arrive a full six months earlier than he in fact did. Arriving in November instead of March, however, presented an entirely different situation, but orders were orders and a further delay of five months until the following April in no way deterred the *Bounty's* captain from his intention of carrying out his orders. Bligh's first plan, after having anchored in Matavai Bay, was perfectly sound. He decided that once the shoots were gathered, planted and thriving, he would refurbish the ship and then set out on a minor voyage of exploration to other island groups in the Pacific, while awaiting the right moment to enter the Torres Straits.

After a good period of shore leave on the 16th November,

Bligh ordered the crew to begin repairing the rigging and sails and to bring aboard extra loads of stone ballast. At the same time more provisions were laid in, mainly salted pork, and also additional fresh water and wood supplies.

Another part of harbour routine which was common to all long-distance voyages was the spreading out and drying in the sun of mouldy ship's biscuits and damp powder. Since the *Bounty* was also anchored several hundred yards off shore, at least half a dozen sailors were more or less permanently engaged in rowing backwards and forwards with visitors and provisions. But despite the generally trying and tiring duties imposed upon them, the crew continued to enjoy their existence, and numerous sketches in the ship's log of gifts, evening entertainments and dancing girls bear witness to this. It was, of course, the breadfruit party who really had the best of everything, even more so when the gathering was finished, and all that was required of them was to sit around and ensure that the shoots flourished in their tubs.

But a man of Bligh's energy and drive was not the person to sit back and let nature take her course, and it was not long before, on one of his inevitable inspection tours, he decided that several of the shoots were withering. He immediately ordered Nelson to replace them, and in due course two hundred and thirty-nine shoots had been pulled up and replaced with fresh ones. Only then was he forced to admit against his will that in fact, 'only one of the plants was found really dead. . . . although while all the others were shooting at the roots they looked so bad that we thought it not advisable to trust them any longer.' At the same time he took another totally unnecessary measure, which was to order the carpenters to make a number of extra tubs. How it was going to be possible to find room for these on board was a matter which could be considered later.

Despite the time and care spent in tending his breadfruit shoots, Bligh nevertheless found time every day to drink with, and play Father Christmas to, the innumerable chieftains. The most shameless cadger among these continued to be Teina, who now possessed such an enormous pile of 'gifts' that he was obliged to ask Bligh to have a large chest made for him to store them in. Bligh subsequently ordered his carpenters to make a chest so large that Teina and Itia could both sleep on the lid in order to ensure the safety of the treasures inside. At the same time, however, Bligh did his best to dispense the benefits of civilization as widely as possible among the islanders. Among other things he had Nelson plant maize, in the sincere hope that in years to come the Tahitians would be able to enjoy the yields of proper crops. But the islanders proved to be just as conservative in their feeding habits as people elsewhere, and even now, nearly two hundred years later, they still have not developed a taste for maize.

Neither did Bligh have much success in encouraging the Tahitians to raise livestock. Convinced that the finest thing he could do for these barbaric folk was to introduce them to the benefits of English beef and milk, Captain Cook had taken a whole farmyard of livestock with him on his last South Seas voyage, and of course Teina had duly acquired three cows and a bull. Bligh had been personally responsible for keeping these animals alive during the voyage, and now naturally enough he was anxious to find out what had become of the breeding animals. But there was no sign of any cattle either in Haapape or Pare-Arue, and in the end Teina was shamefacedly forced to admit that his enemies had grabbed the animals and made off with them. There were now two cows on Moorea, while the third one was on the west side of Tahiti and the bull on the east side. Bligh proceeded to buy back the cow, to which apparently the natives did not attach much value, and somewhat later he succeeded in reuniting her with an understandably impatient and very ferocious bull.

Busy as he was with his shoots and his cattle-raising plans, Bligh scarcely had time to keep a check on the ship's working parties, which were tending to stray further and further from the bay for every day that passed. Consequently it is hardly surprising that after a time discipline should begin to slip. The first serious hitch occurred on the 4th December, and once again the guilty party was the incorrigible trouble-maker Purcell. Hitihiti had asked Bligh for some help with a grindstone which he was making, and when Bligh ordered his senior carpenter to give a hand the latter refused, claiming that the work involved would damage his tools. Bligh contented himself with giving him guardroom arrest for a few days, which was a mild punishment for such an offence, and it was probably this which next day led to another case of 'insolence and disobedience'. This time, to be on the safe side, Bligh punished the offender, Matthew Thompson, with twelve lashes.

Some sort of break in the daily routine was quite evidently needed, and this came rather startlingly on the 5th December. Just before sunset the wind swung round from east to northwest and began to blow straight into the unprotected bay. By seven in the evening the ship was rolling and pitching at her moorings so violently that all the hatches had to be lashed down while the crew were forced to remain on deck. Since it was impossible under the circumstances to get the ship into any sort of shelter, they had no choice but to seek what protection they could on deck and wait for the wind to abate. It continued to blow all night and the next morning dawned stormy and rough.

Things were no better ashore where the stream which ran along Venus Point had swollen, and was now threatening to burst its banks and wash away the improvised greenhouse which contained the precious shoots. While Bligh stood gazing anxiously towards the shore a number of natives suddenly appeared between the palms bearing a small outrigger canoe. Quite undeterred by the fury of the weather they waded out into the surf, launched their boat and began to paddle in the direction of the *Bounty*. Several times it looked as if this mad gesture was going to end in disaster, but to the astonishment of everybody on board the *Bounty* the canoe came safely alongside, and Teina, Itia and another chieftain called Moana clambered aboard carrying fresh coconuts and breadfruit. They embraced Bligh with tears in their eyes, and informed him that they had braved the elements in their canoe to wish him goodbye before the ship was driven ashore and everybody on board drowned. A few hours later, when the worst of the storm was over, Nelson paddled out in another canoe and reported that they had managed to save the greenhouse by digging a channel and diverting the swollen stream in another direction. After yet another wild night the wind finally moved back to its usual quarter, and the inevitable host of taio friends immediately reappeared, paddling and swimming towards the ship.

Neither hull nor rigging had been seriously damaged by the heavy weather, but on the other hand there was a death on board, and this in itself must have affected the morale of the crew to some extent. The casualty, not entirely unexpected, was the drunken ship's surgeon Huggan. He had been needed ashore on the 9th December, but when the officer of the watch went to look for him he found him so helpless that it was obviously a case of something more serious than an ordinary drunken stupor. With the best of intentions he immediately had Huggan moved to the big after-cabin, thinking that a little fresh air might help. But this was fatal, for no sooner was Huggan brought up on deck than he began to fight for breath and subsequently lost consciousness. A short while later he died. Without pretending to any great sorrow Bligh had the dead man buried on Venus Point, and thereupon appointed his reserve, Ledward, as ship's surgeon.

By this time Bligh had questioned the natives sufficiently on the weather conditions to know that these violent north-westerly winds were by no means uncommon during the rainy season between November and April. He therefore decided to move as quickly as possible to the neighbouring island of Moorea, where he knew from his previous visit with Cook that there were a number of well protected bays on the north side. Teina became quite desperate when he heard Bligh's decision. The Moorea people were his worst enemies, and it was they who had carried out the recent devastating attack on his kingdom and caused him to flee for his life. Another reason for his in-dignation was that there were still various highly desirable objects on board which he was planning to acquire in due course. Among other things there were a number of muskets which he had been half promised, and with the assistance of which he hoped to be able to defeat his arch enemies on Moorea, and probably, if the truth were known, make himself absolute monarch of all Tahiti. With selfrighteous anger and grief Teina now deplored the treachery and lack of gratitude of Parai. How could his friend treat him in this way? Did he not realize that he was hazarding the life of both himself and all his crew if he accepted the hospitality of the rascally people of Moorea? Why not move the ship elsewhere around the coast of Tahiti? There were plenty of protected places on the west side and the best of these, of course, was Taaone Bay in Teina's own kingdom.

Bligh was sufficiently moved by Teina's lamentation to promise to look at the bay in question, and he did inspect it on December 13th. The bay amounted to little more than an opening in the reef and was consequently not much safer than Matavai. Between Matavai and Taaone, however, there was another break in the reef which led into a small but deep bay, well sheltered from the westerly winds by a broad point of land. Bligh named this bay Toaroa after a great hump of coral in the entrance channel. Finally he returned to the ship without having made any definite decision, and gave orders for all the necessary work to be carried out as quickly as possible so that the *Bounty* would be ready to leave Matavai before the next westerly gale swept in.

As a further warning that it was time to leave , the sea became exceedingly rough for a few hours on the morning of the 19th. Bligh continued to hesitate between Moorea and Toaroa, but finally decided on the latter after having walked over to it from Matavai. The following description reveals the extraordinary way in which he made this decision :

'All the people of Matavai, I saw, were much concerned at my intention of going to Eimero, and took every opportunity to prejudice me against the people of that island; to which I paid very little attention, as their motive was obvious. Their expressions of friendship and affection for me, however, I could not disregard, as I had no doubt of their being genuine and unaffected; and I felt my unwillingness to leave these kind people so much increased that the next day I sent the master of the launch to re-examine the depth of water between this bay and Toahroah harbour. He returned in the evening and acquainted me that he found a good bottom with not less than sixteen fathoms all the way. The harbour of Toahroah appearing everyway safe I determined to get the ship there as quickly as possible, and I immediately made my intention public which occasioned great rejoicing.'

The best solution of course would have been to pay no more attention to the Admiralty's orders and to sail directly to the West Indies and home via Cape Horn. But such a step was unthinkable for Bligh. Meanwhile there were other alternatives, the soundest of which would have been to make for another group of islands nearer the Torres Straits, for example the Tongas. In this manner it would have been possible to gain valuable experience concerning the care and behaviour of the breadfruit shoots at sea. Furthermore, had any of the shoots died during this stage of the voyage, it would have been an easy matter to replace them on the Tonga Islands. Oddly enough, Bligh does not seem to have considered any such plans, nor apparently had he considered moving *Bounty* into any other bay, even though there were several others on Tahiti which were certainly safer and more desirable than Toaroa. The reason for this was, of course his susceptibility and sentimentality, two weaknesses in the character of William Bligh which have probably never been admitted before.

The move to Toaroa began badly, so badly in fact that anyone who believed in omens would have had good reason for apprehension. Once the seven hundred and forty-four breadfruit shoots were on board and the launch had been loaded with the tent and other camping equipment and sent on its way, the *Bounty* weighed anchor and prepared to move out at 10.30 in the morning. On Bligh's orders the launch should await the ship at the entrance to the bay and then take her in tow to an anchorage which had already been decided upon. But when the *Bounty* came in, the crew of the launch were so slow that the ship had moved on past them before they could get a line aboard. She was now in a very precarious situation and everything depended for the moment on the masthead lookout. To be on the safe side, Bligh had sent none less than Fryer aloft to be on the look out for coral reefs and shallows. But for some inexplicable reason Fryer failed to keep a proper lookout, and before they had time to drop the large bower anchor the *Bounty* was hard aground on the Toaroa shallows. Admittedly there were no leaks as a result of this, but the episode nevertheless tended to increase the confusion on board, and certainly did not improve the captain's already edgy temper. The only way to get the *Bounty* afloat again now was to lay a couple of anchors astern and try to drag her off by means of winches. Bligh, whose patience was by this time near breaking-point, went himself into the boat to lay the bower anchor, while Fryer took charge of the kedge anchor routine. Before the bower anchor was in place, however, Fryer's men had managed to kedge the ship off, but unfortunately they forgot at the same time to pull in the other anchor line, and as a result this got entangled in the reef. The rest of the day was thus spent in retrieving the anchors and untangling the line.

On the following day, on the instigation of Teina, the holy men of the district organized a sort of Te Deum or thanksgiving ritual for Bligh. Without being unjust, it is fair to claim that it was Teina himself who had most reason to be thankful, in so far as his friend Parai's bounteous *Bounty* now lay in Teina's own waters, which meant that he would continue to be assured of the lion's share of the valuables which were still to be cadged from the ship. Bligh for his part was so satisfied with his new anchorage and the reception he had been given that he immediately ordered full-scale Christmas celebrations. For the further entertainment of his guests he organized a gunnery shoot with the ship's cannons and all other available firearms, which, of course, greatly increased Teina's desire to own a number of muskets, even though he still found the noise terrifying.

Generally speaking the routine here was much the same as it had been at Matavai. Fletcher Christian and his party went ashore and erected their tent in the vicinity of the big hut that Teina had had put up as a greenhouse, while Peckover re-established his shop for barter trade nearby. Christian's shore patrols were now, if anything, even more pleasant and leisurely; nor were the seamen on board required to exert themselves overmuch, since by this time the ship was in perfect order and fully ready to put to sea at immediate notice. In view of all this Bligh gave permission for two men to take shore leave each day while he himself went ashore much more frequently.

But this paradisic existence was bad for discipline, and sure enough at four o'clock in the morning, on the 5th January 1789, the watch relief found Midshipman Hayward asleep at his post and the ship's launch missing. As soon as Bligh was informed of this he roused everyone on board and organized a roll call. It subsequently emerged that three men were missing: Bligh's steward William Muspratt, a seaman called John Millward and the marine corporal Charles Churchill. Despite the fact that all the weapons on board were locked in a large chest, the key of which was held by Fryer, the three men had nevertheless contrived to get away with eight muskets. This fact alone was a fair indication that the deserters must have been in league with some of the Tahitian chieftains, who in all probability had promised to hide them in exchange for the weapons.

As has already been pointed out Teina coveted these muskets above everything else, and thus it may well have been he who was behind the flight.

Bligh knew perfectly well that it would be easy for the deserters to remain hidden until the ship had sailed, particularly if they were helped by the natives, and consequently the best thing he could do was to persuade the chieftains to take his side. In circumstances such as these it had been Cook's practice to hold a number of chieftains on board until the men were returned. In principle Bligh had no scruples about adopting Cook's measures, realizing as he did how serious the consequences could be if he were forced to sail without three of his crew. But at the same time he knew that this would not be entirely practical, since if he held some of the chieftains as hostages it was quite possible that the natives would attack and destroy his breadfruit shoots as a reprisal. After careful consideration, therefore, he decided to go ashore himself and persuade some of the chieftains to help him. Once ashore he encountered Moana, Teina and Ariipaea, who had already learned what had happened, and who now informed Bligh that the fugitives had abandoned the launch in Matavai Bay and continued by sail-canoe to Teturoa, a small coral island thirty miles north of Tahiti. Teina was singularly uninterested in the hunt, possibly on account of his inherent timidity, but Moana and Ariipaea declared themselves ready to leave at once for Teturoa. Bligh decided that it would be unnecessary to give them any arms, and advised them, 'to collect around them as friends and then to seize on them and their arms and bind them with chords and show no mercy to them if they made resistance'. Ariipaea and Moana listened and promised to follow the instructions to the letter. Thereupon Bligh put Midshipman Hayward in irons and made the following entry in the log:

'Such neglectfull and worthless petty officers I believe never was in a ship as are in this. No orders for a few hours together are obeyed by them and their conduct in general is so bad that no confidence can be reposed in them.'

To Bligh's intense annoyance the weather was now so bad that the departure of Ariipaea and Moana was delayed a whole week, and they were still away on Teturoa when the next in-

cident occurred on the 17th January. On this particular day
Bligh had ordered that a number of topsails stowed in one of
the stores compartments should be brought out for airing on
deck. Preferring not to depend upon Fryer he took the precaution of examining these sails himself, and was horrified to
find that they were not only mouldy but actually rotten in
parts. There is no greater crime on a sailing vessel than the
neglect of sails, and Bligh immediately flew into another rage,
scribbling furiously in the log; 'If I had any officers to supercede
the master and boatswain, or was capable of doing without
them, considering them as common seamen, they should no
longer occupy their respective stations.'

In view of all this it is perhaps not surprising that Bligh
relied more upon his Tahitian friends than upon his petty
officers where the recovering of the deserters was concerned.
That he did not make the trip to Teturoa himself was due to the
fact that he dared not leave the ship in anybody else's charge
for several days, and not, as is often suggested, because he did
not have the courage. Bligh possessed courage all right, and in
good measure too, as was to emerge when the final act of the
desertion drama was played out on the 22nd January. Neither
Ariipaea nor Moana had yet returned, and Bligh received the
first concrete information on the whereabouts of the deserters
through a Chief Tepahu from the neighbouring easterly kingdom of Tefana. According to Tepahu the three men had just
landed there. Even though night had fallen when Bligh received
this news he did not hesitate for a moment. He had the launch
manned and set out himself to bring the deserters back. Unfortunately the coast of Tefana proved to be surrounded by a
broad, unbroken coral reef so that Bligh and his faithful hench-
man Hitihiti were forced to leave the boat some distance from
Tepahu's village and make the rest of the journey by foot. No
sooner had they landed than they were surrounded by a gang
of natives who were clearly after their clothes and possessions,
but Bligh drew his pistol and quickly dispersed them. By this
time Hitihiti was all in favour of giving up the chase, but Bligh
was determined to go through with it and made straight for
the house where, according to Tepahu, the men were hiding.
Just as he had anticipated, no sooner had he made his presence
known than the three deserters came out and gave themselves

up without any resistance. They later explained why they had given up so easily. Apparently their canoe had capsized just before landing and their muskets and powder had thus been swamped and rendered useless. What might have happened had their weapons still been in good order Bligh evidently never considered, resolved as he was to carry out his duty and retrieve his men. Deciding now that it would be foolish to attempt to navigate the innumerable shallows and coral reefs in the dark Bligh kept watch on his prisoners for the rest of the night and returned with them to the ship the following morning.

The deserters, who were immediately put in irons, insisted that Ariipaea and Moana had persuaded them to change their minds about deserting, and that they had set off again voluntarily to give themselves up on board the *Bounty*. The captain was by no means prepared to accept this story, and needless to say it emerged that they had, in fact, contrived to give Ariipaea and Moana the slip, and were on their way to Moorea or one of the other islands when the canoe capsized and they were forced to seek refuge on Tefana. Muspratt and Millward were both sentenced to twice two dozen lashes, while for some unknown reason Churchill got away with twice a dozen lashes, administered within an interval of twelve days. After pronouncing sentence Bligh addressed the crew on the subject of punishment, and his remarks here explain to some extent the relative mildness of the sentences which the deserters had received. In his view the three seamen were not entirely responsible for their behaviour, and without mincing his words the captain laid a great deal of the blame for the entire affair on the shoulders of his petty officers who, he said, instead of setting a good example to their subordinates were continually slacking and neglecting their duties and responsibilities.

This unfortunate attempt at desertion led indirectly to a mysterious occurrence about which Bligh never actually learned the truth. On the morning of the 6th February it was found that the *Bounty's* anchor hawser had been almost severed at waterlevel. It was evident that this was deliberate mischief on someone's part, presumably in the hope that the ship would break her moorings, drift on to the reef and founder. Bligh had difficulty in believing that any of the inhabitants of Haapape or Pare could have been responsible for such a mean trick, and decided finally that it must have been done on the instigation of a jealous chieftain from another part of the island. We now know, however, thanks to information received by one of the crew on Tahiti after the mutiny, that the guilty party was Teina's youngest brother Vaetua. Vaetua's motive might seem odd in our eyes, but was quite natural from the point of view of the islanders. In this way he hoped to be able to liberate his taio friend Midshipman Hayward, who was still in irons for being caught asleep on watch.

Despite all these distractions and difficulties, Bligh still found time to carry out a series of detailed observations in at least two different fields. In the first place he made a proper chart of Matavai Bay and Toaroa harbour, and took regular sun altitudes in order to establish the exact position of Tahiti. To his annoyance he only found time to calculate the island's position some fifty times, which in his opinion was quite inadequate to make a final and really accurate fix. From these fifty computations, however, he worked out a precise mean latitude and longitude. Secondly he studied with great care the habits and customs of the Tahitians, and his logbook is thick with notes on such varying subjects as their burial rites, methods of child delivery, family terminology, lunar calendars and even pudding recipes. In his spare time he also worked on a Tahitian dictionary. The majority of Bligh's ethnographic notes are of immense value on account of their detail, completeness and accuracy. Apart from all his other qualities Bligh had definite talents in the field of science, and along with Cook he must be regarded as a true pioneer in South Seas research.

At the end of February Bligh made the first preparations for departure by carrying out a series of sorties against cockroaches and rats to protect his precious plants on the way home. As an extra precaution he had mustered as many cats as could be found and let them run loose on board. Finally he put up all the yards, had more tubs made and turned the chicken house on board into an improvised greenhouse. But before he had time to bring the remaining provisions and equipment on board, not to mention all the additional breadfruit shoots, a tremendous tropical deluge began. Bligh was sufficiently experienced to know that, incongruous though it may sound, anyone exposing himself too long to one of these downpours ran the risk of contracting pneumonia. Unwilling to risk the health of his crew so soon before the voyage home was due to begin, he gave orders to stop work until the rain passed. But this pause lasted ten full days, since the rain continued steadily until the middle of March. On the 25th March after a week or more of furious activity the captain issued his sailing orders. These were as follows:

1) All cats ashore immediately.
2) Sailors souvenirs to be limited in quantity to what can be stowed in their ship's chests.
3) The ship to be searched in case of stowaways.

The time had now come to bring aboard the next batch of breadfruit shoots, and once this operation was successfully completed Bligh was able to note down that he had with him a total of over a thousand thriving shoots, that is to say, more than twice the number necessary. Finally those parts of the ship which were not occupied by shoots were filled with pens containing twenty-five pigs and seventeen goats.

The bad weather continued to hinder *Bounty's* departure, and it was not until the 4th April that the breeze was at last suitable for her to leave the harbour at Toaroa. Teina, who together with his wife was permitted to stay on board until the last moment, was inconsolable, chiefly no doubt because he feared that as soon as his protector had sailed off his enemies would move in and relieve him of his collection of treasures. In fact it was more than likely that he would have to pay with his life for his arrogance and deceit during the past months. In final desperation he asked to be allowed to stay on board and return with Bligh to England. Bligh, who during the last few weeks had at last begun to see through Teina, nevertheless felt a certain responsibility for him, and gave him two muskets, two pistols and a thousand shots per weapon. He departed from the *Bounty*, as he had first approached her, in the ship's launch and clutching his final presents in his arms: the two ship's dogs, Venus and Bacchus. Bligh's final laconic entry in the log before leaving Tahiti was as follows: 'At 5 o'clock the boat returned and being hoisted in, we bade farewell to Otaheite, where for 23 weeks we were treated with the greatest kindness and fed with the best meat and finest fruit in the world.'

CHAPTER IV

VOLCANO ON THE HORIZON

DESPITE the fact that the crew of *Bounty* had enjoyed an almost perfect existence on Tahiti no one seems to have had any serious regrets over leaving. Anyone who has been away for a long time, no matter how restless and full of the spirit of adventure he may be, is bound to be pleased at the thought of returning again to family, friends and familiar surroundings. Nor was the *Bounty's* crew any exception to this, a fact which is borne out by the notes of the diligent Boatswain Morrison:

'Everybody seemed in high spirits and began already to talk of home, affixing the length of the passage and counting up their wages. . . .and one would readily have imagined we had just left Jamaica instead of Taheite so far onward did their flattering fancies waft them.'

The distance from Tahiti to the Society Islands is only about one hundred nautical miles, and by the morning of the following day the most easterly of the group, Huahine, appeared over the horizon. Either on the spur of the moment or else in accordance with a preconceived intention, Bligh decided to make a brief halt here in order to call on an old acquaintance. This was no less than Mai, the Rousseauesque 'noble savage' whom Cook had taken with him to England in 1775, and who had made a great stir in court and society circles with his urbane and witty manners. Some years later Cook had returned his savage to the latter's island, and had a house built for him there in the English style, in the hope that in due course he

82

would perhaps open the eyes of his backward fellow natives to the benefits of civilization and make them aware of the dignity and power of the English nation. It was quite understandable that Bligh, who had helped to reinstate Mai on Huahine twelve years previously, should now be curious to find out how he had fared. But as soon as they were close enough to be able to see with a ship's glass that Mai's house had been razed to the ground, it became evident to Bligh that something had gone wrong somewhere. A couple of natives who appeared in a canoe a few hours later confirmed his suspicions. Mai had very soon become thoroughly unpopular with everyone on board through his overbearing behaviour and his indiscriminate use of the firearms which he had brought back. He, along with the two Maoris and the monkey whom he had brought back with him, were long since dead—disposed of in a manner not specified. There was no point in wasting further time there, reflected the captain, and the *Bounty* was on her way again before sunset.

Ever since leaving Tahiti, Bligh had insisted that the ship's routine should be resumed according to normal practice, and he took great care to ensure that proper discipline was maintained. This was not an unreasonable demand, but after the excessive freedom which the crew had enjoyed for a full five months, they found it difficult to readjust themselves to the required routine. Fletcher Christian in particular, who had been his own master entirely during the long stay ashore, now found it extremely trying to be back under the captain's thumb again. To make matters worse, the friendship between these two men had begun to cool even before the *Bounty* had left Tahiti. It is difficult to find a specific reason for this, although it is not entirely improbable that Bligh's change of heart may have been the result of his having, consciously or unconsciously, become jealous of Christian for the much freer and easier existence that the latter had been able to enjoy there. The captain's efforts to re-establish discipline on board were, needless to say, accompanied by constant slanderous tirades in all directions. The crew were 'scoundrels, rascals, hellhounds, beasts and infamous wretches', and time and time again he threatened that before they reached the Torres Straits he would 'kill one half of the people and make the officers jump overboard'. According to one reliable witness, Christian and his companion Stewart were in the end 'so much afraid of Endeavour Straits, as any child is of a rod'.

There was a welcome diversion early in the morning of the 9th April when a waterspout was seen moving across the face of the sea in the direction of the ship. Despite the fact that it approached and passed the *Bounty* very quickly Bligh nevertheless observed it with the utmost attention and has left us a most detailed description of this remarkable phenomenon. He wrote as follows:

'As nearly as I could judge it was about two feet diameter at the upper part and about eight inches at the lower. I had scarce made these remarks when I observed that it was advancing rapidly towards the ship. We immediately altered our course, and took in all the sails except the fore-sail; since after which it passed within ten yards of our stern, making a rustling noise, but without our feeling the least effect from its being so near us. The rate at which it travelled I judged to be about ten miles an hour going towards the west in the direction of the wind. In a quarter of an hour after passing us it dispersed. The connection between the column, which was higher than our mastheads, and the water below, was no otherwise visible than by the sea being disturbed in a circular space of about six yards in diameter, the centre of which, from the whirling of the water round it, formed a hollow; and from the outer parts of the circle the water was thrown up with much force in a spiral direction, and could be traced to the height of fifteen or twenty feet. At this elevation we lost sight of it, and could see nothing of its junction with the column above.'

Two days later, quite unexpectedly, an unusual looking atoll was spotted. The charts showed only open water here and the atoll was thus regarded as a new discovery. All dissatisfaction and boredom was forgotten for the moment as everybody strained their eyes in search of the inevitable native canoes. It was not until the following day, however, that the first canoe showed up, and much to the general disappointment there was not a single female on board. The four men manning the canoe spoke a Polynesian dialect which was closely allied to Tahitian, and it was therefore not difficult for Bligh to establish that his newly-discovered island was called Aitutaki. (Today this island, which is part of the Cook Islands group, still has the same name.) Since there were still plenty of provisions on board—the crew were enjoying daily pork, bananas, yams and bread-fruit—and insomuch that the islanders did not seem particu-larly friendly, the *Bounty* continued on her way the same even-ing.

Nothing outstanding happened after this until the 17th April, when Bligh decided that it was up to him to make a slight detour and check that Cook's recently discovered Niue or Savage Island really was in the position given on the charts. He found, somewhat disappointedly, that the position given was correct, and from there he set course for the Tonga Islands which would be the *Bounty's* last stop before leaving the Pacific. The breadfruit shoots were flourishing, thanks to careful watering by Nelson and Brown, and thus there seemed to be no necessity to go into the Tongas as originally planned, to replace dead shoots. But water supplies were getting low, particularly on account of the large quantities needed to keep the shoots fresh, and once again, thanks to his experience from his voyage with Cook, Bligh knew that there was an excellent spring on an island called Nomuka.

Before the ship reached Nomuka Christian again felt the lash of Bligh's tongue, and on this occasion he lost his patience and replied spiritedly:

'Sir, your abuse is so bad that I cannot do my duty with any pleasure. I have been in hell for weeks with you.'

One can only guess what Bligh's reply may have been.

No sooner had the *Bounty* dropped anchor in one of Nomuka's bays on the 23rd April than she was surrounded by numerous canoes manned by powerfully-built natives. A care-ful inspection of the breadfruit shoots now revealed that one had died and that two or three were somewhat withered. Even though the remaining thousand odd were strong and fresh, Bligh nevertheless could not conceive of reaching Jamaica with fewer plants than he had had on leaving Tahiti, and he there-fore sent Nelson ashore the next morning to collect more fresh shoots. At the same time Peckover resumed his trade with the natives.

On the 25th April it was the turn of Christian and Elphinstone to go on shore duty. Christian was ordered to supervise a force of eleven seamen in filling water casks, while Elphinstone was sent off with a team of four to collect wood. Bligh gave strict orders that all weapons should be left in the boats, forbidding the patrols to use them except in the direst emergency. After the splendid reception that everyone had received in Tahiti, no one thought for a moment that the Tonga natives, who were closely akin to the Tahitians, would be other than kind and cooperative. Had not Cook, after all, christened these the Friendly Islands? It quickly became clear, however, that the Tonga natives were not at all of the same disposition as the Tahitians, for no sooner had the shore patrols landed than they were surrounded by a threatening crowd who did their best not only to steal the sailors' gear but also their clothes. Before the astonished Christian had had time to take any defensive measures, the natives had made off with an adze and an axe. When this loss was subsequently reported to Bligh he replied acidly that the episode obviously could have been avoided if Christian had had the sense to make the natives keep their distance. He then went on to express his surprise that an armed English officer should allow himself to be intimidated by a handful of naked savages. Christian immediately replied:

'The arms are of no use while your orders prevent them from being used.'

This remark must have made some sort of impression upon Bligh, because when the next working party was sent ashore the following day an extra petty officer went with them with orders to remain in the launch and to intervene should the necessity arise. Since this seemed a fairly simple task Bligh sent Fryer, and, of course, Fryer once again contrived to make a fool of himself, insomuch that while he was in the launch a number of natives succeeded in stealing the boat's anchor from right under his nose. It must be admitted, however, that they were very cunning in this operation. While two men splashed in the water around the launch to stir up the bottom a third swam in unobserved and cut the anchor rope. At the same time, so as not to give the game away by letting the rope dangle, a fourth native held on to it under the water while his companion got safely away with the anchor. Fryer, instead of pursuing the thieves, went dutifully back and reported the incident to the captain. What was worse, with his usual stupidity he tried to soothe Bligh by assuring him that the loss was not so great since there were plenty of anchors on board.

'The loss is not very great, sir? By God if it is not great to you it is great to me,' bellowed Bligh.

Furious with rage and frustration, Bligh now ordered that all the chieftains on board should be held as hostages until the anchor was returned. But for once this unpleasant though usually effective means of blackmail was of no avail, since the thieves were from another island and had already returned there in triumph with their loot. When Bligh learned this he hastily put things aright by begging the pardon of the chieftains involved and presenting them all with gifts of atonement. Wood and water supplies were now well topped up, and Bligh decided to get away from the persistent confusion and trouble by sailing the same evening.

Since Nomuka was to be the *Bounty's* last South Seas port of call, everybody on board had taken advantage of the opportunity to dispose of the remainder of their barter goods and acquire in exchange large quantities of coconuts, yams, fruit, live pigs, native clubs and spears and other souvenirs. Besides all these private purchases there was also a great quantity of fresh provisions for general feeding purposes on board. These included a large pile of coconuts which had been heaped up on the halfdeck between the gun mountings. Before going to his cabin at the close of this eventful day, Bligh specially ordered the watchkeepers to keep a careful eye on this pile.

Nevertheless the following morning, when the captain reappeared on deck, the pile looked considerably smaller. He immediately turned to Fryer and said:

'Mr Fryer, don't you think those coconuts are shrunk since last night?'

The unfortunate Fryer was forced to agree that the heap no longer reached the level of the ship's railing, but suggested that perhaps they had been more carefully stacked by the crew so that they should take less room. Bligh, however, was quite convinced that some of the nuts had been stolen. As has already become apparent, the *Bounty's* captain was no supporter of the time-honoured cliché 'speechless with anger'; in fact his verbosity tended to increase with the deterioration of his temper, and on this occasion the fury of his abuse reached an unprecedented level. For some obscure reason he had decided that Fletcher Christian was the guilty party, and he now rushed over to him and bellowed:

'Damn your blood, you have stolen my cocoa nuts!'

'I was dry,' admitted Christian, 'I thought it of no consequence. I took one only, and I am sure no one touched another.'

'You lie you scoundrel, you have stolen one half.'

Christian was deeply hurt and upset.

'Why do you treat me thus, Captain Bligh?' he asked.

'No reply,' screeched Bligh and shook his fist in Christian's face. 'A damned thief, that's what you are.'

Thereupon Bligh questioned all the other petty officers in turn if they had seen any of the crew stealing coconuts. No one had.

'Then you must have had them yourselves,' insisted Bligh viciously.

Still absolutely determined to find the guilty parties, the captain now ordered each man to produce his own private store of nuts. Once all the nuts had been assembled each individual was questioned in detail about the number of coconuts he had purchased for his own personal use and how many of these he had consumed so far.

When it was Christian's turn to be interrogated he replied bitterly:

'I do not know, sir, but I hope you don't think me so mean as to be guilty of stealing yours.'

'Yes you damned hound, I do. You must have stolen them from me or you could give a better account of them,' was Bligh's reply.

Furious and frustrated over not being able to clear the matter up, Bligh had to content himself with heaping more invective upon the miserable crew, and then ordering the petty officers to keep an eye on the men and the men in their turn to keep an eye on the petty officers.

He then called out his clerk, Samuel, and ordered him to stop the rum ration of everybody on board, and to cut the yam ration from one and a half to three-quarters of a pound. Finally, according to an unconfirmed report, he is reputed to have confiscated the entire supply of coconuts.

There can be no denying that Bligh had good reason for being dissatisfied with his incompetent petty officers, and it is fairly safe to claim that the coconut episode was the last straw in a whole series of irritating incidents. Nevertheless it must be admitted that Bligh went altogether too far when he pronounced this extensive collective punishment for such a petty matter. The gentlemen on board, in particular, took a very poor view of the captain's behaviour, and agreed to demonstrate their disapproval by refusing in future Bligh's invitations to dine at his table.

Later the same day there was a further clash between Bligh and Christian. What it was all about this time is not known, but one thing is certain, that shortly afterwards, when Bligh's arch enemy Purcell happened to run into Christian, the latter had tears in his eyes.

'What's the matter, Mr Christian?' asked Purcell.

'Can you ask me and hear what treatment I receive?'

'Do I not receive as bad as you?'

'You have something to protect you,' sighed Christian, referring to Purcell's rank which ensured him against corporal punishment, 'and you can speak again, but if I should speak to him as you do he would probably break me, turn me before the mast, and perhaps flog me; and if he did it would be the death of us both, for I am sure I would take him in my arms, and jump overboard with him.'

'Never mind, it is but a short time longer,' said Purcell consolingly.

Christian seemed not to hear him and went on:

'In going through Endeavour Straits I am sure the ship will be hell. I would rather die ten thousand deaths than bear this treatment. I always do my duty as an officer and a man ought to do, yet I receive this scandalous usage. Flesh and blood cannot bear this treatment.'

At this point Boatswain Cole appeared and did his best to comfort Christian and persuade him to forget what had happened. But Christian, who had apparently been stripped of all his pride, replied simply:

'To be counted a thief is more than I can bear.'

And then to Fletcher Christian's utmost astonishment, shortly afterwards, Bligh sent him an invitation to dinner. Presumably the captain was feeling remorseful over his behaviour, and thought that an invitation of this sort might ease the situation somewhat. But if he really did think that then he did not know Fletcher Christian very well, and obviously had little idea how deeply he had been hurt. It may also be that Bligh, thick-skinned himself, thought that Christian had already forgotten what had happened. But whatever the case may have been Christian declined the invitation. Midshipman Hayward, on the other hand, to whom the invitation was now extended, accepted with alacrity, anxious as he was to re-establish himself in the captain's favour.

Admittedly Bligh conducted himself very badly on this unfortunate day, but it is evident that Christian likewise entirely lost his sense of proportion as a result of what had happened. True, he had been very shabbily treated, but he should nevertheless have realized that Bligh was the victim of his own temper and that his bark was worse than his bite. Furthermore, Christian ought to have derived some comfort from the knowledge that the crew were all on his side. But now, instead of trying to forget the matter, he became gradually more and more preoccupied with it. It would be months before the *Bounty* reached England, and he was convinced that it would not be long before the captain humiliated him again. It was this idea above all that he could not get over, and in the end he became obsessed with the thought of getting out of the whole business by one means or another. Suddenly he hit upon what he felt must be the only real solution. First he systematically destroyed all his letters and records, muttering to himself as he did so that no one was ever going to be allowed to read them. Next he gave away all his souvenirs from Tahiti, and when his companions asked him what exactly he was up to he revealed that it was his intention to build a raft and desert ship under cover of darkness. Sure enough shortly afterwards he built himself a crude raft out of some poles and planks, a contrivance incidentally which was anything but seaworthy. The fact that the sympathies of the rest of the crew were with Fletcher Christian emerges quite clearly here, since although they knew of his plans and preparations no one made any attempt to give him away to the captain.

Despite his almost insane determination and anxiety, however, Christian did not leave the ship as soon as the raft was completed, but resolved to wait until they should pass the next island. This was Tofua, which consisted of little more than the peak of a volcano, the fiery gleam of which vaguely illuminated the night sky. And now suddenly the wind died down, which in its turn made it questionable whether or not the *Bounty* would reach Tofua before dawn.

Fryer had the first watch. A fine rain had been falling when he went on, but by 10 p.m. this had eased off and the cloud was clearing, leaving a pale moon and a quiet sky over a gently heaving sea. In due course Bligh appeared on deck to give his usual final orders before turning in. Fryer seems to have been in a good mood this evening, since he turned politely to the captain and said gently:

'Sir, we have got a fine breeze and a moon coming on, which will be fortunate for us when we come to the coast of New Holland.'

'Yes, Mr. Fryer, so it will,' replied Bligh amiably.

Having delivered his orders Bligh descended through the after hatchway to his cabin. He usually left the door ajar at night so that the duty officers could call him if anything unusual happened, and since it was exceptionally warm on this particular evening he left the cabin door wide open.

At midnight Peckover came up to take over the middle watch. The slight breeze had died almost entirely and they were still some twenty miles from Tofua. As the night wore on Christian became increasingly impatient, and at half past three he gave up all hope and crawled disconsolately into his bunk. His mind was in a state of furious unrest and all his pent-up hatred against Bligh was as close to exploding as was the lava-filled crater of Tofua's volcano.

CHAPTER V

THE DAY OF THE MUTINY

SHORTLY before 4 a.m. Midshipman Stewart, who was in Peck-over's watch, went down to wake Fletcher Christian for the morning watch. The latter had apparently had no sleep whatever and seemed, according to Stewart, 'much out of order'. Stewart, although much younger, was Christian's closest friend on board, and he now did his best to console him and dissuade him from going through with his desperate desertion scheme. In his efforts to pacify his friend Stewart indicated that there were many other and better means of getting his own back, and was imprudent enough to add that there were others on board who had had enough of Bligh's tantrums and that these men were 'ripe for anything'. According to another version of the conversation, Stewart is reputed to have stated flatly:

'When you go, Christian, we are ripe for anything.'

With these words ringing in his ears, Christian went up to take over the watch from the good-natured but phlegmatic Peckover who immediately went below to his bunk. Christian posted the eight men in his watch: one at the helm, one as lookout and the other six standing by for sail duties. Besides these eight men the watch also included two midshipmen, Hayward and Hallet. Even though Hayward was ambitious and dreamed of swift promotion in the Navy, he often grossly neglected his duties, as when for example he had had the night watch at Tahiti and slept while two seamen made their getaway with a ship's boat. Bligh had kept him in irons a whole month for this crime, and consequently he ought to have been on his best behaviour afterwards and done all he could to restore the captain's confidence in him. Apparently he did his best, but he appears to have been chronically somnolent, and on this particular morning he had no sooner reported for duty than he found a deserted spot, curled up and immediately went to sleep. The other midshipman failed to show up at all.

Under normal conditions Christian would have made it his business to rout out Hallet and shake Hayward out of his sleep (unless perhaps everybody on board habitually took their duties lightly when Bligh was not about?). Obsessed as he was with his feelings of hate and revenge, however, Christian's only concern now was how to escape from his present miserable predicament. Standing alone on deck he began to realize the significance of Stewart's casual remarks, and it was not long before he was actually toying with the idea of seizing the ship instead of making an ignominious getaway on his own. Christian knew perfectly well that Midshipmen Hayward and Hallet were among the few on board who would certainly remain loyal to the captain, and their absence at this moment was thus almost a good omen. There were one or two of the petty officers as well who would more than likely take Bligh's side, but the majority of the crew, as Stewart had pointed out, would undoubtedly follow Christian.

The final decision was made abruptly and without consideration for the consequences, and Fletcher Christian's first gesture, once his mind was made up, was melodramatic enough to show how desperate and unbalanced he was on that fateful morning. With all the histrionic zeal of a light opera hero, he hung a heavy lead weight around his neck inside his shirt with the intention of jumping overboard and being dragged down into the depths in the event of the mutiny proving a failure. What course of action he would take if the mutiny were successful he had not stopped to consider.

His next step was to distribute the seamen in his watch throughout the ship so that he could talk to them one at a time without being overheard. It was five o'clock by this time, and while the men cleared the decks and made ready for the morning scrub-down, Christian approached Isaac Martin, the only American on board. Christian's reason for tackling Martin first was in no way connected with the fact that the latter was an American, but rather that he had been flogged on Bligh's orders in Tahiti, and thus could hardly be expected to harbour any feelings of affection or loyalty for his captain. Martin listened carefully to what Christian had to say—and then refused to have anything at all to do with a mutiny! Not even when Christian showed him the lead weight inside his shirt and accused him of being a coward would be consent.

All at once Christian's position had become perilous. The mere act of trying to incite a man to mutiny was a serious offence, and if Martin went to Bligh, Christian would unquestionably finish up on the gallows. Fortunately for Christian, however, Martin's sense of loyalty was not so pronounced as it seemed, since after further discussion he suggested that Christian should try Quintal, one of the most reckless men on board and another victim of Bligh's flogging orders in Tahiti. Quintal agreed enthusiastically to the plan, and immediately offered to go below and recruit further valuable and reliable assistance in the form of the ship's marine corporal, Churchill. Churchill was a cocksure and choleric character who, ever since the unsuccessful desertion attempt in Tahiti (for which he too had been flogged), had hated Bligh. Christian agreed to Quintal's proposal, and sure enough, a few minutes later, Churchill came rushing up accompanied by his boon companion Thompson.

Churchill was wildly excited over the plan, and proceeded to offer Christian a great deal of more or less valuable advice before dashing back to the forecastle to recruit the rest of the off-duty men, while Christian continued to work on his own watch. All whom he now approached fell in with his plan, but he evidently felt that Norman, one of the carpenter's mates, would have misgivings, and consequently did not bother to inform him of what was happening. By a stroke of good fortune, however, Norman's attention was completely occupied at this time by the presence of a shark which was following the ship, and he was therefore apparently quite unconscious of what was going on around him.

A few minutes later Churchill returned to report that all the seamen in the forecastle, including Brown the gardener, were prepared to take part in the mutiny. If the project were to succeed, however, it was vital that the mutineers made a prisoner not only of the captain but also of those petty officers who could be expected to remain loyal to him, and this would be impossible without weapons. All the ship's muskets, pistols and cutlasses were stowed in a large wooden chest which stood on top of the main hatch at the after end of the forecastle, where the five midshipmen, master's mate Elphinstone and Christian had their bunks. The keys to this chest were entrusted to Fryer, but as everyone on board knew, he had handed them to Coleman, the armourer, in order to avoid being troubled every time someone wanted a musket or a cutlass. Christian now went directly to Coleman, woke him and demanded the keys on the pretext that he needed a musket to shoot the shark which was following the ship. This was presumably not the first time that Coleman had been woken up for such a reason, and he handed over the keys without demur.

Anxious lest the master's mate and midshipmen might wake too soon, they crept quietly and cautiously over to the weapons chest. But as they approached it it looked as if the whole scheme were doomed, since there, sound asleep on top of the chest, was the missing midshipman Hallet. Hallet had apparently discovered that during the warm nights it was more agreeable to sleep here than in his bunk. Christian hesitated for a moment, and then roughly roused the sleeping midshipman and asked him what the devil he meant by being asleep when he was supposed to be on watch. Scared out of his wits, Hallet scuttled off without giving any thought in his confusion to the curious fact that the ship's second-in-command had awoken him accompanied by half a dozen men, several of whom belonged to the off-duty watch. Before Elphinstone and the remaining cadets knew what was happening, the mutineers had opened the chest and armed themselves with half a dozen muskets. Thompson now stood guard over the chest while Christian and Churchill hurried off to arm the rest of their accomplices, who were waiting farther forward in the forecastle. Even Isaac Martin had by now changed his mind and accepted a weapon.

Bligh and Fryer both had their cabins next to the main greenhouse cabin, one deck down astern. Yet another deck down, and immediately below them, slept Bligh's most trusted assistant, Peckover and also Ledward the young surgeon, and Samuel the clerk, all of whom Christian had decided he must make prisoners. The only entrance to this part of the ship was directly abaft the main mast, and thus it presented no major tactical problem to gain complete control of the *Bounty*. All that now remained was to render harmless the two midshipmen, Hayward and Hallet, the carpenter's mate Norman and the few other seamen on deck who were not aware of the plan, before they had time to warn Bligh and his followers.

Without wasting any more time in waking the half dozen or more men who were still asleep below decks in their hammocks, the mutineers dashed up through the forecastle hatchway. Three bells in the morning watch had just been rung (in other words it was half past five), and by this time it was almost broad daylight. All in all, on the face of it, things on board appeared to be fairly normal. Three newcomers had arrived on deck: ship's cook Hall and his assistant Muspratt, who were chopping wood for the galley stove, and shortly afterwards Byrne the fiddler, who came up to complain about the din that the woodchoppers were making at this ungodly hour. The off-duty watch, on the other hand, were apparently in no way disturbed by the chopping. Helmsman Ellison and Mills, the lookout, remained unconcerned at their posts, and Norman still only had eyes for the shark. Hayward had admittedly woken from his dormouse slumber, but his attention too was riveted by the presence of the shark escort. Hallet, like Hayward, was either disinterested, or else had not noticed that the majority of the duty watch were nowhere to be seen, and he continued conscientiously to keep an eye on a solitary seaman who was engaged in plucking a number of chickens for the evening meal.

In due course, however, the appearance of a number of seamen with muskets made some sort of impression on Hallet's slow mind, so that he actually confronted one of them:

'What are you about, are you going to exercise already?'

'Yes, I don't know the captain's reason for it, he has ordered to exercise at daylight,' was the terse reply.

By this time Midshipman Hayward had begun to grow somewhat suspicious, and he started to edge away sternwards. At the same instant, however, Christian appeared on the scene with a cutlass in his hand, and put a stop to the play-acting for once and all by brusquely ordering both the young midshipmen to keep their mouths shut and stay where they were. Whereupon he selected two seamen who were to have the honour of accompanying him below decks to arrest the captain. The two men he chose were Churchill the corporal and a sailor named Thomas Burkett, who had been one of the breadfruit group ashore on Tahiti and who was a particular favourite of Christian's. At the same time he ordered Quintal and Sumner, who

had been among the first to join him this morning, to look after
Fryer, while Alex Smith should guard the important stern
hatchway abaft the main mast.

When Christian and his two assistants strode in through the
open cabin door the captain was sleeping serenely and soundly,
respectably and properly clad in nightshirt and nightcap.

'Mr Bligh, you are my prisoner,' said Christian ceremoniously.

Bligh was wide awake in an instant, and immediately began
to bawl for help at the top of his voice. He refused to stop
shouting even when Christian walked over and put the blade of
the cutlass at his throat. Finally, knowing perfectly well that
the likelihood of anyone coming to the assistance of the captain
was minimal, and having no particular desire to murder him,
Christian put aside his cutlass and resolved to truss him up
instead. It now transpired that no one had thought to bring a
rope with them, and it was not until Churchill had bellowed
and cursed at the mainhatch guard for several minutes that a
sounding line was finally thrown down to them.

Meanwhile Sumner and Quintal found themselves with a
much more simple task to perform, since when they woke
Fryer, who was sleeping on top of his seaman's chest, he was so
confused and distracted that he completely forgot his two
pistols lying close at hand. Before he had time to gather his
wits, Churchill had come in and seized the pistols—not apparently, that they would have made much difference, since
according to a subsequent statement by Fryer, neither of the
pistols was loaded. Sumner and Quintal knew that Fryer had
no love for the captain, and consequently treated him quite
reasonably. Fryer now tried, without success, to dissuade the
mutineers from going through with their plan, and finally asked
them what they proposed to do with the captain.

'Damn his eyes, put him into the boat and let the bugger see
if he can live on three-fourths of a pound of yams a day,' was
the savage reply.

On the deck below the captain's cabin Nelson, the botanist,
awoke at once when Bligh began to shout, and rushed up the
ladderway to see what was going on. Sumner and Quintal, who
were at the top of the ladder with Fryer, promptly shoved
Nelson down again, stating flatly that this was a mutiny. At the
same moment Peckover came stumbling out of his cabin, and

when Nelson told him that the ship had been captured his first remark was:

'But we were a long way from land when I came off deck.'

When Nelson patiently explained to him that the ship had not been taken by a hoard of bloodthirsty savages from the Tonga Islands, but by Bligh's second-in-command Fletcher Christian, Peckover immediately started to mount the ladder. But Sumner and Quintal were still there, and, faced with a brace of cutlasses, Peckover was forced to rejoin Nelson, whereupon the pair of them sat down to consider how they might take the ship back again.

While all this was going on, Bligh had been taken up above decks with his hands bound behind his back and stood against the mizzen mast. The first thing he noticed up here was that Ellison, the helmsman, had left his post, and he immediately began to upbraid him for this. Ellison, who had sailed with Bligh before and who had joined the *Bounty* on the recommendation of Duncan Campbell, had so far refused to join the mutineers. Bligh's stream of invective at this moment, however, lost him another supporter, for Ellison flew into a violent rage, armed himself with a cutlass and immediately volunteered personally to stand guard over the captain. Isaac Martin, on the other hand, who had also been detailed off to guard the captain, was by this time beginning to regret having joined the mutineers and, in fact, showed himself so well-disposed towards Bligh that Christian decided it would be safer to replace him.

There was now obviously no point in continuing to shout for help, but Bligh refused to keep quiet. He became if anything more voluble than ever, and cunningly endeavoured, even at this stage, to have them change their minds. attempting to terrify them with the grim punishment which awaited them if they were caught. Christian, recognizing the danger of this kind of talk, finally lost his patience, prodded Bligh in the tummy with his cutlass and roared:

'Mamu, sir! Not a word or death is your portion.'

Bligh must have seen the danger in Christian's eyes at this moment, because he promptly did as he was told and kept quiet for a long time afterwards. There is no doubt at all that at this stage of the mutiny Christian was both nervous and unpredictable, and he is reputed by witnesses from the time to have been

a strange sight with his flowing hair, desperate eyes and wild, ·
distracted expression.

Mamu is a Tahitian expression, and one of the various words
which the crew of the *Bounty* continued to use long after they
had left the island. The psycho-analyst would undoubtedly
interpret Christian's use of this expression in such a critical
situation as a deep-rooted subconscious desire to return to
Tahiti, a conclusion which the rest of us are bound to accept,
irrespective of any psychological considerations.

Christian's original plan, approved by the other mutineers
before they made their *coup*, was to dispose of Bligh and his
closest associates in one of the ship's boats, and then return to
Tahiti and put ashore the remainder of the non-mutineers
(unless, in fact, as Christian quite evidently believed, everyone
on board would then agree to follow him). As far as the
mutineers themselves were concerned, it was their ultimate intention to settle on some isolated and inaccessible South Sea
island where life in general was as agreeable as it had been on
Tahiti.

The individuals on board whom the mutineers generally
detested were, apart from Bligh, the two cadets Hayward and
Hallet and Samuel, the clerk, who had had the thankless job of
acting as assistant purser. Thus the smallest of the ship's boats,
the jolly, should have been adequate for the purpose the
mutineers had in mind. Bligh and the two cadets were already
up on deck, and Christian now sent below for Samuel who had
been confined to his cabin all this time. At the same time
Churchill, who from the beginning had taken a leading part in
the organization of the mutiny, ordered the shark-watcher
Norman and the hen-plucker Muspratt to get to work and
remove the large pile of yams which were stowed in the ship's
jolly.

The equally active Quintal now remembered that there were
still one or two of the crew below decks in the fore ends who
had not yet been woken up. He immediately went down and
roused leading seaman Cole and the ship's carpenter Purcell
with the following words:

'Mr Purcell, you and Mr Cole go on deck and do as you think
proper, for we have mutinied and taken ship, and Mr Christian
has the command. The captain is confined, all resistance will

be in vain, if you attempt it you are a dead man.'

In company with the sailmaker, Lebogue, who had been sleeping by the hatchway ladder, Cole and Purcell came on deck to see if Quintall really were speaking the truth. It soon became evident that he was, and they promptly retreated below decks again to report the news to the half dozen men who, oddly enough, were still in their hammocks. These consisted of quartermasters Simpson and Linkletter, Bligh's steward Smith, able seaman Millward, carpenter's mate McIntosh and boatswain's mate Morrison. By this time the mutineers must have been getting somewhat careless, since all at once Elphinstone, the master's mate, the three midshipmen Young, Stewart and Heywood and the ship's boy Tinkler, contrived to dodge their guards in the forecastle and come up on deck. At this point, Midshipman Young appears to have decided to join the mutineers, apparently (judging from the remarks which followed) on account of the rations which he had been receiving.

'This is a serious affair, Mr Young,' growled Bligh, having realized the attitude of his midshipman.

"Yes, sir, it is a serious matter to be starved. I hope this day to get a belly full!' was Young's bitter reply.

Altogether, on the upper deck and in the forecastle, there were now some fifteen loyal men, the majority of whom were not even being guarded. The mutineers, who were approximately equal in numbers to the loyalists, were admittedly armed, but at the same time were generally unwatchful and undisciplined; there is little doubt that had the loyalists had a determined and resourceful leader they could at this point have crushed the mutiny. The two men who might be expected to have taken the initiative were Elphinstone and Cole. The former apparently made no move whatever, while the latter was so completely devoid of ideas that his only thought was to go and seek the advice of Fryer which, astonishingly enough, the mutineers permitted him to do. Fryer informed him that it was his intention to remain on board and try to retake the ship, and advised him to be patient and await the right moment. Cole seems to have been satisfied with this, and he subsequently returned to the upper deck to rejoin his equally unimaginative companions and see what would happen.

The considered opinion of the boatswain's mate James Morrison, who incidentally was as non-plussed as everyone else, was that:

'the behaviour of the officers on this occasion was dastardly beyond description, none of them ever making the least attempt to rescue the ship, which would have been affected had any attempt been made by one of them, as some of those who were under arms did not know what they were about. . . Their passive obedience to Mr Christian's orders even surprised himself and he said immediately after the boat was gone that something more than fear had possessed them to suffer themselves to be sent away in such a manner without offering to make resistance.'

Meanwhile from below decks Fryer had persistently badgered Christian to be allowed to come on deck, and after refusing him several times Christian finally gave his consent. When Fryer emerged from the hatchway Christian had just picked up a cutlass again, apparently with the intention of putting a stop once and for all to Bligh's persistent efforts to talk the mutineers into giving up their idea. According to Fryer's description, Christian's eyes were burning with hate, and he was brandishing the cutlass threateningly and violently in front of the captain.

'Mr Christian,' cried Fryer rushing forward, 'consider what you are about!'

'Hold your tongue, sir,' shouted Christian in reply, 'I have been in hell for weeks past. You know, Mr Fryer, that Captain Bligh has brought all this on himself!'

Fryer now attempted, as had been his intention ever since he first heard of the mutiny, to play the role of mediator. He appealed to Christian with all the feeling and conviction he could summon:

'You and Mr Bligh's not agreeing is no reason for your taking the ship Mr Christian, you and I have been on friendly terms during the voyage, therefore give me leave to speak. Let Mr Bligh go down to his cabin and I make no doubt that we shall all be friends again in a very short time.'

'Hold your tongue and I'll not hurt you. I have told you that it is too late,' was Christian's terse reply.

Fryer now put forward the extraordinary proposal that Christian should assume command of the *Bounty*, and sail her back to England according to schedule with the captain as prisoner on board, so that ultimately the issue could be settled in the courts. But Christian was not so gullible as to believe that any court would exonerate him from the crime of mutiny, even if it did go so far as to find the captain guilty of breach of duty. This was quite apart from the fact that if he changed his mind now he would immediately have all the mutineers against him. He therefore told Fryer that if this was all he had to say he might as well get below to his cabin again and keep quiet. Not to be outdone, Fryer now suggested that the least the mutineers could do would be to give Bligh and his companions a larger boat to put to sea in, but once more Christian refused to listen to him.

This was the end of Fryer's attempts at mediation, and none of the mutineers seems to have bothered with him any more. Nevertheless he apparently managed to get near enough to whisper to Bligh that it was his intention to remain on board, to retake the ship in due course and then to return and pick up the men who were to be set adrift in the ship's jolly. Bligh, on the other hand, produced another plan which was more in keeping with his spirit. He urged Fryer to strike Christian down without further delay, pointing out that this would spread confusion among the other mutineers and enable the loyal crew to regain the upper hand quickly and effectively. Unfortunately, however, Christian must have heard the captain's advice to his master, because he is reputed to have advanced promptly upon Fryer, threatened him with his cutlass and said:

'Sir, if you advance an inch further, I will run you through,' whereupon Fryer was escorted down to his cabin again, closely guarded.

While these unsuccessful attempts at arbitration were going on around the mizzen mast, a number of the mutineers had succeeded in getting the jolly boat over the side and into the water. Norman, the carpenter, loyal to the captain from the very outset, immediately demonstrated his allegiance by clambering over the side and settling down in the jolly. He had not been there more than a few moments, however, before he was obliged to clamber out again, and very hurriedly at that, since the small boat was so rotten and worm-eaten that it began to sink rapidly. The two midshipmen, Hayward and Hallet, were extremely alarmed by this spectacle, and they at once began to appeal miserably to Christian to give the captain the cutter instead. This in its turn led to violent discussion among the mutineers, some of whom growled wrathfully that 'the jolly boat is too good for them', while others, with menacing gestures in the direction of Bligh, who was still bound to the mast, argued that the safest and easiest way out would be to get rid of him and his companions on the spot. But Christian was still in command, and being just as much opposed to bloodshed on deck as he was to deliberately drowning them by setting them adrift in the jolly, he ordered the cutter to be emptied of its load of yams and coconuts and launched in place of the jolly boat.

Launching the cutter proved to be a much more difficult business, and required the efforts of ten or more men plus various ropes and pulley tackle. Christian thus called on the idle carpenters and boatswains and ordered them to give a hand in the operation. In due course the cutter was bumping and heaving alongside the *Bounty*, and this time, to the astonishment of everyone on board, it was the half-blind fiddler Byrne who was the first over the side.

Anxious to bring the whole disagreeable business to an end as quickly as possible, Christian now ordered Hayward, Hallet and Samuel to collect some provisions and clothing and get down into the boat as fast as they could.

'Why, Mr Christian, what harm did I ever do you that you should be so hard on me? I hope you won't insist upon it,' said Hayward with tears in his eyes.

'I hope not, sir!' enjoined Hallet, equally desperately.

Christian quickly made it evident that he was perfectly serious, and sent the two midshipmen scuttling away below to collect their belongings.

The majority on board had by now had time to consider the whole situation a little more carefully. Christian and his closest associates had long since made their irrevocable decision, since even if they were to lay down their arms and return the ship to the captain at this juncture, they would surely be hanged for mutiny in due course. Meanwhile more than half of the crew who so far, although refusing to join the mutineers, had been but passive onlookers, now had to make their choice. According to the laws on mutiny there was no such thing as neutrality : any man on a ship who did not clearly demonstrate his loyalty to the captain was condemned as a mutineer. The only way now in which Cole and the others could indicate their loyalty was by taking to the cutter with the captain, and this is what they decided to do. But the cutter was only designed to carry ten men, and since the loyalists were now far in excess of this number Christian was once again approached, this time to replace the cutter with the launch which was considerably larger. Even Bligh, who so far seems to have asked no favours of the mutineers, joined in this appeal and finally, ironically enough, it was Purcell, Bligh's arch enemy, who swayed the decision. Dramatically he pointed out to Christian that it would be sheer murder to send them away in such a small boat.

'I have done nothing that I am ashamed or afraid of; I want to see my native country again,' he ended pitifully.

Once more Christian's sense of reason must have prevailed, and knowing perfectly well that Bligh and his companions could not hope to survive in the cutter, he ordered this boat in its turn to be replaced by the launch.

Once the launch was in the water all those who had elected to go with it were sent off to collect their personal belongings before boarding it—all, that is, except Bligh, whom Christian had no intention of letting out of his sight. Instead he sent the captain's steward, Smith, below to collect a pair of trousers and a uniform jacket. At this point, while the loyalists were about their business, Christian sent below for a bottle of rum from Bligh's private store, and the mutineers toasted the success of their project.

In the matter of assembling belongings Samuel, the clerk, seems to have shown the most initiative, since he slipped unnoticed into the captain's cabin and seized both the latter's documents of authority and the ship's logbook. He also prepared to take with him Bligh's personal diaries, his Tahitian dictionary and a number of original drawings for different charts. Unfortunately, however, the guards stopped him, and consequently these valuable papers were lost to posterity. Cole contrived to lay his hands on a compass and Purcell filled a bucket with nails of various sizes. None of the loyalists seems to have been in any hurry, and it is perhaps understandable that the hotheads Churchill and Quintal should have deplored Christian's indolence and done their best to make the loyalists hurry themselves.

It was not until a quarter to eight in the morning that an irresolute and extremely depressed Christian could compose himself sufficiently to get the launch away. The first ones to be ordered off the ship were Hayward, Hallet and Samuel, all of whom were singularly unpopular on board. Next it was the turn of Fryer, who was escorted right up to the ship's side by his guards. At the last moment he turned to Christian and said :

'I will stay with you, if you will give me leave.'

'No sir, go directly into the boat,' replied Christian briskly.

Fryer tried yet again :

'You had better let me stay, Mr Christian, for you'll not know what to do with the ship.'

'We can do very well without you, Mr Fryer,' grated Christian icily.

It is very possible that Fryer, as he later claimed, wanted to stay on board in order subsequently to retake the ship. At the same time, however, it must have been evident to him that this scheme was now out of the question, since the men who were to have helped him had by this time all elected to go with Bligh in the launch. Bligh must have been equally as unrealistic about the matter as Fryer, or else he simply did not want to have him in the boat at all, because at this point, to everyone's surprise, he turned to the master and ordered him point blank to remain on board. This was more than Christian could stand, and he brandished his cutlass again and roared at Fryer :

'By God, sir, go into the boat or I will run you through !'

Under the circumstances Fryer seems to have had no choice, but even so he contrived to persuade Christian before making his final exit to be allowed to take with him his young brother-in-law Tinkler, and also to collect various personal belongings.

The remaining men from abaft, Peckover, Nelson and Ledward, had been brought up on deck at the same time as Fryer, but unlike the others no one made any attempt to force them aboard the launch, and they were given complete freedom of choice. As Christian had anticipated, however, these three were loyal to the captain, even though somewhat confused and unsure of themselves. About half a dozen other men were already in the launch by this time, including, oddly enough, the

American Isaac Martin and also Lamb, who at the outset had been on the side of the mutineers and had actually armed himself on their behalf with a musket. When Churchill caught sight of Martin, he immediately accused him of treachery and ordered him at gun point to get back aboard the *Bounty* again, but allowed Lamb to stay where he was. At the same time the watchful Quintal noticed that Purcell was quite casually preparing to take his large chest of tools with him, and he shouted warningly:

'Damn them, if we let them have those things they will build a vessel in a month.'

Christian did nothing whatever about this, while Purcell stubborn as usual, persisted in his intention and finally, despite the furious opposition of Churchill, clambered down into the waiting launch accompanied by his precious toolchest.

By this time the ship's boat was beginning to get very low in the water, but still the loyalists continued to climb down into her. In the end Bligh, who was to be the last man on board, called anxiously:

'You can't all go in the boat my lads, don't overload her, some of you must stay in the ship. Never fear, my lads, I'll do you justice if ever I reach England!'

Christian was now becoming alarmed that all the properly trained warrant and petty officers were apparently preparing to desert him, and he subsequently ordered Norman, the ship's carpenter, and Coleman, the armourer to remain on board. A further inspection of the men in the launch revealed that McIntosh, a carpenter's mate, also planned to leave the ship, and he, too, was ordered back on board. Purcell, on the other hand, skilled craftsman though he was, was permitted to remain in the launch, possibly because Christian realized how much he and Bligh detested each other. By general request the half-blind fiddler Byrne was also detained, but there was no difficulty over this as he was still sitting quietly in the cutter, unaware that the loyalists were now boarding the launch.

Among the remainder who were held against their will were the two midshipmen George Stewart and Peter Heywood. Despite the fact that Stewart was Christian's closest friend on board, his home, parents and career still meant more to him, so that he had resolved at an early stage of the proceedings to remain loyal to the captain, come what may.

Heywood, however, was less resolute than his young colleague. The problem as far as he was concerned was whether or not the occupants of the open boat were likely to survive in the tremendous wastes of the Pacific, and for this reason he was delaying his decision until the last moment. Now that Christian was making his selection of useful crew, however, Churchill went over to Heywood who was standing at the rail and said:

'What is you going to do Mr Heywood?'

Heywood replied cautiously that Churchill was quite wrong if he thought that he was on the side of the mutineers, and then added with naive straightforwardness that it was nevertheless his intention to stay on board the *Bounty* where he felt the chances of survival were better. As he said this, Stewart happened to be passing on his way below to collect his gear. He heard Heywood's remarks and turned to him saying:

'Peter, don't think of it; for if you stay, you'll incur an equal portion of guilt with the mutineers, though you have no hand in the mutiny. Come down to the berth with me, let us get two or three necessaries, and go to the launch with the captain.'

It is evident that Churchill had taken it for granted from the very beginning of the mutiny that Stewart and Heywood would be on the side of their friend Christian, and he now said reproachfully:

'Why, Mr Stewart, I thought you had been a man of more spirit.'

Stewart replied that he knew perfectly well what Churchill meant, but that he had absolutely no intention of bringing disgrace upon himself just for the sake of getting his own back on Bligh, whereupon he strode resolutely away towards the after hatchway. Stewart's firm attitude obviously gave Heywood something to think about, and after a moment's hesitation he followed his companion's example. But on account of their knowledge of navigation these two young men would be of considerable value to the diminished crew of the *Bounty*, and it did not take Churchill more than a few moments' reflection before he decided to keep them on board whether they liked it or not. He therefore ordered Thompson, who was still guarding the weapons chest, to keep an eye on the after hatch and prevent the two midshipmen from coming up again.

When they were duly informed of Churchill's decision and refused permission to show themselves on deck again Stewart, who unlike Heywood fully realized the gravity of their situation shouted up to Churchill:

'If you won't let us go I desire you'll inform the captain that we are detained by force!'

'Aye aye,' retorted Churchill ironically, 'I'll take care of that'—obviously without the least intention of doing anything of the sort.

One other man on board who shared Heywood's opinion that the chances of survival in the open boat were negligible was the boatswain, James Morrison. When he informed Fryer of his intention to remain on board the latter encouraged him to do so, pointing out that he might later be able to muster enough supporters to retake the ship. Despite Fryer's encouragement, however, his conscience still worried him to such an extent that he turned to Cole and told him what he proposed to do. Cole merely shook him by the hand and wished him luck, an act which apparently reassured him and helped to convince him that he was doing the right thing.

Now at last the sheep were separated from the goats, seventeen men waited in the overloaded launch, and the time had come for William Bligh to make his departure from the scene.

Christian is reputed to have been deeply moved when he now addressed his erstwhile commander:

'Come, Captain Bligh, your officers and men are now in the boat and you must go with them. If you attempt to make the least resistance you will instantly be put to death.'

At this point Bligh seems to have lost some of his composure, because quite unexpectedly he appealed pathetically to Christian.

'I'll pawn my honour, I'll give my bond, Mr Christian, never to think of this if you'll desist. Consider, I have a wife and four children in England, and you have danced my children upon your knee!'

But Christian remained resolute:

'No, Captain Bligh, if you had any honour, things had not come to this, and if you had any regards for your wife and family, you should have thought on them before and not behaved so much like a villain.'

For the moment it looked as though Bligh would continue to argue the point, but he was brusquely interrupted by Christian. Boatswain Cole now attempted to talk Christian round. The latter confided to Stewart subsequently that at this juncture he had begun to regret deeply his actions, although he had realized that it was too late to change his mind. He therefore replied to Cole regretfully:

'It is too late. I have been in hell this fortnight past and I am determined to suffer it no longer. You know, Mr Cole, that Captain Bligh has treated me like a dog all the voyage.'

'I know it very well, Mr Christian,' said Cole, 'we all know it, but drop it, for God's sake.'

Bligh now humiliated himself even more by saying almost desperately:

'Can there be no other method taken?'

Churchill, who by this time was beginning to grow uneasy over Christian's obvious uncertainty, broke in brusquely, saying:

'No this is the best and only method.'

His words were followed by a roar of assent from the rest of the mutineers, and this expression of common feeling must have convinced Bligh that there was no point in further discussion, because as soon as his hands were untied he climbed down into the waiting boat without another word. Still deeply worried by his bad conscience Christian now hurriedly handed down his own sextant and nautical tables to the captain.

'There, Captain Bligh, this is sufficient for every purpose. You know the sextant to be a good one.'

In the same instant Bligh's steward Smith dashed forward, and before anyone could prevent him he had leaped down into the boat to join his lord and master.

With nineteen men on board the launch now had scarcely more than eight inches of freeboard, and it was on this account that Fletcher Christian has many times been accused of having deliberately sent Bligh and his companions to a certain death. But this is not true. In the first place the island of Kotu was so close by that it could be seen from *Bounty's* mast-top, in the second place there was practically no wind and the sea was mirror calm, while in the third place, improbable as it may sound, Christian had offered to tow the launch as far as Kotu.

Bligh apparently accepted Christian's unexpected offer of a tow, and once a line had been made fast the launch was allowed to run out astern of the *Bounty*. Shortly afterwards Christian sent down further supplies of pork, bread and water to keep the loyalists going during their first few days ashore. In order to make room for these additional provisions, Bligh gave strict orders for all the hammocks which had been so optimistically brought on board to be dumped over the side and, encouraged by Christian's obvious generosity, he now went so far as to ask for a few muskets.

Despite the violent protests of the mutineers, Christian went half way to meet Bligh in this matter, and sent down four cutlasses. Meanwhile the men on board the *Bounty* jeered and shouted mockingly:

'What use have you for firearms on the Friendly Islands where you have so many friends?'

In the middle of this uproar Coleman, the armourer, was heard to shout to the loyalists that he would be grateful if someone would contact Mr Green in Greenwich, if they reached London, and inform him of what had happened. Peckover was distressed about having no shirt, and one of the mutineers went below to fetch one for him. Churchill, however, demanded that in return for the shirt Peckover should hand back Midshipman Heywood's pocket watch which the former had borrowed sometime ago, and despite Peckover's reluctance to part with the timepiece the exchange was finally made. The *Bounty* men now began to cheer for Tahiti, with the exception, that is, of the two ship's carpenters Norman and McIntosh and the half-blind fiddler Byrne, all of whom loudly protested their innocence and deplored being kept on board the *Bounty* against their will.

By degrees, however, the enthusiasm of the mutineers became transformed into a feeling of violence directed at the captain in the launch. Insult upon insult was hurled over the stern and, inevitably, the moment came when someone shouted:

'Blow the bugger's brains out.'

The next instant a shot was fired 'for fun' over the heads of the defenceless men in the small boat. It now became evident to Bligh that the privilege of the tow was not worth the risk of their proximity to the ship, and he therefore gave orders to cast loose. It was now eight o'clock, three hours since the mutiny had begun, and still there was no sign of a morning breeze. In view of the situation the loyalists decided to take to the oars, which was by no means an easy business, loaded down as the ship's boat was. They pulled well away from the *Bounty* as quickly as possible, careful to keep dead astern of her, knowing as they did that the mutineers might easily decide to turn the ship's cannon on them, and that as long as they remained in line astern they were safe.

On board the *Bounty* Fletcher Christian stood motionless at the rail, gazing out after the receding launch. One of his remarks from this time has been recorded. Speaking to someone who was standing beside him he said that he would 'readily sacrifice my own life if things could be returned to normal and the persons on the launch all safe in the ship again'. To someone else he admitted that his heart practically failed him when Bligh mentioned his wife and children, adding dramatically that he would willingly have jumped overboard if he had thought that such an action would change the course of events.

Thanks to the fact that Bligh continued to keep his logbook after leaving his ship, we know today what he felt and thought as the launch drew away:

'I had scarcely got a furlong on my way when I began to reflect on the vicissitudes of human affairs; but in the midst of all I felt an inward happiness which prevented any depression of my spirits, conscious of my own integrity and anxious solicitude for the good of the Service I was on. . . .What man's situation could be so peculiarly flattering as mine twelve hours before? I had a ship in the most perfect order and well stored with every necessary both for service and health; by early attention to those particulars I had acted against the power of Chance in case I should not get through Endeavour Straights as well as against any accident that might befall me in them, and to add to this I had very successfully got my plants in the most flourishing and fine order, so that upon the whole the voyage was two thirds completed and the remaining part no way doubtful.'

Bligh was particularly preoccupied with the actual cause of the mutiny, and his conclusions were as follows:

'I can only conjecture that they have ideally assured themselves of a more happy life among the Otahetians than they could possibly have in England, which joined to some female connections has most likely been the leading cause of the whole business. The chiefs have acquired such a liking to our people that they have rather encouraged their stay among them than otherwise, and even made promises of large possessions. Under these and many other attendant circumstances equally desirable it is therefore not to be wondered at tho' not possible to be foreseen, that a set of sailors, led by officers, and void of connections, or if they have any, not possessed of natural feelings sufficient to wish themselves never to be separated from them, should be governed by such powerful inducements but equal to this, what a temptation it is to such wretches when they find it in their power, however illegally it can be got at, to fix themselves in the midst of plenty in the finest island in the world where they need not labour and where the alurements of disipation are more than equal to anything that can be conceived.'

Bligh maintained this attitude for the rest of his life, and succeeded furthermore on his return to England in convincing everyone there that Christian and his accomplices had carefully prepared the mutiny beforehand, and had carried it out solely with a view to returning to Tahiti. But it must surely be evident from what has been stated in this chapter that in fact Christian acted on an impulse, and that few, if any, mutinies in the British navy have ever been so badly organized and carried out. One possible explanation for Bligh's conclusion that the mutiny had been planned in secret beforehand is that, with his exaggerated sense of order and system, it was inconceivable that anyone could act so impulsively and capriciously as Fletcher Christian had done.

But apart from Christian's hysterical behaviour, there was another more deep-seated reason behind the mutiny on the *Bounty*; the intense resentment of the entire crew over the iron discipline and the constant stream of invective which they had had to put up with after leaving Tahiti for the Tonga Islands. They seem to have been particularly incensed over the collective punishment which the captain had handed out on the 27th April following the absurd coconuts controversy, and incongruous though it may seem there is good reason to believe that this small incident in itself was an important factor in the actual development of the mutiny.

In conclusion, remembering that this was 1789, and that a

similar pattern of events was developing on a larger scale elsewhere, it might be interesting briefly to review the mystery in
its historical and social perspective. It will thus be observed
that each one of the fourteen sailors who had the dangerous
and arduous deck duties on board took part in the mutiny. On
the other hand, those who remained loyal to king and captain
were nearly all in positions of authority (the only important
exceptions being Christian and Young). Thus the mutiny on the
Bounty can be interpreted almost as a class struggle; a revolt
of the oppressed, neglected, poverty-stricken and homeless seamen against a privileged and overbearing gentleman-class, the
chief representative of which in their eyes was Captain Bligh.
Had not the leader of the mutiny himself been a gentleman it is
more than likely that the latent hatred which existed among
the wretched seaman-class for their superiors at this time would
have resulted in a bloody massacre rather than the astonishingly quiet and courteous affair that the mutiny in fact was.

CHAPTER VI

IN SEARCH OF A HOME

ONCE the launch was out of sight Christian pulled himself together, and ordered his twenty-four men to assemble on the upper deck. During the course of the mutiny a number of the crew, who had hitherto been little more than anonymous figures on board, emerged as individuals with distinct person-alities and characters. These men, whose behaviour and attitudes were to play an increasingly important role in the weeks and months to come, can be divided into two groups, first those who had taken an active part in the mutiny:

Midshipman Edward Young
Marine corporal Charles Churchill
Gunner's mate John Mills
Gardener William Brown
Seaman and cooper Henry Hillbrant
Seaman Matthew Quintal
Seaman Matthew Thompson
Seaman Isaac Martin
Seaman Alexander Smith
Seaman Thomas Ellison
Seaman John Sumner
Seaman John Millward
Seaman William Mickey
Seaman William Muspratt
Seaman John Williams
Seaman Richard Skinner
Seaman Thomas Burkett

The second group consisted of the seven loyalists who had refused to have any part in the mutiny, but who had nevertheless been forced to remain on board. These were:

Midshipman George Stewart
Midshipman Peter Heywood
Boatswain's mate James Morrison
Armourer Joseph Coleman
Carpenter's mate Charles Norman
Carpenter's mate Thomas McIntosh
Seaman Michael Byrne

Having assembled his men, Christian asked them to elect a leader, pointing out that if they so desired he was willing to hand over the command to someone else. It is very possible that by this time Christian would have been only too pleased to hand over the burden of responsibility to another, but on the other hand, knowing as he did that it was now too late to renounce the cause, he may well have taken this step in order to assert his position once and for all, and to indicate to people like Churchill that he was the leader by common assent. Thus, as Christian probably anticipated, no one came forward, and he was unanimously elected captain of the *Bounty*.

His first move now was to split the crew into two watches, one of which he put under the command of Midshipman Stewart. A number of men immediately protested, complaining that it was unfair to make a loyalist virtually second-in-command on board, and that if it had to be one of the midshipmen then they preferred the more popular Heywood. But Christian was adamant, orders were made to be obeyed, and so long as he was captain they would be. Next, chiefly with a view to demonstrating his position, Christian moved into Bligh's cabin, and gave orders for the breadfruit shoots to be thrown overboard. Finally he gathered up all the personal belongings left by the men in the launch, and distributed them by lots among the mutineers.

The next problem for Christian and his men was to decide where to go. Their original, hastily resolved plan had been to make for Tahiti after the mutiny, and put ashore the loyalists who had been forced against their will to remain on board, and then to seek an isolated island where they could settle down without risk of being discovered. Upon further consideration, however, they decided that the loyalists with them were all skilled and capable men, and that consequently they would be a valuable asset to the new colony. Thus, without even bothering to consult the unfortunate loyalists, they decided not to return to Tahiti but start searching instead for a suitable island home.

In an account of one of Cook's voyages, in the ship's library, Christian had found a short description of a small rocky island called Tupuai, some three hundred nautical miles south of Tahiti. Cook had discovered this island on his third South Seas voyage in 1777. Neither Cook nor any of his companions had gone ashore there but a number of natives had come out to the ship by canoe, and apparently both in customs and language these were closely akin to the Tahitians. Christian had therefore every reason to believe that he and his men would be just as well received here as they had been on Tahiti. Tupuai was situated on the 23rd parallel of latitude, which meant that the climate would be pleasantly cool compared with Tahiti and yet not too cold to prevent the cultivation of tropical vegetation and fruit. He now made his findings known to the crew, suggested that the island might well suit their purposes, and again put the matter to the vote. The mutineers agreed promptly and unanimously, evidently without fully realizing that Tupuai would thus be the island where they would settle down for the rest of their lives, and the *Bounty* was duly swung round on a southerly course in the general direction of Tupuai.

According to Boatswain Morrison, he and the other loyalists on board were constantly making new plans for retaking the ship, but these were foiled time and time again by the watchful mutineers. There is doubtless a good deal of truth in this claim since Churchill in particular kept constant watch on the weapons chest and slept on the lid of it every night. But the loyalists must nevertheless have had plenty of opportunity to meet in secret and lay their plans, their movements being completely unrestricted on board. Consequently one is forced to assume that they were, in fact, quite content with their lot and on the best of terms with the mutineers, a fact which is verified by Midshipman Stewart's obvious willingness to cooperate in the general routine on board. The only person on the ship who was not content seems to have been Fletcher Christian who was becoming steadily more melancholy and dejected. Time and time again, according to witnesses who survived the adventure, he was found in his cabin with his head in his arms, not bothering even to look up when anyone entered or addressed him. But these depressions were only short-lived, and otherwise he carried out his duties and disciplined his crew with a degree of thoroughness and severity which Bligh himself would surely have approved of had he still been on board.

Shortly before arriving at Tupuai, Christian ordered his men to make themselves a simple uniform from sail cloth, clearly with the intention of instilling some sort of respect in the natives when they reached the island. This may seem slightly absurd but it should be remembered that in those days the only ranks who wore uniforms in the British fleet were officers and marines. As no other ship had stopped at Tupuai since Cook's brief visit there eleven years previously, the natives could hardly be expected to appreciate what exalted creatures uniformed English mariners were when the *Bounty* came gliding in to anchor at Tupuai on the 28th May after a month's sailing. From the outset the Tupuai islanders were extremely suspicious of the visitors, and when Stewart began to sound the only break that existed in the coral reef surrounding the island, a crowd of armed warriors immediately set out in a large outrigger canoe to see what he was about. They did not like what they saw, and in the naive belief that they had the upper hand on account of their superior numbers they prepared to board the cutter. Alarmed and surprised by this hostile behaviour, Stewart and his companions immediately opened fire on the natives with the two pistols they had with them. Despite the fact that one pistol refused to function properly, while the other was inaccurate and shot wide of its mark, the attackers were nevertheless extremely frightened by the noise and made off in a hurry.

On the following morning, when the *Bounty* dropped anchor in the lagoon inside the coral reef, it seemed that the natives had decided that uniformed sailors were after all something to be respected, because for the rest of the day they kept well away. Finally, after holding council all night, they apparently resolved to sue for peace for they sent aboard a very venerable old gentleman carrying a banana branch, which is the Polynesian equivalent to our olive branch or white flag. Apart from the fact that this ancient messenger of peace was scared out of his wits by the various animals on board, the negotiations were carried through without a hitch, and he subsequently paddled ashore again, well content with the variety of valuable gifts which the mutineers had given him. Shortly afterwards another canoe left the shore of the lagoon, and as it approached the *Bounty's* crew were delighted to see that it contained no less than eighteen girls, 'all young and handsome, having fine long hair which reached their waists in waving ringlets'. The girls swarmed aboard just as willingly and happily as their Tahitian kinsfolk had done, and were received by the waiting sailors 'with civility', as Boatswain Morrison so discreetly put it. Fortunately, however, one or two of the mutineers still found time to keep an eye on the next group of natives who were approaching, and the nearer these came the less the sailors liked what they saw. There were several canoes this time, containing some fifty or more men; powerful athletic looking fellows who despite their guile were unable successfully to conceal the large numbers of spears and slings which they had with them. Christian now realized that the messenger of peace had been no more than a spy on board and that the girls had been sent merely to divert the attention of the sailors from the warlike preparations which were going on ashore. Without a moment's delay he cleared the females off the ship, armed his men and posted them around the railings. The warriors, realizing that their plot had been detected, immediately cut the *Bounty's* anchor rope and began their attack. It was obvious to Christian by this time, reluctant though he may have been, that there was nothing for it but to teach these islanders a proper lesson, and he promptly ordered Mills to fire a four-pounder cannon ball in the midst of the canoes. The crash of the explosion and the tremendous force of the ball terrified the natives and they fled in confusion, closely followed by the ship's boat manned by armed mutineers who shot several of them down by musket fire. As a result of this rather sanguinary action the lagoon was afterwards known as Bloody Bay.

The mutineers' first attempt at colonization could scarcely have begun more disastrously. Yet first encounters between South Seas natives and Europeans had many times been similar to this, without seriously affecting subsequent relationships. Even on Tahiti itself the original discoverer of the island,

Wallis, had in the beginning been attacked and forced to defend himself with firearms. As a rule, however, the natives would forget such incidents astonishingly quickly, and often became the faithful friends of their victors even after the most bloody and devastating defeats. Thus for a man who knew the South Seas and the ways of the natives as well as Christian, it was by no means unreasonable to hope that he and his men could shortly win the friendship of the Tupuai islanders. With this in view, as soon as it became apparent that the natives had fled temporarily to the hilly district in the centre of the island, Christian proceeded to demonstrate their peaceful intentions by making extended trips ashore and leaving tools, nails, glass pearls and other gifts of atonement in every hut they came upon.

These diplomatic missions also enabled Christian to examine the island more closely, and the more he saw of it the better he liked it. The hills in the centre were only a few hundred feet high, and there were numerous broad plains. Judging by the profusion of cultivated fields and plantations the soil was very fertile. Here and there crystal streams bubbled down towards the sea, so that there was obviously no fresh water problem. Another important factor was that the island was small and difficult to locate, and that Bloody Bay with its one entrance through the coral reef was the only possible anchorage place, consequently it was most improbable that any passing ship would be likely to put in there. If the *Bounty* were stripped of everything of value on board and the hull then burned no one would ever discover their hiding place.

The one thing that did disturb Christian somewhat was the lack of any sign of livestock on the island. This can only have implied that they simply did not exist on Tupuai, a fact borne out by the fear of the erstwhile peace messenger when he had caught sight of the ship's pigs and goats. In view of all this Christian proposed to his companions that before settling down for good on the island they should return to Tahiti and acquire a good supply of livestock there. The mutineers, who had no desire whatever to become total vegetarians, had another good reason for wanting to revisit Tahiti first. It had become fairly evident to one and all that the Tupuain women were unlikely to be as affectionate and accommodating as their Tahitian counterparts and, in fact, several of the crew made it quite clear that as far as they were concerned the acquiring of womenfolk on Tahiti was far more important than the question of pigs and goats. Christian, himself deeply attached to a beautiful Tahitian girl, agreed with his men, and it was unanimously resolved to set off for Tahiti without further delay in order to procure these various vital necessities.

For a number of reasons this was a risky decision to make. In the first place it was extremely likely that if the *Bounty* returned so soon to Tahiti without her captain and with such a small crew the islanders there would become suspicious, and one or another of the chiefs, guessing the truth, might even decide to seize the ship and imprison the mutineers. Secondly, the loyalists on board would probably take advantage of the opportunity to desert, and finally, there was the danger that one of the crew might let it slip that they intended to settle on Tupuai, information which would undoubtedly be passed on to the next English or European vessel which visited Tahiti.

Much to the surprise of everybody, however, the brief visit to Tahiti went through without a hitch. When on the 6th June Chief Poino and various of his delighted subjects came aboard in Matavai Bay with their usual gifts of welcome, Christian was ready with a most ingenious explanation. He told them that shortly after they left Tahiti they had met Captain Cook and that the latter had transferred Bligh, the rest of the crew and all the breadfruit shoots to his own ship, and then ordered Christian to return to Tahiti to take aboard supplies of livestock and plants for a newly-founded colony called Aitutaki in Australia.

This extraordinary yarn was accepted without question by the natives—assuming, of course, that they understood the gist of Christian's stumbling Tahitian. As far as the loyalists were concerned, and the rest of the mutineers too for that matter, Christian had threatened them with flogging and keel-hauling if they attempted to desert or tell the Tahitians the truth.

In the space of one week Christian contrived to procure no less than four hundred and sixty pigs, fifty goats, Bligh's bull and one cow, innumerable chickens and two cats and two dogs. With the exception of Christian's girl, Mauatea, and a couple of other faithful mistresses, the Tahitian girls showed not the slightest desire to accompany the *Bounty* back to Tupuai. On the contrary, they did everything possible to persuade their respective lovers to remain on Tahiti instead. During the return journey the situation improved somewhat when two female Tahitian stowaways emerged, but this balance was subsequently outweighed again with the appearance of a number of male stowaways, including the incorrigible Hitihiti. When the *Bounty* again dropped anchor in Bloody Bay the Tahitian complement amounted to nine men, eight boys, ten women and one small girl, which can hardly have said to have solved the problem of the balance of sexes. The bull had died during the voyage, but the cow and all the other livestock were in the best of health, so that the excursion was all in all anything but a failure.

It so happened that the unwelcome Tahitian male stowaways were to prove of great value to the settlers, since in no time at all they persuaded the Tupuains that their English friends were of peaceful intent, and they continued to act as excellent interpreters and mediators. Chief Tamatoa who ruled over the entire western half of the island, including Bloody Bay, went as far as to become a name brother with Christian, and this advantageous pact was duly celebrated with great solemnity and ceremony. Thus by a stroke of good fortune the situation was completely changed, and the future of the little colony looked bright and promising.

Tamatoa offered the colonists a large piece of land adjacent to Bloody Bay, but for some obscure reason this did not suit Christian who had his heart set on another district farther to the east. In point of fact the best soil on Tupuai was to be found in Tamatoa's kingdom, and had Christian taken the trouble to examine the conditions a little more carefully there is no doubt whatever that he would have accepted Tamatoa's offer and settled on this beautiful, fertile and well-watered part of the south coast. The mutineers, as usual, made no objections when Christian insisted that they ought to settle the northeast corner of the island, but Tamatoa protested loudly and bitterly, and with every good reason since the district which Christian had in mind was in the kingdom of Tamatoa's arch enemy Chief Taaroa. To desert his name brother and go and live in the kingdom of his worst enemy was, as far as the natives were concerned, a deadly insult. Christian, although he had lived ashore on Tahiti for nearly five months and ought consequently to have known better, apparently thought that he could be name

brother with two chieftains at the same time, and he subsequently offered Taaroa the same honour. The latter needless
to say was overwhelmed with delight at the prospect of securing the alliance of this powerful, well-armed stranger, and
immediately accepted Christian's offer. From that moment
onwards Tamatoa became the sworn enemy of all the
mutineers.

Fletcher Christian's choice in this matter was extremely
unfortunate since Taaroa's kingdom was only half the size of
that of Tamatoa, and he had only half the number of subjects.
In addition to this the island's third chieftain, Tinarau, whose
kingdom bordered on Taaroa's in the south, was an ally of
Tamatoa, which meant that the mutineers now had more than
threequarters of the island's population against them. Furthermore most of the warriors who had died in the Bloody Bay
battle when the *Bounty* first anchored there had come from
Tinarau's kingdom, which is one of the reasons why this chieftain had hated the newcomers violently ever since their arrival
on the island.

Scarcely had Christian succeeded in moving the *Bounty*
round inside the coral reef to an anchorage off Taaroa's kingdom than the difficulties began. First two of the crew, Sumner
and Quintal, went off on a twenty-four hour excursion ashore
without leave from Christian. When Christian reprimanded
them for this they replied that the ship was now in harbour
and that they were thus their own masters. Under the present
circumstances it was more important than ever for the mutineers to hold together and avoid internal disputes, and without
attempting to refute the argument that the mutiny had made
them all free and equal, Christian resolutely drew his pistol and
ordered the two offenders to be put in irons. Having considered
their situation during the course of the night, the two men
asked Christian's pardon the following morning and were subsequently released without further punishment.

Meanwhile the mutineers could not live for ever on board
the *Bounty*, particularly since they had already agreed to strip
her and then burn her so that she might not be sighted and
betray their presence. But in view of their perilous position,
following the dispute with the other island chieftains, they felt
that it would be inadvisable to get rid of the ship until they
had established an equally well-protected place to live ashore.

The best solution to this was obviously to build a fortress, and in the middle of July Christian selected a pleasant glade surrounded by thickets about three hundred yards from the shore. He appears to have had in mind a veritable castle, the sort of thing that all boys dream of building, complete with ramparts, turreted lookout towers at the corners, a moat and a drawbridge! As soon as the location and general plan of the fortress had been agreed upon Christian organized the work as follows.

Brown, the gardener, with a Tahitian to assist him, was detailed off to plant vegetables and root crops for their future needs, while Coleman and Mickey were put to making spades and mattocks. Hillbrant was made cook for the entire company, and Byrne and Ellison were given the job of ferrying from the ship people, livestock and goods. The remaining eighteen of the crew, loyalists included, and the Tahitians were put to work on the fortress under Christian's command, and here Christian set a good example by taking a spade himself and joining in the rudimentary digging.

During the early stages of this hard and tiring work Christian realized that his plans for the size of the fortress were altogether too ambitious, and he was reluctantly obliged to reduce the intended dimensions by half. In spite of this, the work progressed very slowly indeed, and in due course other setbacks occurred. Ever since the breach between the *Bounty* men and the chieftains Tamatoa and Tinarau, the latter had boycotted the mutineers by the simple means of forbidding their people to supply them with foodstuffs. Consequently the mutineers had been forced to content themselves with whatever fruits and vegetables they could find in Taaroa's little kingdom. Now to make matters worse, the few natives that did turn up at the working site with supplies were not particularly impressed by the barter goods which they were offered, and even went so far as to suggest that their own indigenous stone tools and bark cloths were much better than the European iron and cotton goods. Worst of all, however, was the fact that the girls, who seemed to delight in tantalizing the men during their daily toil, flatly refused to spend the nights on board ship.

Time and time again Christian tried to regain the friendship of the two alien chieftains, and even went to the extent of making a tour of the coast in the ship's boat with gifts of appeasement. It is probable that in the end he would have succeeded in his endeavours, had he not made the foolish and completely irresponsible mistake of allowing his four hundred and sixty pigs and fifty goats to run wild over Tapuai. (The building of styes and stalls for these animals was a difficult and demanding operation which the mutineers had apparently failed to consider while they were so enthusiastically collecting them on Tahiti.) Since these were the first livestock ever to have set foot on the island there were no fences anywhere and consequently, once the animals were set loose, they were able to roam at liberty among the crops and plantations. This, combined with the fact that the mutineers trespassed wantonly and deliberately both to help themselves to root crops and fruit and to retrieve their animals, led inevitably to open conflict. The first serious trouble occurred on the 25th August when one of Tinarau's men was killed. The chieftain planned a reprisal by sending out pretty female decoys whose task it was to lure the unsuspecting sailors deep into the palm woods. The first victim of these Mata Hari tactics was Alexander Smith who was fortunate enough to survive with no more than a bad scare and the loss of his clothes. In return for this, Christian had the hut burned down where the treachery had taken place, and he also confiscated a number of grotesque religious idols which were greatly valued by Tinarau. The only result of these counter measures was that Smith's seductress, frightened for her own safety, fled to the *Bounty* and remained on board.

Tinarau now adopted different tactics. Accompanied by a large team of bearers carrying enormous quantities of food-stuffs, he appeared at the half-finished fortress on the 2nd September, and announced that he was seeking a truce and that there should be peace between them on condition that Christian returned the idols. One of the Tahitians had fortunately noticed, however, that the bearers had concealed some weapons in the nearby undergrowth before announcing their arrival. The boy had warned Christian of this, and Christian in his turn had armed and alerted his own people. In the middle of the bogus peace negotiations Tinarau observed that the sailors were armed, realized that his plot had been foiled and hastily dissolved the meeting. A well-aimed shot from one of the *Bounty's* cannons sent the entire band of hostile natives rushing headlong back to the woods again.

Christian was by no means dismayed or discouraged by

Tinarau's efforts to dislodge or eliminate the settlers; instead he gave orders for the work on the fortress to be hurried up, the sooner to establish proper protection against similar attempts. But several of his companions had already had more than enough of the whole business, and were far from happy about the prospect of being obliged to spend the rest of their days on Tupuai, and a few days later, when Christian announced that the time had now come to strip the *Bounty* and burn the ship, he was met by a storm of protest. After a great deal of discussion the mutineers agreed to settle on Tupuai, on one condition only, this being that each and every man be provided with a woman forthwith. The only way to procure women here would be to kidnap them, and this was such a risky and undesirable method that Christian refused even to consider it. Then the only thing for it, replied one of the men, was to go back to Tahiti where there were plenty of willing and friendly females to be had. Christian tried desperately to dissuade them from this insane project, pointing out that they were mutineers and criminals, and that if they returned to Tahiti and were caught they would finish up on the gallows, everyone of them. But neither side would give way, and the palaver continued for a full three days. The only outcome of the seemingly endless discussions was that several of the men became exceedingly thirsty, and when Christian refused to give them rum they broke open the spirits chest and helped themselves. In despair Christian now issued extra rations all round, and once again appealed to the opposition for their own sakes and for the sake of their companions to forget the insane idea of returning to Tahiti.

But as a result of all this Christian had lost a great deal of prestige, and he was fully aware now that if he tried to force his will upon them any further it would only lead to another mutiny, a mutiny furthermore which in all probability would not be so bloodless as the previous one. Very reluctantly he put the matter to the vote. The result was a complete defeat for him—sixteen hands were raised in favour of returning to Tahiti. Fletcher Christian now made a final appeal, in his characteristically melodramatic way.

'Gentlemen, I will carry you and land you where ever you please, I desire no one to stay with me, but I have one favour to request, that you will grant me the ship, tie the foresail, and give me a few gallons of water, and leave me to run before the wind, and I shall land upon the first island the ship drives me to. I have done such an act that I cannot stay at Otaheite. I will never live where I may be carried home to be a disgrace to my family.'

But these histrionics had some effect because scarcely had he finished speaking than Midshipman Young cried out: 'We shall never leave you Mr Christian, go where you will!'

Another seven men, Brown, Mills, Martin, Mickey, Williams, Smith and Quintal, followed Young's example. This is hardly surprising, however, since these men were all original mutineers with everything to gain and nothing to lose. The loyalists naturally all voted in favour of Tahiti, but the extraordinary thing is that they should have been allowed to take part in the negotiations at all since without their votes the figures would have been 9:9.

Loading back on board the gear which had been used for the fortress-building project did not take long. But then there arose the problem of the valuable livestock, which the mutineers had no intention of leaving behind as a parting gift to the islanders. Recapturing these was going to be a difficult business, wandering as they were half wild throughout the length and breadth of the island. Matters became even more complicated when Alexander Smith's girl revealed the mutineers' plans to Tinarau, who immediately seized and hid as many of the animals as he could lay his hands on. The most coveted prize was the unfortunate cow, and when a group of the mutineers finally found its tracks on the 12th September and set out in pursuit of it they were duly set upon by a band of Tinarau's men and beaten so thoroughly that they were lucky to get away with their lives. This incident seems to have infuriated Christian to such a degree that he immediately set off at the head of a large expedition, grimly determined to punish Tinarau and his followers for such an insult.

Tinarau was ready and waiting for the thirty *Bounty* men with a force of no less than seven hundred warriors. To begin with the Tupuaians had the advantage, since they had cunningly taken up positions in a rocky and forested area where the attackers were unable to use their firearms to full effect.

The campaign quickly developed into a very uneven hand-to-hand struggle, and in due course Christian gave orders for his men to retreat, regrouping subsequently on open ground. The natives very unwisely went into the attack again, and were now met by murderous, concentrated fire. Stone slings and spears were no match for this sort of opposition, and when Tinarau's men finally retired they left sixty dead and injured on the battlefield. Remarkable as it may seem, only one of the *Bounty* men was injured, and then only very slightly. Finally, as a sort of grotesque anticlimax to the battle, the triumphant sailors slaughtered the object of the conflict, the cow, and ate her with great relish.

And so at last, a few days later in the middle of September, greatly to the relief of both the islanders and those on board, Fletcher Christian sailed his ship skilfully out through the shallows and the reef into the open sea, and once more set sail for Tahiti. Apart from those who had arrived in her, besides most of the animals and a large variety of plants, the *Bounty's* crew now included a young relation of Taoroa called Taaroamiva and two other Tupuaians of lowlier birth, all three of whom, on account of their friendship with the mutineers, had decided that they would be safer on the ship than remaining on the island.

Like Bligh, Christian went well up to windward of Tahiti in preparation for his approach, and then hove to in the vicinity of Meetu, so that the two parties could decide upon how best to divide up the ship's remaining supplies between them. Early on the morning of the 22nd September, Christian and his twenty-four companions were back again in Matavai Bay for the third time in twelve months.

Christian promptly sent ashore the sixteen separatists, as they might be termed, and also Taaroamiva, Hitihiti and the remainder of the Tahitian stowaways, all of whom were glad to get back to their own peaceful island. Thanks once more to the friendly and uninquisitive co-operation of Poino, the personal belongings of all those who were going ashore had been ferried off and landed before nightfall.

The unsuccessful attempt at colonization on Tupuai had taught Christian, and possibly also some of his companions, two things: first, that it was difficult, if not impossible, in the long run to avoid misunderstandings and quarrels with the natives on an inhabited island, and that consequently the only solution would be to settle an island which was uninhabited and also, if possible, isolated and inaccessible; secondly, that wherever they went they should take with them an adequate supply of good-natured and accommodating women.

For the moment there was no point in considering how and where they were going to find the sort of island they needed, while on the other hand the business of women had to be settled here and now before they left Tahiti. The question was how to go about this. Their earlier attempts to recruit Tahitian women for the colonization of Tupuai had shown that, generally speaking, the latter were not particularly keen on leaving their own exquisite island; even the ones who had been persuaded to go to Tupuai and had remained there at their men's sides had, with but two exceptions, fled gratefully ashore again on their return to Matavai Bay.

Christian was finally forced to agree to the same infamous plan as the mutineers had put forward back at Tupuai, i.e. to kidnap the required number of women. They thus resolved to remain at Tahiti a couple of days longer than originally intended, ostensibly for the purpose of taking aboard fresh supplies of water and provisions. Christian now proceeded to invite aboard a whole band of womenfolk for departure celebrations, and he also managed to get Coleman, the armourer, to return on board for the evening fun and games. Once the party was in full swing and the guests sufficiently intoxicated, the mutineers cut the anchor rope, raised the sails and steered out to sea. Coleman immediately grasped the situation and was over the side and swimming ashore before anyone had time to stop him. The women, for the moment, however, were not unduly alarmed since the crew managed to persuade them that they were only moving the ship to another anchorage at Pare. It was not until the *Bounty* began to heave in the long offshore swell outside the coral reef that they really understood what was going on, and then only one of them had the courage to follow Coleman's example and jump over the side.

The nine mutineers waited until the following day to take a proper look at their catch. All in all there were now eighteen Tahitian females on board, besides two Tupuai males and a young Tahitian male, who had been permitted at their own request to remain on the *Bounty*. Each of the twelve men was now permitted to choose the female which appealed to him most, and when this business had been concluded without dispute the remaining six women, needless to say the oldest and plainest, were dumped ashore on the neighbouring island of Moorea. Shortly afterwards, however, the numerical balance was again upset when three Tahitian male stowaways emerged on to the upper deck. Apparently the mutineers decided that the three newcomers had only themselves to blame, since instead of being sensible about the matter and returning to Moorea to put them ashore they continued on their way.

Four months were to elapse before the vagrant sailors finally found their ideal island. Oddly enough, until very recently, no one has known what route the *Bounty* took during this critical and important stage of their South Seas adventure, and only now, 173 years afterwards, has this serious gap in the history of the *Bounty* episode been filled in by the Australian historian Henry Maude. Professor Maude has built up his report from a multitude of documents—both newly discovered and long extant (though previously ignored) accounts. The most valuable of these accounts was delivered many years later to an inquisitive captain by a Tahitian woman known as Jenny who had been one of the girls kidnapped in Matavai Bay. Thanks to Professor Maude's diligence and ingenuity it has been possible to piece together, stage by stage, the long and trying voyage which the *Bounty* finally made.

After their third departure from Tahiti, Christian first began to consider the Marquesas Islands some seven hundred nautical miles northeast of Tahiti. Further research in the ship's library revealed, however, that this group was inhabited by a race of singularly bloodthirsty cannibals, and Christian thus turned his attention to two other groups of islands which had also been discovered by the Spaniard Mendana. These were the Solomons and Santa Cruz islands, and on the face of it they looked as if they might be suitable. The others immediately agreed to the proposal, none of them having even the vaguest knowledge of Pacific geography, and the *Bounty* was brought round to a westerly course.

A few degrees south of Aitutaki, a week or two later, a rocky island of much the same size and character as Tupuai appeared over the horizon. There was no sign of this island on the charts, and the *Bounty* men sailed in towards it full of expectation. As the ship approached a canoe containing a few peaceful looking natives with gifts of coconuts and suckling pigs came out to meet them. After some hesitation one of the men came aboard the *Bounty* and was soon engaged in lively conversation with the Tahitians. They seem to have understood each other without any trouble at all, but then according to Jenny's chronicler the following incident occurred:

'One of the natives was much delighted by the pearl shell buttons on the Captain's Jacket. The Captain in a very friendly manner gave the man the Jacket. He stood on the ship's gunwale showing the present to his countrymen when one of the mutineers shot him dead. He fell into the Sea. Christian was highly indignant at this. He could do nothing more, having lost all authority, than reprimand the murderer severely: the other natives in the canoe immediately picked up their murdered companion, placed the body in the canoe and paddled towards the shore with loud lamentations.'

After such a provocative and brutal murder there was of course no longer any question of settling on this island, and the *Bounty* left hurriedly without even having discovered what it was called. It is fairly certain, however, that this must have been Rarotonga, one of the largest of the Cook Islands group.

And so the weeks went by. It is obviously impossible to say just where the *Bounty* went, but it is very likely that they cruised backwards and forwards in order to cover as large an area as possible. Mendana had discovered numerous islands, and several of these were much larger than Tahiti, so that it should have been possible to sight them from a great distance. But despite a keen and careful lookout system the great ocean appeared totally empty in all directions. Today, knowing as we do the tremendous magnitude of the Pacific, this does not seem surprising, but it must have been a terrifying and demoralizing experience for the wretched mutineers in the little ship. We now know, too, that Mendana had made an unfortunate error in fixing the position of his island groups, and had placed both the Solomons and the Santa Cruz islands some two thousand miles east of their true position.

By the middle of November provisions and fresh water were beginning to run short. It was now almost two months since the *Bounty* had left Tahiti, and everyone on board was in the worst of spirits, particularly Christian who by this time was more obsessed than ever by his guilty conscience.

According to the charts the nearest island to their present position was Tongatabu in the south Tongas. Christian decided that in the circumstances the best thing they could do would be to make for this as quickly as possible and reprovision. Apparently they had the good fortune to be well received here, and found no difficulty at all in bartering for all the fresh vegetables and fruits they required. It is very probable, too, that they replenished their reserves of livestock, since it is unlikely that many of the wretched animals could have survived the confinement of the months which had passed since they had been put aboard at Tupuai. Ironically enough, Tongatabu was only a few hundred miles away from the scene of the actual mutiny some seven months before, and here they were, with no more achieved than when they had seen Bligh and his followers slip away astern of them in the ship's launch. To have attempted to settle on one of the Tonga group would have been sheer madness, however. In the first place the Tongalese were known for their treachery and brutality, and in the second place, when the Admiralty sent a ship out to hunt for the mutineers, as they undoubtedly would do, the first area that would carefully be combed would be the Tongas. Thus the mutineers were faced with no choice but to continue their maritime wanderings in the hope that one fine day their dream island would simply appear out of the sea.

The next island to appear was an unusually high and fertile atoll. This was spotted a few days after leaving Tongatabu, and once again the hopes of everyone on board were raised. But the very black and woolly haired savages who promptly appeared dispelled any ideas they may have entertained of landing here. With the sparse information available it is difficult to say for sure which island this might have been, but it must anyway have been one of the Lau group south of Fiji, the inhabitants of which were just as fierce and cannibalistic as the Tonga natives.

By this time Christian was beginning to realize that some definite decision would have to be made soon, and again he resorted to the ship's library in a last desperate attempt to find something which might suit their purposes. He now picked out a large handsome volume bound in fine leather and containing the account of a circumnavigation by one Captain Carteret, 1766-69, who had sailed in company with Wallis when the latter discovered Tahiti. Apparently at one point Carteret had lost contact with Wallis, and it was then that he came upon an isolated rocky island in the south Pacific. Christian read the following with growing hopes:

'We continued our course westward till the evening of Thursday, the 2nd of July, when we discovered land to the northward of us. Upon approaching it the next day, it appeared like a great rock rising out of the sea: it was more than five miles in circumference and appeared to be uninhabited, it was, however, covered with trees, and we saw a small stream of fresh water running down one side of it. I would have landed upon it, but the surf, which at this season broke upon it with great violence, rendered it impossible. I got soundings on the west side of it, at somewhat less than a mile from the shore, in twenty-five fathoms, with a bottom of coral and sand, and it is probable that in fine summer weather landing here may not only be practical but easy. We saw a great number of sea birds hovering about it, at somewhat less than a mile from the shore, and the sea here seemed to have fish. It lies in latitude 20° 2′ south: long. 133° 21′ west. It is so high that we saw it at the distance of more than fifteen leagues, and it having been discovered by a young gentleman, son to Major Pitcairn of the marines, we called it Pitcairn's Island.'

Even though it was by no means certain that Pitcairn Island was uninhabited, it nevertheless seemed the perfect place as far as Christian could judge, and without more ado he altered course and began to make for it. The direct distance from the Lau islands to Pitcairn was some three thousand nautical miles, but unfortunately it was impossible to sail straight there due to the unchanging easterly trade winds, and consequently the *Bounty* was forced to go south and then swing round in an arc, which added at least another five hundred miles to the initial distance. This explains why the last leg of the *Bounty's* final voyage took almost two months to complete, particularly since additional days were undoubtedly spent in finding Pitcairn; Carteret having made an error of two hundred miles in its position. Jenny reported to her chronicler that at this time, 'all on board were much discouraged; they therefore thought of returning to Otaheite.'

The *Bounty's* travel-weary crew finally sighted Pitcairn Island at sunset on the 15th January, 1790. Christian hove to that evening, going in closer the following morning and sailing round the island several times in succession. With its high, steep cliffs it looked like some enormous fortress, with only the odd crevice and ledge here and there to relieve its unassailability and offer access to the high plateaus and fertile valleys in its interior. Even though there was only a moderate wind, the base of the thousand-foot cliffs were white with foam and spray, and the roar of the breakers seemed to warn the mariners that they would find no peaceful haven to anchor in here. But on the other hand, once ashore, it was doubtful if a more secure and easily defended hiding place could be found in the whole of the South Seas.

It was two days before the sea became calm enough to risk a landing, and then, accompanied by Brown, Williams, Mickey and three of the natives, he set off towards the cliff face in the ship's cutter. After a few anxious minutes they contrived to land, drag the boat up on a rocky ledge and begin the ascent of the perpendicular rock wall.

The first thing they spotted when they reached the top were groves of breadfruit trees and banana and yam plants. They all of them knew that these must have been planted and, concluding that the island must be inhabited after all, they hastily loaded their muskets. The next sign of human presence was a number of Polynesian idols and stone altars of the type which they had seen on both Tahiti and Tupuai, but these were covered in moss and it was not long before the explorers were able to comfort themselves with the knowledge that whoever might have lived here had long since departed.

Arriving back on board, Christian learned to his anger and dismay that while the patrol had been ashore the remaining mutineers had been on the point of weighing anchor and returning to Tahiti while leaving the shore party to manage as best they could. In view of this attitude he decided that it would be wise to get the stores ashore as quickly as possible, and he thereupon set everyone to work. The plants which they had tended so carefully all this time were evidently superfluous now, since there was all they needed in this respect ashore. But the surviving animals and extensive stores would mean a major operation, and the one remaining ship's boat was by no means adequate for this. Christian rather ingeniously got over the problem by lowering the hatch covers into the water and using these as rafts.

By January 23rd all the animals and stores and the greater part of the yards, rigging and sails had been taken off the ship and landed at a little inlet between the cliffs, which was somewhat unimaginatively christened Bounty Bay. At this juncture there were still a number of valuable articles left on board, but Christian must have been obsessed with the fear that his colonization plans would be broken up a second time, because the very same evening, when everyone had retired, he sent one of his most dependable men back aboard to fire the ship, and minutes later when the alarm was raised the *Bounty* was already ablaze from stem to stern. According to Jenny, 'they were all in tears at seeing her in flames. Some regretted exceedingly they had not confined Capt. Bligh and returned to their native country, instead of acting as they had done.'

Thus the colonization of Pitcairn Island began, and the mere fact that Christian alone of the nine remaining mutineers was the only one who was genuinely determined and anxious to begin a new life here was in itself anything but a promising token for the future.

CHAPTER VII

EIGHTEEN MEN IN A BOAT

UNLIKE the sequence of events which preceded and led up to the mutiny, the developments after it took the form of series of episodes involving different individuals and different places. Consequently it is impossible to maintain any strict chronological order in this narrative, and we must now return again to the morning of the mutiny in the vicinity of Tofua, and follow the fate of Bligh and his eighteen men as they pulled away from the *Bounty* in their overloaded ship's boat on the 28th April, 1789

When the mutineers and the loyalists parted company, Christian took it for granted that the latter would make for one of the nearby Tonga islands, there to relax and await the inevitable arrival of a European trading vessel. But the idea of waiting idly and indefinitely on some alien shore for rescue was hardly likely to be entertained by a man of William Bligh's energy and enterprise. Thus no sooner had the *Bounty* disappeared from view than he began to ponder over the quickest means of getting back to England, where his first move would be to organize an expedition to hunt down and bring to justice the 'pirates', as he now termed the mutineers. The obvious solution would be to make for a place visited regularly by European ships. Bligh was well aware that two years ago the British government had despatched a military mission to the east coast of Australia to found a penal colony, but on the other hand he had no idea whether or not the project had been successful, and he was of too cautious a nature to chance it. The only place where he could be sure of finding a ship was at one of the Dutch or Portuguese trading posts in the East Indies. The nearest of these was on the island of Timor, and despite the fact that it was three thousand five hundred miles away Bligh nevertheless decided that it would be wisest to aim for there.

If they were to have any chance at all of succeeding they must first land somewhere to overhaul their boat and replenish their water and food supplies. When Bligh had visited the Tongas with Cook in 1777, he had become particularly good friends with a powerful chieftain called Pouleho who lived on Tongatabu, and he now resolved to go there before leaving for the East Indies. But once again Tongatabu was over a hundred nautical miles from their present position, and Bligh realized that they ought first to land quite locally in order to get some proper rest and straighten up the boat. The nearest island, Kotu, was an atoll, and Bligh knew from long experience that these coral islands were as a rule not only devoid of vegetation but also often without much fresh water. Therefore he set course instead for the volcanic island of Tofua which was about thirty miles to the north and which could be seen from far off on account of its column of smoke. Nevertheless, despite hard and steady rowing, it was not until the following afternoon and helped by a fresh following wind that they first caught sight of the fifteen hundred foot peak, and it was dark by the time they had rounded the southern point of the island and found sheltered water.

By now the stiff wind was lashing the darkened shore line with heavy breakers. Simpson, the quartermaster's mate, dived over the side with great courage and swam ashore to investigate the landing chances. His report on returning was emphatic, landing before daylight was out of the question, they would have to lay by until morning. This was a great disappointment to the tired and cramped sailors, particularly since, the water being too deep to lower an anchor, they would have to take turns at the oars all night to keep the boat off shore and within sheltered waters. Bligh now issued an extra ration of rum all round and the miserable assembly settled down to get what sleep they could.

There was not much sleep for anybody that night, but they nevertheless woke the next morning in good spirits, comforted as they were by the thought of probable habitation ashore. Shortly after sunrise they left the bay again, and began to row slowly along the coast, inspecting it carefully as they went. But as the hours passed their intense hunger began to assert itself, until finally Bligh was forced to drop anchor in another well-sheltered bay and send a patrol ashore under Samuel's command in search of food.

In anticipation of the patrol's return, well-furnished with fruit, nuts, eggs, game and pork, the remaining sailors landed on the shore of the bay and proceeded to build a large fire in preparation for the vast cooking operations which were to take place. To their utter despair, however, Samuel and his companions returned almost empty handed. They reported that the island seemed to be uninhabited, although there were certain indications that at one time or another natives had at least called there. Thus the only returns from the patrol's trying excursion were a few pints of fresh water, so once again the starving *Bounty* men were forced to make a meal of a piece of ship's biscuit and a cup of wine per head, since Bligh was absolutely resolved not to squander the existing rations until he was quite certain of being able to replenish his supplies.

Shortly afterwards Bligh ordered everyone on board the launch again, and they continued the survey of the island by water. A little farther on they caught sight of a number of coconut palms growing at the top of a steep cliff, but once more the surf made it impossible to land, and there was nothing for it but to send a couple of men over the side to swim ashore. After a perilous climb up and down the cliff face the men returned with about a score of fresh coconuts.

By now Bligh had given up all hope of finding adequate reserves of provisions on Tofua, and resolved to set off for Tongatabu without further delay. They sailed almost immediately, but as soon as they left the sheltered water it became obvious that the wind was too strong and they were forced to turn back again and spend another miserable night in the small bay where they had lain the night before.

The following morning they made a second attempt to put to sea, and were again obliged to retreat to their bay on account of high wind and seas. By now the food situation was beginning to become critical, supplies were diminishing instead of increasing, and each man's ration for breakfast that morning was limited to a small piece of ship's biscuit and a spoonful of rum.

Bligh now took Samuel and Nelson with him and went off himself to explore the island. They soon picked up a track which led right up to the crater of the volcano in the centre of the island, and there to their astonishment they came upon a couple of native huts and a number of banana trees. In addition to this they also discovered a proper fresh water spring, and when they finally staggered back to the launch they had with them not only three hands of bananas but also some ten gallons of drinking water. The effort of this excursion must have been too much for Bligh because just as the three men reached the water he fainted and would undoubtedly have drowned had his companions not succeeded in grabbing him and heaving aboard the launch. However, the men who had remained aboard had been totally unsuccessful in their efforts to catch fish, and consequently the midday meal was no more stable than breakfast had been. On the other hand, everyone's spirits had been raised by the news that the island was quite definitely inhabited, particularly since this meant that they might not even have to go to Tongatabu but carry out their preparations for the East Indies voyage here instead. It was thus generally agreed that they should stay for a few more days and thoroughly explore the island.

Everyone needed proper rest and sleep before any extended excursions ashore could be undertaken, and the question was how to go about it. The problem was solved when someone spotted a low cave at the far end of the bay, and the entire crew, with the exception of Fryer and a couple of assistants who were to look after the boat, settled down in it to spend a more comfortable night sheltered from the wind and rain.

Early the following morning a patrol went out and returned a few hours later with the glad news that they had actually encountered a number of apparently friendly natives. The natives in their turn were not long in informing their friends and neighbours of the presence of the white men, and soon some thirty or more of them had descended into the cave. Bligh made every effort to befriend them and it appeared that he had succeeded, thanks chiefly to his excellent knowledge of Tahitian which was obviously closely related to their language. At his urgent request they returned to their settlements to fetch breadfruit and bananas, and shortly afterwards lively bartering was in full swing. The one thing that was worrying Bligh at this juncture was just what answer to give if the natives questioned him about his ship. Sure enough in due course one of them did, and Bligh very inadvisedly replied that they had been shipwrecked and that the rest of the crew had perished. What he should have done to retain the respect of the natives was tell them that his well-armed and well-manned ship was not far off and would shortly be coming to collect them. It seemed, nevertheless, that the natives had not fully grasped what he said, since they continued to trade with the white men quietly and apparently unconcerned with what had happened. So far so good, but the fact remained that when Bligh counted up the results of the day's trading in the evening, it emerged that the returns had been very meagre, with the result that the evening meal had to be limited to a coconut and a quarter of a bread-fruit per man. In view of all this Bligh once again considered the Tongatabu project, particularly since there was a sudden and marked improvement in the weather, and he retired to the cave for the night to ponder the final decision.

The following morning, while a number of the crew were ashore fetching supplies of fresh water, large numbers of natives began to appear, and in due course canoes also entered the bay, one of which contained an elderly cheiftain named Makakavau. Makakavau showed great interest in the launch and seemed particularly inquisitive about the contents of Fryer's tool chest. When Fryer attempted to convince him that the chest contained muskets, Makakavau demanded to be allowed to see them and finally became so aggressive in his manner that Fryer lost his nerve and opened the chest. The chieftain, realizing that the white men had a lot of valuable articles with them but no firearms to defend themselves with, now brusquely demanded a saw as a present and turned very nasty indeed when Fryer refused him. At the same time, several other chieftains, accompanied by their warriors, arrived over the rocks. One or two of these chieftains immediately recognized Bligh, since they had been at Nomuka and Tongatabu when he had visited those islands previously with Cook. One of them in particular was an even more recent acquaintance, having been among the chieftains held as hostages by Bligh during the anchor incident at Nomuka only a few weeks previously. Now, either as a reprisal for the indignity suffered by this chieftain, or else purely and simply with the intent of laying their hands on the white men's treasures, the assembled chieftains began to behave in a most threatening and unpleasant manner. Furthermore they had evidently sent for reinforcements, because by noon there were some two hundred natives surrounding the cave and the launch, all clapping rather sinisterly with small sling stone ammunition. The situation was extremely disagreeable for Bligh and his small band of followers, particularly since they could hardly attempt a retreat before the water carriers had returned. Time and time again the chieftains insisted that they were Bligh's friends and tried to persuade him to sit down with them. But this only increased his suspicion and put him more on his guard, and instead he retreated into the cave where he coolly settled down to describe the events in his logbook.

All at once a number of the natives seized the mooring line of the launch and began to drag it in towards the shore. The only weapons which the *Bounty* men owned were the four cutlasses which Christian had given them, and two of these were in the launch while the other two were in the cave. Although the situation looked hopeless Bligh immediately grabbed a cutlass, dashed over to one of the chieftains and threatened to cut his throat unless he ordered the men to release the mooring line at once. Amazingly enough the chieftain hurriedly did as he was told, whereupon Bligh returned quickly to the cave where at least he was safe from an attack from the rear.

Just before noon the water carriers returned with a mere four gallons of water, and Bligh now handed out a more substantial meal to each man, consisting of a coconut and a whole breadfruit. While they ate he made the following entry in his log:

'As our situation could be no worse, I told every one I would wait until sundown, that by that time perhaps something might turn in our favour, and they might be induced to leave us as they had done before, that if we attempted to go at present we must fight our way through which we could do more advantageously at night, and that in the meantime we would endeavour to get off to the boat what we had bought.'

For the time being the loyalists were permitted to wander backwards and forwards between the cave and the shore more or less as they pleased, but when the natives realized that they were making preparations to leave they began to obstruct them.

One or two of the more aggressive warriors actually used physical force, and when Bligh sent someone down to stow his logbook on board they made a determined attempt to seize it, obviously assuming that it was a particularly valuable article. The *Bounty* men were becoming extremely worried by this time, since more and more warriors were appearing, both overland and in large war canoes. Meanwhile the nerve warfare was intensified through the regular, sinister clapping of hundreds of pairs of small sling stones.

No further direct action was taken, however, except that towards evening the assembled islanders began to light fires here and there, clearly indicating that they intended to stay for the night and possibly launch their expected attack. As far as Bligh and his men were concerned, the only thing to do was to take a chance and deliberately pull out. Having agreed upon this they got their belongings together and began to make their way slowly down towards the launch where Fryer and his companions were waiting anxiously. The chieftains now barred the way, and Makakavau asked with studied surprise why they were not going to stay the night. Bligh replied gruffly that it was his custom always to sleep on board, but that he would willingly come ashore again in the morning to continue trading. He also tried to give the impression that it was their intention to remain on Tofua until the weather improved sufficiently to permit their departure for Tongatabu. Makakavau's reply was brief and to the point:

'You will not sleep on shore! Then we will kill you.'

Bligh now decided to try the hostage tactics again and without warning he seized Ngakitikiti in a powerful grip and shouted at his men to get aboard the launch as quickly as possible. As they dashed out into the shallow, however, Ngakitikiti tore himself loose, whereupon the entire native assembly closed in to the attack, screaming wildly. Bligh turned and followed his men for all he was worth, and succeeded in reaching the boat miraculously enough without once being struck by the barrage of sling stones. He was subsequently lugged aboard in a most undignified manner by Fryer, and now while the two men proceeded to indulge in an absurd and thoroughly incongruous argument on how best to manoeuvre the boat out, a tragedy occurred. Norton, noticing that the natives had grabbed the mooring line with the intention of hauling the launch and her crew ashore, bravely but very rashly leapt out and attacked the mob single-handed. He was promptly savagely attacked thrown to the ground and battered to death with stones. As soon as Bligh realized what had happened he pulled out a knife and hacked off the mooring line. But their troubles were not over yet because it was now found that the bow anchor had fastened in the bottom, and this only finally came loose when one of the prongs snapped off. Six men were sitting with their oars poised and the moment the launch was freed they pulled desperately out towards the open sea.

The action thus turned into a sea battle, since several large war canoes, rapidly manned by crews of powerful natives, paddled after the launch and were soon close enough to begin stoning it. Bligh now made a last desperate attempt to delay his bloodthirsty pursuers. He ordered his men to strip off their clothes and throw them into the water, one or two garments at a time. As he anticipated the canoes immediately slowed down while their occupants fished for the precious articles, and this gave the *Bounty* men just the additional lead they needed. By now it was getting dark, and since they were so far out to sea that the island no longer provided any shelter against the high wind that was blowing the natives evidently decided to give up the chase.

The eighteen men in the boat had managed to escape with their lives, but their position was still anything but hopeful as they huddled together in the open boat which pitched and rolled violently in a heavy sea. Bligh tentatively proposed that they should stick to their original plan of making for Tonga-tabu for fresh provisions before the long voyage to the East Indies. By this time the matter of reprovisioning had become a dire necessity, since their existing supplies consisted of no more than 150 lbs. ship's biscuits, 20 lbs. pork, 28 gallons water, 5 quarts rum and 3 bottles of wine.

In reply to Bligh's proposal, Boatswain Cole expressed the opinion that it would be sheer madness to expect that they would be received any better at Tongabatu, and that so far as he was concerned it would be far more sensible to make straight for Timor in the East Indies.

Bligh protested that the natives of Tongatabu were a different kind of people, whereupon Fryer interrupted politely:

'Pray, sir, had you any words with the natives of Tongatabu

when you was there with Captain Cook?'

'Yes, we had several of them in confinement for theft.'

'Then, if that is the case, sir, they will play us some trick.'

'Well then, Mr Fryer, what is best to be done?'

Fryer answered without hesitation:

'Sir, providence may heave us on some friendly shore, by making a fair wind of it sooner than working to windward.'

Since there was a bow wind to Tongatabu and a following wind to Timor, it was obvious whose side Fryer was on, and it soon emerged that practically everyone else on board was more inclined to risk the long sea voyage at once rather than put their lives in the hands of a crowd of completely unpredictable Tonga natives.

Bligh now pointed out the tremendous disadvantages of such a project. In the first place they must bear in mind that the distance as the crow flies was three thousand five hundred miles, that they possessed no charts over this part of the Pacific, that the voyage might easily take as much as two months and that the likelihood of renewing their supplies of provisions en route was negligible. Existing on the provisions in hand would imply a ration of an ounce of ship's biscuits a day, while the fresh water could not possibly last more than two weeks, which meant that unless there was regular rain they would in all probability die of thirst.

It is likely that after the adventures on Tofua it was Bligh's definite intention to sail directly for the East Indies, but that he had astutely manoeuvred his subordinates into actually making the proposal so that they would not be able to blame him individually for the hardships and misfortunes which they would almost certainly have to put up with.

To be on the safe side, Bligh once more asked Fryer if he were quite certain of his decision, and the latter replied that he definitely was.

'Well lads,' said Bligh addressing the crew at large, 'are you all agreeable to live on one ounce of bread and a gill of water per day?'

'Yes, sir,' was the unanimous retort.

In a spirit of general enthusiasm and relief the launch's sail was now set and the crew split up into two watches. The launch handled remarkably well under the circumstances, but as the hours passed the sea became so rough that she lost steering headway every time she descended into the trough of the waves, while she was time and time again in danger of capsizing as she hung on the crest of one of the great rollers. In addition she was continually shipping water so that most of the crew had to bail for dear life to keep her afloat. When the first scowling red dawn broke Bligh wrote laconically in his log:

'. . . .a situation equally horrible perhaps was never experienced.'

During the course of the morning, despite the frenzied bailing, Bligh realized that as much weight as possible would have to be got rid of if the launch were going to survive, and in due course they dumped overboard a spare sail, a large coil of rope and all the clothing and personal belongings which were not absolutely essential. Meanwhile what really saved them was the absence of the unfortunate Norton, since the presence of one more man on board, particularly as he had been the largest and fattest of them all, would undoubtedly have caused the little boat to founder. Thus there was a certain element of macabre good fortune in the fate of Quartermaster Norton.

During his previous visit to the Tongas Bligh had heard mention of another group of islands to the northwest of these, called Viti or Fiji. Lying in the general direction in which they were bound, Bligh could not resist the temptation of looking for these islands and charting them, even though they lacked the physical condition, time and equipment for such a project. On the 4th May he sighted the first of this group, and during the following days he made so many new discoveries that he entirely forgot the grimness of their plight. His companions, however, were by no means as enthusiastic, and were extremely anxious over what might happen if they were spotted by hostile inhabitants. They were particularly alarmed when Bligh deliberately steered down the straits between two thickly populated islands knowns as Viti Levu and Vanua Levu. Nevertheless everything went well until they passed the last of the Fijis, the Yasawa group, when two large sail canoes suddenly left the shore and began to bear down on them. After the recent adventures at Tofua the *Bounty* men had not the slightest desire to make the acquaintance of these islanders, and they now plied their oars to give themselves extra speed. Thanks to a fresh following breeze, which seemed to spring up just at the right moment, the launch managed to keep well ahead of the native canoes, and after a while the islanders gave up the chase and turned back. Just what the intentions of these natives were is not known, but the *Bounty* men had every good reason to suspect the motives of what were reckoned to be some of the most treacherous and bloodthirsty savages in the South Seas.

The weary rowers were rewarded for their efforts a few hours later when a veritable cloudburst enabled them to collect some six gallons of water, so that they were permitted to quench their thirst properly for the first time since the mutiny. The following day dawned grey and cloudy, and Bligh did what he could to divert the attention of his shivering men by telling them all he knew of the islands and weather conditions in this part of the Pacific. He even drew a rough map which was handed round for their general enlightenment, and he then continued to hold their interest by constructing a crude scales upon which to weigh out the daily rations. These scales consisted of two half coconut shells suspended from a bar by pieces of thin string, while for weights he used a couple of pistol bullets. After many computations and experiments Bligh came to the conclusion that one meal's ration amounted to a ship's biscuit or the weight of one bullet. It has subsequently been established that one of these bullets weighed three fifths of an ounce. This then was the total food ration per man, since Bligh had very wisely made up his mind to reserve the salt pork for a final emergency. It was discovered that the best method of eating this meagre ration of characterless biscuit was to soak it in sea water, which gave it a little added flavour, and then to eat it slowly, carefully chewing each minute mouthful.

The following day Bligh kept his men occupied raising the gunwales of the launch by the addition of spars and sailcloth, thus giving everybody a little extra protection against wind and waves. Unfortunately the few remaining pieces of sailcloth were insufficient to rig up any sort of overhead awning against the steady downpour of rain which continued to fall day after day. In order to keep themselves a little warmer, Bligh advised everyone to remove their clothes, dip them in the sea and then put them on again, the idea being that the sea water was much warmer than the rain. But this was a very difficult procedure in such crowded conditions, and very tiring too in the long run.

The persistent heavy rain kept two men fully engaged in bailing, while the sea was still so rough that the launch was in constant danger of capsizing. Another difficulty with which the helmsman had to contend was the shifting wind that kept swinging round to the south and which in the long run could result in their missing the Torres Straits and having to go round via the north of New Guinea. Thus, despite the increased risk involved in having the wind on their beam, they continued to keep to their original course.

Ever since the beginning of the voyage from Tofua they had kept a fishing line over the stern, but to their intense disappointment they never got a bite, presumably because they had the wrong type of hook and bait to catch any of the large numbers of tropical mackerel and tunny which abound in these waters.

On the 14th and 15th May, when the launch was just north of the New Hebrides, a number of high, rocky islands suddenly appeared over the horizon. Bligh dutifully christened these Banks Islands after his patron Sir Joseph, but refused to run the risk of going ashore there, despite the temptation of possible food and being able to get off of the boat for a while. The men were now urging Bligh to let them eat the pork, arguing that this was the only way in which they could recover sufficient strength to continue the journey. But he resolutely refused to part with this vital reserve, and got round his men instead by prescribing a teaspoonful of rum, a spiritual magic which never failed to help.

Nevertheless by the 20th May everyone was close to despair and Bligh wrote as follows in his log:

'At dawn of day some of my people were half dead. Our appearances were horrible, and I could look no way but I caught the eye of someone. Extreme hunger is now evident, but thirst no one suffers, or have we an inclination to drink, that desire is satisfied through our skin. What little sleep we get is in the midst of water and we wake with severe cramps and pains in the bones.'

As usual Bligh continued to do his utmost to keep up the courage of his men, arguing without much conviction that they were better off under these conditions than if the weather had been fine. A day or two later, however, he could no longer be bothered to trump up any new form of encouragement and wrote simply:

'Our distresses are now extremely great. We are so covered with rain and sea that we can scarce see or make use of our eyes. Sleep, although we long for it, is horrible, for my part I seem to live without it. We suffer extreme cold and everyone dreads the approach of night.'

On the 22nd May everyone was still alive and Bligh made the following entry:

'If ever men experienced the power of goodness, of Divine providence, we do at this instant in a most eminent degree, and I presume to say that our present situation would make the boldest seaman tremble that ever lived. We are obliged to take the course of the Sea, running right before us and breaking all over us. Watching with the utmost care as the least error in the helm would in a moment be our destruction.'

Twenty-four hours later the end seemed very near, and it was only with the greatest effort that Bligh was able to scribble down the next entry:

'The misery of this day has exceeded the preceeding. The night was dreadful. The sea flew over us with great force and kept us bailing with horror and anxiety. At dawn of day I found everyone in a most distressed situation, and I now began to fear that another such night would produce the end of several who were no longer able to bear it.'

That same evening the sea began to ease off and to everyone's delight the sun appeared. Clothes were immediately hung up to dry and when Bligh handed out an ounce of pork in addition to the biscuit and water ration the atmosphere became almost festive. But Bligh was not the person to indulge in false optimism, and he now took advantage of the more favourable conditions to recheck the provision supplies. This check revealed that if he continued to hand out the three-fifths of an ounce ration, the ship's biscuit would last another twenty-nine days. If all went well they ought to reach Timor within that time, but on the other hand bad weather or misfortune might easily delay them considerably longer. For example they might be forced to continue right through to Java. Bligh therefore decided to cut the biscuit ration from three times to twice daily so that the supplies would last six weeks if necessary. It needed a great deal of courage and tact to announce this to his companions and expect to get away with it, but he nevertheless managed to put it over so casually and smoothly that the matter was settled and accepted without one single voice being raised in protest.

The same day a number of birds approached the boat and began to circle around it. These were a form of tern, known as noddies on account of their reputed stupidity; they will alight on a ship and remain where they are until actually chased off. The *Bounty* men had encountered these birds often enough on the way out from England, and they now waited patiently for one of them to come down within reach. It was not until the following day, however, that they finally succeeded in grabbing a noddy. This was immediately torn to pieces, divided up into eighteen portions, innards and all, and devoured raw. Shortly afterwards the same day they managed to catch a gannet, which is somewhat larger than the noddy and reputedly even more careless and clumsy. This time the blood was run off and given to the three weakest men, whereupon the flesh was eaten by the rest. The next day two more noddies were nabbed, and when these were cut open undigested octopus and flying fish was found in their stomachs, but the fish went the same way as the fowl.

The warm sunny weather persisted, and it was not long before everyone in the boat was beginning to long for rain again, the more the better. In their weak state, as Bligh fully realized, they were less capable of enduring the tropical heat than the tropical rainstorms, and from the 26th May onwards the voyage developed into a desperate race with death for the crew of the launch. Fortunately by this time they had almost reached the Great Barrier Reef.

At three o'clock in the morning on the 28th May, Fryer at the helm was suddenly alerted by a dull heavy roaring, and when he peered ahead he was able to make out a tremendous surf only a few hundred yards in front of them. Bligh immediately gave orders for a change of course, which was fortunately an easy matter since the wind was in the southeast, and thus blowing parallel with the direction of the reef. With his usual thoroughness he also ordered the crew to man the oars, but they were far too weak to do this, and as soon as the launch had been sailed out of the danger zone they hove to and awaited daylight.

The main question now was how long it would take to find a break in the reef and an island inside where they could go ashore to rest and recover. Captain Cook was the only man who had ever been known to sail through the Great Barrier Reef into the treacherous waters between it and the east coast of Australia, and the one or two openings in the reef which he had discovered were well south of Bligh's present position. Meanwhile, during the early morning hours the wind had swung round to the east so that there was a risk of the launch being blown in and pounded to pieces on the reef itself.

But this risk was insignificant compared with the terrible prospect of dying from hunger, thirst and heat, and in view of this Bligh very resolutely steered in towards the reef again as soon as it was full daylight. To his relief he discovered an opening not more than a mile to the north. At the same time he caught sight of a small round island lying in the calm waters on the other side of the reef, and they now swept in towards this under the full force of the following wind.

But it was something like twenty miles to this island, and before they reached it they noticed a larger and more fertile island which was nearer and they decided to land there instead. It was dark before they finally got ashore, and it was not until the following morning that they were able to ascertain to their intense relief and delight that it was uninhabited and that the shore abounded in fine large mussels. A fire was immediately started and they made a huge pot of mussel stew which was subsequently eked out by several ounces of ship's biscuits. Bligh christened this island Restoration Island, partly because it was here that they were all restored to health and vigour, and also apparently because he happened to remember that this day, the 29th May, was the one hundred and twenty-ninth anniversary of the restoration of Charles II.

During the past few weeks the one and only problem in these men's lives had been that of survival, and yet now, as soon as a certain degree of wellbeing and safety had been restored to them, ridiculous trifles began to lead to puerile and nonsensical disputes. The crew of the launch had gone with Bligh either out of a sense of duty or else on account of their fear of being apprehended and charged with mutiny. They were thus a very mixed bunch and, of course, included Bligh's two traditional enemies Fryer and Purcell. These two had scarcely recovered before they began to complain over the way in which the captain made the mussel stew, and the general atmosphere was in no way improved when it was found that someone had stolen the pork reserves.

Bligh was anxious to lay in a good store of mussels for the continuation of the voyage, but his men were so weak and apathetic that he decided it would be better not to drive them too hard for the present. Therefore, after having cooked one more pot of stew he gave orders to break camp and resume the voyage northwards. At dawn on the 31st March they discovered a new island which they called Sunday Island, and here again Bligh sent a party ashore in search of mussels. It was here that trouble began again between Bligh and Purcell. Whatever the argument may have been about, Bligh apparently felt that the rest of them should have been grateful to him for their survival, and he turned harshly on Purcell saying:

'If I had not been with you, you would not have been here now!'

Purcell, who, like many of his companions, considered that the mutiny had been Bligh's fault from the very beginning, replied insinuatingly:

'Yes, sir, if it had not been for you we should not have been here.'

Bligh grasped his meaning and roared:

'What's that you say?'

Purcell repeated with facetious innocence:

"I said, sir, that if it had not been for you we should not have been here.'

'You damned scoundrel, what do you mean?'

Purcell now lost his temper too and answered hotly:

'I am not a scoundrel, sir, I am as good a man as you in that respect.'

Purcell's behaviour was now dangerously close to open mutiny, and Bligh, like Christian, was absolutely determined to maintain his authority whatever the circumstances might be. Nevertheless he now did a very peculiar thing. He seized one of the cutlasses and curtly ordered Purcell to prepare to defend himself. But the suddenness of this grim challenge apparently had the desired effect because Purcell's courage seemed to desert him, and he backed away muttering:

'No, sir, you are my officer.'

At this point Fryer returned from his mussel-collecting sortie, and instead of taking his captain's part he laughed jeeringly at the situation and shouted rudely to Bligh:

'No fighting here. You are both under arrest!'

Whether the remark was a joke or not, Bligh now turned fiercely on Fryer and growled:

'By God, sir, if you offered to touch me I would cut you down.'

Fryer tried to make Boatswain Cole take his side but Cole, recognizing the danger of the situation, refused to commit himself so that Fryer too was forced to change his tone. His next remark was milder and more respectful:

'Sir, this is a very wrong time to talk of fighting.'

Bligh pointed at Purcell with his cutlass:

'Didn't you hear the fellow tell me that he is as good as I?'

By this time Purcell obviously thought it best to follow Fryer's example, and he broke into a conciliatory tone:

'When you called me a scoundrel I told you that I was not, but as good a man as you in that respect and when you said that you had brought us here I told you that had it not been for you we should not have been here.'

Bligh was anything but satisfied with this snide apology, but on the other hand he realized that if he pursued the matter it would only make the situation worse, and he brought the episode mildly to a close with the comment:

'Well then, if you had not any meaning in what you said, I ask your pardon.'

From that day onward Bligh never went anywhere without his cutlass, and he remarked gratefully and piously in the log-book that, 'the Almighty has seemed pleased to give me sufficient strength to make use of it'.

As they sailed on past the coast they several times caught sight of natives on the mainland, and when on the 1st June they encamped on a small island for the night, Bligh gave strict orders that only one small fire should be made and that this should be kept well sheltered. Shortly afterwards on the same evening, when he was out inspecting the island, he glanced behind him and was horrified to see a huge blaze lighting up the camp. He rushed back and found that, contrary to his orders, Fryer had made his own fire and fallen asleep beside it. Bligh's remarks to Fryer on this occasion were not recorded, and even if they had been it is doubtful that they could be included here. Meanwhile another party had been sent off to catch noddies, and when they returned they had a mere twelve birds with them, remarkably few in view of the large numbers of these birds which were roosting on this small, sandy island. Nelson duly explained that Lamb, the ship's butcher, had rushed in among the sleeping birds and frightened them before the others could make a fair catch. This was apparently more than Bligh could stand, for, without another thought for his dignity and rank, he rushed at the hapless butcher and gave him a tremendous clout on the ear. Had the captain but known it, this was more than deserved since long after the voyage was over it emerged that on this particular evening Lamb had, in fact, seized and devoured no less than nine birds.

At dawn they sailed on again. Bligh's plan was to follow Cook's route, swinging west at the northernmost point of York Peninsula and slipping out into the Torres Straits by Prince of Wales Island. As a matter of fact Bligh continued even further out to the north, since he mistook the island for part of the mainland, and as a result of this, without realizing it, he discovered a very satisfactory new passage through the labyrinth of channels which makes up the Torres Straits. By the 4th June they were out again in the open waters of the Arafura Sea.

The island landings inside the Great Barrier Reef had certainly restored the *Bounty* men both physically and mentally, but on the other hand the only addition to their food supplies amounted to a few dozen dried mussels, and there was still a good ten days sailing ahead of them. Fortunately however, they continued to capture the odd seabird, and on the 5th June they managed to seize a black tern, whereupon the blood was fed to the weakest men before the flesh was divided up among the rest. The following day Bligh also increased the biscuit ration from two to three helpings a day, but nevertheless there was not a man who was not suffering from exhaustion, sleeplessness and swollen legs. The condition of Ledward and Lebogue was particularly serious, and the general state of health was by no means improved by the unremitting downpour of rain. The one and only thing that they had to be grateful for was a strong steady following wind which was driving them along at the rate of nearly four knots.

On the 11th June someone managed to capture another black tern, and Bligh decided to keep it until the following day. This decision irritated Fryer in particular, but fortunately his and everyone else's attention on board was diverted before a proper dispute could arise by the sudden appearance over the horizon of a rocky coastline. They knew at once that this must be Timor in the East Indies, but the island is three hundred miles long, and all Bligh could say for certain was that they were somewhere off the south coast. He vaguely remembered, however, that the Dutch garrison town of Kupang was situated in the southwest corner, and he therefore began to sail slowly along the palm-lined shore in this direction.

When night fell they had seen nothing beyond a few small Malayan villages, and Bligh decided to heave to for the night rather than run the risk of missing Kupang. At noon the next day, when they had still not found the Dutch town, they dropped anchor to fix their position. The launch was now only a few hundred yards off shore, and there was not a man on board who was not sorely tempted by the sight of the profusion of coconuts and fruit growing there. The restrained themselves, however, comforted by the knowledge that they were now very near indeed to Kupang. The only two who were not prepared to wait, of course, were Fryer and Purcell who insisted upon being allowed to go ashore at once. In the end Bligh sailed right in close and told them to get ashore, at the same time forbidding anyone else to leave the boat. Faced with the prospect of being left behind, the two men again relented, and Bligh sailed on as soon as he had taken the sun altitude. In the absence of a chronometer, he was only able to fix their latitude but this alone was sufficient to assure him that they must be in the immediate vicinity of Kupang, and sure enough a few hours later they reached the southwest point of the island where a friendly Malay villager offered to tow them the last bit of the way. Despite the fact that there were only a few miles left, it is questionable whether or not they could have managed without this tow, since there was no wind in these sheltered waters and none of them was capable of rowing more than a couple of hundred yards.

At two o'clock that night they heard the sound of a cannon shot, and just before dawn on the 14th June their Malayan pilot announced that they had arrived. Thus all in all, according to Bligh's own careful calculations, with the loss of only one man he had sailed the overloaded, open ship's boat for forty-two days, covering a total of three thousand seven hundred and one nautical miles of unknown ocean. His comment in the log at this juncture was as follows:

'Thus happily ended through the assistance of Divine Providence without accident a voyage of the most extraordinary nature that ever happened in the world, let it be taken in its extreme duration and so much want of the necessities of life.'

On their arrival, despite the fact that everyone on board was desperately in need of care and attention, Bligh, acting in accordance with naval etiquette formally raised a distress pennant and waited for the local commandant to wish them welcome and grant permission to land. Fortunately they were spotted at once by the garrison guards, and a few minutes later Captain Bligh staggered ashore. The first person he encountered was an English sailor who immediately took him to his own commander, a certain Captain Spykeman who had spent many years in Dutch service. Spykeman promptly organized a proper English breakfast in his home, complete with tea, and requested Bligh to send for his men without delay. Bligh did this, though he rather spitefully gave orders for Fryer to remain on board as ship's guard.

He was deeply moved as he sat at the breakfast table, nor was he ashamed to admit this emotion in his logbook. He wrote:

'The abilities of the most eminent artists perhaps could never have more brilliantly shone than in a delineation of two groups of figures that at this time presented themselves, and where one might be so much at a loss to know which most to admire, whether the eyes of famine sparkling at immediate relief, or the preserver horror-struck at the spectres of men. For anyone to conceive the picture of such poor, miserable beings, let him fancy that in his house he is in the moment of giving relief to eighteen men whose ghastly countenance, but from the known cause, would be equally liable to afright as demand pity, let him view their limbs full of sores and their bodies nothing but skin and bones habited in rags, and at last let him conceive he sees the tears of joy and gratitude flowing over their cheeks at their benefactors. With the mixture of horror, surprise and pity that his mind will be then agitated, were the people of Timor on giving us relief.'

The Dutch governor put a comfortable and roomy house at Bligh's disposal, but when the latter heard that on account of shortage of space his men would have to live either in the garrison hospital or else on board Captain Spykeman's ship, he immediately made room for them in his house, even though he would surely have preferred to keep clear of the majority of them for a few days. Bligh's next move was to submit a full list of the mutineers' names to the Dutch authorities before finally settling down to the unattractive task of writing a full report on the mutiny and subsequent events to their lordships at the Admiralty. At the same time he began making enquiries about the quickest way he and his men could get back to England. To his annoyance he learned that Batavia was the only place in the Dutch East Indies from which ships sailed directly to England, and furthermore that he would have to get there by October or wait until the next sailing which would be in January. Another complication was that there were no regular communications between Kupang and Batavia, nor was there any chance of hiring a suitable vessel for this trip. Finally Bligh purchased a small schooner which he christened *Resource*.

Sailing a forty-foot schooner eighteen hundred miles from Kupang to Batavia would be no pleasure cruise, and Bligh realized that he would have to wait until his men were fully recovered before he could even consider beginning the voyage. But this too was going to take time though he found it impossible to remain idle. Consequently he filled side after side of his logbook with notes on such varied subjects as market prices, slave trade, Chinese burial ceremonies, the history of Timor, the best means of cultivating rice and the health and general characteristics of the Malayan natives. Nelson the botanist seems to have been the only other member of the crew who

was as energetic as Bligh, and he daily made long botanical excursions and even succeeded in collecting a number of breadfruit shoots. Tragically enough, however, his activities were
short-lived because within a month of their arrival he con-
tracted an 'inflammatory disease' and soon died.

Where his men were concerned Bligh was just as strict and
impersonal as ever, but that this whole attitude was a facade
and that he was, in fact, lonely and greatly oppressed by the
misfortunes which he had suffered emerges very clearly from
the following letter which he wrote to his wife shortly before
sailing from Kupang:

My dear, dear Betsy,
I am now in a part of the world that I never expected; it is,
however, a place that has afforded me relief and saved my life,
and I have the happiness to assure you I am now in perfect
health. That the chance of this letter getting to you before
others of a later date is so very small, I shall only just give you
a short account of the cause of my arrival here—what an
emotion does my heart and soul feel that I have once more an
opportunity of writing to you and my little angels, and particularly as you have all been so near losing the best of friends,
when you would have had no person to have regarded you as I
do and you must have spent the remainder of your days without knowing what was become of me, or what would have been
still worse, to have known I had been starved to death at sea or
destroyed by Indians—all these dreadful circumstances I have
combated with success, and in the most extraordinary manner
that ever happened, never despairing from the first moment of
my disaster but that I should overcome all my difficulties.
Know then, my own dear Betsy, I have lost the *Bounty*. . . .
The secrecy of this mutiny is beyond all conception, so that I
cannot discover that any that are with me had the least knowledge of it. Even Mr Tom Ellison took such a liking to Otaheite
that he also turned pirate so that I have been run down by my
own dogs. I, however, have every expectation to get the better
of everything. . . . My misfortunes I trust will be properly
considered by all the world. It was a circumstance I could not
foresee. I had not sufficient officers, and had they granted me
marines, most likely the affair would never have happened—I
had not a spirited or brave fellow about me, and the mutineers

treated them as such. My conduct has been free from blame, and I showed everyone that, tied as I was, I defied every villain to hurt me; Hayward and Hallet were midshipmen of Christian's watch, but they alarmed no one, and I found them on deck seemingly incerned (unconcerned) until they were ordered into the boat. The latter has turned out a worthless impudent scoundrel, but I beg of you to relate nothing of them until I come home. I know how shocked you will be at this affair, but I request of you, my dear Betsy, to think nothing of it, all is now past and we will again look forward to future happiness; nothing but true consciousness as an officer that I have done well could support me. I cannot write to your uncle or anyone, but my public letters, therefore tell them all that they will find my character respectable and honour untarnished. I have saved my pursery books so that all my profits hitherto will take place and all will be well. Give my blessing to my dear Harriet, my dear Mary, my dear Betsy, and to my dear little stranger, and tell them I shall soon be home.

Remember me to your father and Annie Campbell and Mrs C. and give affectionate respects to your uncle and family. To you, my love, I give all that an affectionate husband can give— love, respect, and all that is or ever will be in the power of your ever affectionate friend and husband.

Wm. Bligh.

Having armed the little schooner with four cannons (as protection against the innumerable Chinese pirates in these waters) and also taken on board a collection of plants, including three breadfruit shoots, Bligh sailed out from Timor on the 20th August. Presumably for purely sentimental reasons, and despite the burden it entailed, Bligh also took the launch in tow. Altogether it took *Resource* forty-two days to reach Batavia, that is to say exactly as long as the journey from Tofua to Timor, and although the crew did not suffer in the same way there were nevertheless a number of occasions when the situation looked particularly ominous. The worst of these incidents happened not at sea but in the harbour at Surabaja in the middle of September. During the halt there, Bligh was faced with what almost amounted to another mutiny, and once again the instigators of the trouble were Purcell and Fryer. This time, however, Bligh was able to call on the assistance of Dutch troops who arrested the two men and put them in irons in two other Dutch vessels with which *Resource* was sailing in company to Batavia. At the next harbour Fryer apologized for his behaviour and was released, but Purcell remained in irons until the small fleet reached its destination on the 1st October.

There proved to be very few places available on the European ships leaving Batavia, and consequently the eighteen survivors from the launch were at last obliged to split up. During the wait here the ship's cook, Thomas Hall, died from the notorious local swamp fever, and Bligh too was gravely ill with it. Nevertheless on the 16th October he embarked on an England-bound trading vessel, and after a certain amount of trouble he managed to get permission to take Samuel and his steward John Smith with him. The remainder were left behind under Fryer's command to wait for a later ship. The launch and *Resource* had already been sold for a very small sum.

The voyage home via the Cape of Good Hope took five months, and on the 14th March, 1790 Bligh was once again back in Portsmouth. Of the men he left behind in Batavia, Elphinstone and Linkletter died of fever, Lamb died on the voyage home and Ledward in another vessel was shipwrecked and drowned. Thus, including Norton who had been murdered on Tofua and Nelson who had died at Timor, only twelve of the original nineteen who had left the *Bounty* finally reached England. The remarkable thing about this, however, is that none of the deceased actually died during the nightmare journey from Tofua to Timor, a fact which serves to emphasize the brilliance of William Bligh as a seaman, navigator and leader.

As soon as Bligh's arrival became known, the newspapers began to publish highly imaginative descriptions of the mutiny and the subsequent voyage in the launch, and one of the largest theatres in London quickly produced a dramatization of Bligh's adventures. The billposters give a good idea of the type of production this was:

ROYALTY THEATRE
Well-Street, near Goodman's-Fields.

— — — — — —

This present THURSDAY, May 6, 1790,

will be presented

A FACT, TOLD IN ACTION, CALLED

THE PIRATES!

or

The Calamities of Capt. BLIGH.

Exhibiting a full account of his Voyage from his taking
leave at the Admiralty.

AND SHEWING
The BOUNTY sailing down the River THAMES.

The Captain's reception at Otaheite and exchanging the *British
Manufactures* for the BREAD-FRUIT TREES. With an OTA-
HEITEAN DANCE

The Attachment of the OTAHEITEAN WOMEN to, and their
Distress at parting from, the BRITISH SAILORS.

An exact Representation of
The Seisure of Capt. BLIGH in the cabin of the BOUNTY, by
the pirates.

With the affecting Scene of forcing the Captain and his faithful
Followers into the boat.

Their Distress at Sea, and Repulse by the Natives of One of the
Friendly Islands.

Their miraculous Arrival at the *Cape* of *Good Hope*, and their
friendly Reception by the Governor.

DANCES AND CEREMONIES of the HOTTENTOTS
On their Departure. And their happy Arrival in England.
Rehearsed under the immediate Instruction of a Person who
was on-board the Bounty, Store-Ship.

This extraordinary spectacle was as effective as any tele-vision or publicity programme today in turning Bligh into a popular hero, and the entire campaign reached its zenith in June of the same year when a series of extracts were taken from Bligh's logs, carefully edited and published as a book by the Admiralty.

In accordance with the existing statutes it had to be estab-lished through a court martial who was responsible for the loss of the *Bounty*, and this was duly set up at the end of October as soon as the remnants of Bligh's followers had arrived home from Batavia. First Bligh's own description of the mutiny was read, and then the petty officers were questioned as to whether or not in the days immediately preceding the mutiny they had heard anything which indicated that such an action was being contemplated. They all denied this emphatically, and then the following question was put to Fryer, the master:

'Did Captain Bligh and you others do your best to retake the ship after the mutiny had broken out?'

'All that was within our power,' replied Fryer confidently.

Midshipmen Hallet and Hayward heartily corroborated Fryer's claim that everything possible had been done to reclaim the ship, and then the president of the court asked Bligh if he had any comments or charges to prefer against the men present. Bligh replied that the only one whose behaviour had not been satisfactory was Purcell. Finally the court asked each of the men present if they had any accusations to make against their captain and they all replied that they had none.

Shortly afterwards the court pronounced its findings as follows:

'This court has found that the *Bounty* was taken by force from Lieutenant Bligh by Fletcher Christian and certain other mutineers, and hereby declares that Lieutenant Bligh and those of his petty officers and crew who returned to England and are here present are freed from all responsibility.'

To anyone who is familiar with all the details of the mutiny it is quite evident that a great deal of what happened was con-cealed at the court martial. It is understandable, of course, that the petty officers and midshipmen who had been guilty of dere-liction of duty and cowardice did not give evidence against themselves. But on the other hand, why did Bligh not give a truer picture of all that had happened, and why did he criticize Purcell's behaviour while not mentioning the relatively much more irresponsible conduct of the ship's master, Fryer? The captain's behaviour certainly seems somewhat peculiar. It may of course be claimed that after all they had been through together Bligh's whole attitude had become more amenable. Another, more popular, interpretation is that Bligh was most anxious to avoid anything which might threaten his career, and that he felt that a long trial wherein he might be called upon to answer counter accusations by his men could easily spoil his chances of promotion. All such theories, however, are purely conjectural, and even if they might be correct, one nevertheless has a feeling that there must have existed other concealed reasons for Bligh's remarkably mild attitude. It can be pointed out in this respect that even in the case of Purcell, who was individually tried, Bligh was so conciliatory that he was let off with no more than a reprimand.

However, the mutiny itself was a crime which could not be overlooked, and their lordships thus decided to despatch a warship to the South Seas without further delay to hunt down the mutineers and bring them to justice. This thankless and rather wild project was to be commanded by a certain Captain Edward Edwards who was well known for his severity and strict discipline. At his disposal he had a twenty-four gun frigate, the *Pandora*, with a crew of one hundred and sixty. Midshipman Hayward was appointed second lieutenant on board *Pandora*, a well-advised measure, since, apart from the men who had returned with Bligh, there was no one of authority who had any idea what the mutineers looked like.

Before *Pandora* sailed from England on the 7th November, Bligh had been promoted commander, and scarcely a month later he was given full captain's rank. Sir Joseph Banks' confidence in Bligh was in no way affected by what had happened, and no sooner were the court martial proceedings over than he again began to campaign for a second breadfruit expedition, once more with Bligh in command. George III, who was exceedingly prestige-conscious, gave his full support to the new project and arrangements commenced forthwith. Unfortunately, however, the expedition was prevented from leaving right away on account of the preparations for war against

France, and it was not until August 1791 that the new expedition departed. Their lordships seem to have learned from their mistakes, moreover, since this time Bligh was given three very competent commissioned officers to assist him, besides a contingent of eighteen marines and finally an additional small escort vessel to sail in company with him.

CHAPTER VIII

THE LONG ARM OF JUSTICE

HAVING followed the destinies of the two principal characters and their companions this far, it is time to turn back again and see what happened to the nine mutineers and seven loyalists who went ashore in Matavai Bay on the 22nd September, 1789 when the *Bounty* made her very last visit to Tahiti.

All sixteen of these men had their respective taio brothers either in Poino's kingdom, Haapape or else in Teina's Pare. At the same time of course they also had numerous other male and female acquaintances and friends, while at least half a dozen of them had established permanent mistresses among the island girls. They were thus received as cherished relations and husbands who had now returned after a long voyage. The men themselves, however, without even bothering over the fact that Matavai was the most frequented harbour on the island, and that their presence would be discovered the moment an English ship appeared, accepted with gratitude and delight the offers of local hospitality.

The only person missing from the huge reception committee was 'King' Teina, who incidentally had since changed name again and was now known as Mate. (In order to avoid confusion he will continue to be referred to as Teina in this account.) Shortly after the departure of his protector, Bligh, in April 1789, Teina began to be seriously concerned over the threat of the attack and plundering of his kingdom by the other chieftains, and he therefore decided to withdraw to his brother-in-law Vehiatua's domains on the Taiara peninsula. According to a rumour which soon reached the *Bounty* men, Teina now even employed an armed bodyguard who was said to be an

English naval deserter too. Teina's younger brother Ariipaea, however, who was acting as a sort of regent during the former's absence, and who incidentally was more popular with his people than Teina, did everything in his power to persuade the sixteen well-armed and well-equipped white men to settle in Pare. But to the keen disappointment of the two brothers, only five of them, mutineers Muspratt and Hillbrant and loyalists Byrne, McIntosh and Norman, accepted the Parean offer of a large piece of land and plenty of servants.

The other ten men preferred to remain on Venus Point in the kingdom of the good-natured, easy-going Poino, where they had first been initiated into the pleasant mysteries of Tahitian living. Here the loyalist Morrison, who now seems to have been accepted as the *de facto* leader, was housed by none less than Chief Poino himself. The mutineer Millward also joined the royal household, although this was on account of his having established a liaison with one of Poino's wives. Stewart, the loyalist midshipman, was one of the half-dozen men who had found a regular mistress, which so far as the Tahitians were concerned, was tantamount to being married, and he thus settled down quite naturally with his 'father-in-law', along with his colleague Heywood. The third household consisted of mutineer Thompson and loyalist Coleman, both of whom moved in with the latter's 'parents-in-law'. In a fourth hut lived the three mutineers Burkett, Sumner and Ellison, and here it was Sumner's sociable 'parents-in-law' who prepared their food and kept house for them. Mutineer Skinner was apparently less gregarious because he went off to live alone with his girl. Finally there was the violent and sanguinary Churchill who held court in his taio-brother's house and brooded over Morrison's enviable position as unspoken leader of the group. Generally speaking, however, the sixteen men were not split up as one might have expected into loyalists and mutineers; instead they seem to have formed a reasonably harmonious group with a fairly common bond of friendship among them.

Even though the *Bounty* men must by this time have realized that Teina's position was not so elevated and venerable as they had been led to believe when they first visited Tahiti, they nevertheless still regarded his son Tu as the heir apparent of the entire island. Thus as soon as they had settled down and established their domestic arrangements, they set off together to

Pare to pay homage to the young prince. With the still faithful Hitihiti as spokesman and master of ceremonies they expressed their veneration in true Tahitian fashion by shedding the special bark cloth mantles which they were wearing over their shoulders for the occasion, presented Tu with a fine selection of iron goods and finally, on the instigation of Hitihiti, handed over the fearsome idols which they had seized on Tupuai. To round off their obeisances they fired off a series of deafening salutes with their muskets. The seven year old Tu was understandably vastly impressed by all this, and they were consequently assured that they should consider themselves completely at home no matter where they were on Tahiti. Ariipaea, Tu's uncle, concluded the ceremony by ordering an elaborate feast and presenting each one of the *Bounty* men with a large piece of land, clearly in the hope that this gesture might persuade one or two more of the white men to desert Venus Point in favour of Pare.

To have ignored Tu's father Teina would have been a grave breach of etiquette, and since the latter was still too timid to show himself at Matavai, the *Bounty* men despatched a delegation under Churchill's eager command to pay their respects to Teina on the Taiarapu peninsula. Churchill returned a fortnight later together with Teina's much discussed bodyguard, an Englishman named Brown. Brown stated that he had been left behind by a Swedish warship at his own request about a month before, and then went on to boast of the many great deeds which he had accomplished in the course of his life. He claimed that he had been a sergeant of the marines in Portsmouth, an officer in the army of the Indian Prince Haidar Ali and captain of a ship which he had himself captured. This was all prior to his inexplicable decision to join one of Gustavus III of Sweden's warships as an ordinary seaman. Although many of Brown's stories were clearly the product of a fertile imagination, there is no doubt that he had in fact landed on Tahiti from a ship flying the Swedish flag. The activities of this ship have always been a mystery to maritime historians, but recent investigations have revealed that it was on a naval mission, approved by Gustavus III, and financed by an English merchant named John Henry Cox. Since 1788, Sweden had been at war with Russia, and at his own request Cox had been appointed by Gustavus III to hit the enemy in the rear by attacking his trading posts in

Alaska and Kamtschatka. This absurd project would hardly have been likely to make any difference to Russia, and apparently Cox never made any serious attempt to carry it through. What happened to the expedition is in no way connected with this narrative, but on the other hand it can be mentioned that Cox, without knowing anything about the mutiny of course, had tried to put into Tupuai just before his arrival at Tahiti, and this must have been at the very time when the mutineers were striving to build their stockade there. Since it was late in the afternoon, however, and because there was an offshore wind, Cox apparently gave up after a couple of unsuccessful attempts to land and continued on his way to Tahiti without the slightest idea of the strange state of affairs ashore.

Some time later Poino, who was an extremely sensible man, showed Morrison a letter from Cox addressed to all ship's captains who might put in to Tahiti. It emerged from this that the bold Brown had knifed another member of the crew on *Gustav III* (or *Mercury*, which was the ship's cover name) and had simply been dumped ashore on Tahiti as a punishment for his crime. The majority of the *Bounty* men had disliked Brown from the outset, and it was with a sense of relief that they saw him depart again for Taiarapu to resume his post as bodyguard and military adviser to Teina.

The party had now been on Tahiti somewhat over a month, and had thus had plenty of time to consider their position and to make plans for the future. The nine mutineers must obviously have been the most uneasy, since, even though they might be fairly certain that Bligh and his men could not hope to survive, they must at the same time have realized that in due course the Admiralty would be bound to send out another ship to investigate what had happened to the breadfruit expedition. The wisest move, of course, would have been to follow Christian's example and make for some deserted and inaccessible island as far away from Tahiti as it was possible to get in a native canoe. But none of them seems to have thought of this, probably because they were suffering from a form of the well-known and aptly named disease 'Polynesian paralysis', which manifests itself in a complete inability on the part of the afflicted individual to make the effort to board a homeward bound ship.

The first of the sixteen men to give any thought to how to

get away from the island was the loyalist and tacitly-accepted leader of the group, Morrison. Despite the fact that on the face of things he was as contented with the idyllic island existence as his companions, he nevertheless felt that it was his duty to build some sort of boat and try to get to Timor or Batavia and thence back to England. His first step was to confide in the two loyalist carpenters Norman and McIntosh concerning his intentions. Strangely enough these two men fully supported Morrison's extraordinary plan and promised their complete co-operation. But a team of three was far from adequate for such a project, and they realized that somehow or other they would have to recruit the help of the rest. It was evident to Morrison that the mutineers could hardly be expected to show any enthusiasm for such a plan, since if the loyalists managed to reach England they would be bound sooner or later to acquaint the Admiralty with what had happened and reveal the whereabouts of the guilty men. He thus claimed that he was intending to build a boat for the fun of it, and so that when it was completed they could make pleasure cruises to other island groups in the vicinity. Presumably because they were somewhat bored with having nothing to do, at least ten men immediately agreed to give a hand, and none but the initiated seem to have suspected Morrison's real plan.

The boat-builders were quickly divided up into teams, and they went to work with a will. Even Brown got to hear of it, and made the long trip over from Taiarapu to give advice. Much to the relief of the boat-builders, however, he quickly tired of so much constructive activity and returned to his lord and master Teina.

Force of habit is a potent factor, and it was not long before the boat-builders fell back into their regular ship's routine with watch-keeping and the formal raising and lowering of the flag at forenoon and sunset. At the same time, Morrison began to keep a proper logbook, and here he recorded everything that happened with the same care and accuracy that Bligh had done during the voyage. The group felt nevertheless that they had forgotten something of importance, and in due course they realized that this was Sunday matins. From that moment onwards the service was performed regularly and piously, and to balance it another time-honoured procedure was also resumed. It had become the habit, among the large numbers of natives who gathered to watch the boat-building activities, for one or another of them to purloin the odd tool. The only answer to this, resolved Morrison, was flogging, and thus it became the practice to seize any unfortunate native who was caught stealing and administer the requisite number of lashes. Incidentally this gesture and the other routine procedures should help to dispel the popular claim that the mutineers fled to Tahiti full of Rousseauesque ardour and the desperate anxiety to escape the vileness of European civilization.

The boat-building programme soon produced innumerable knotty problems. The Tahitians themselves, skilled canoe craftsmen, were only too willing to lend a hand, but the vessel that Morrison and his men were planning was unlike anything the islanders had ever seen. The Tahitian canoes, either a long slender hull with an outrigger or else two identical heavy hulls of catamaran design, were built of planks and actually 'sewn' together by means of a heavy raffia-type material. But instead of building a large catamaran type vessel, which would have sailed well and relatively fast, the *Bounty* men obstinately persisted with their plans for a proper clinker-built schooner, and were thus forced to manage in the actual construction work without the help of the natives. Two other major problems were the long, exhausting treks which had to be made up into the hills to find the proper timber, and the lack of a saw large enough to carry out the basic sawing of the long planks. Here, however, the Tahitians were of invaluable assistance with their remarkable technique of splitting the large tree trunks with stone wedges and then smoothing the planks with rough coral stone. Finally the work was seriously delayed by the absence of a forge, and it was not until Coleman contrived with great patience and ingenuity to construct one from stone and clay that the boat-building project really began to make progress.

Despite all these complications they had practically completed the skeleton of the hull when, on the 8th February, 1790, an unfortunate incident occurred which threatened to wreck the entire project. Churchill's accomplice, the unsavoury Thompson, was roundly thrashed by a native for having raped his sister. Shortly afterwards, in a vicious temper after this humiliating experience, he turned on a crowd of natives who were watching the boat-building work and endeavoured to drive them away. They were apparently slow in dispersing, whereupon he seized his musket and fired pointblank into the group. The ball killed a man and the child in his arms and injured two others. All the *Bounty* men, with the exception of Churchill who thought this a good lesson for the savages, were furious over Thompson's brutal stupidity, and feared that Poino and his subjects would lose their patience and avenge themselves on the group as a whole. When this point of view was expressed Churchill immediately offered to organize an effective striking force which would knock a proper sense of respect into the natives for once and all.

This vicious alternative was immediately rejected by the others, and they were busily discussing the best means of making an adequate apology when to their great good fortune it emerged that the dead man was from another part of Tahiti, and therefore had no rights whatever in Haapape or Pare. The *Bounty* men were pleased and relieved to hear this, everyone that is except the barbarous Churchill, who in his frustration recruited his kindred spirits Thompson and Brown and set off for the Taiarapu peninsula, where he hoped that Teina would be more appreciative of his military abilities.

Generally satisfied with the outcome of the unfortunate episode, the boat-builders now returned to work with a will. But it was not long before Churchill made his presence felt again. Scarcely two weeks later a letter arrived from him, a panegyric on life at Taiarapu and the unending goodness and generosity of Teina and his brother-in-law Vehiatua. It concluded by urging the entire group to move over to Taiarapu without delay. But Morrison and his men were sick to death of Churchill, and they did not even bother to reply to the letter. This was a mistake, however, because shortly afterwards Churchill showed up again in person at Matavai, this time with the startling news that Vehiatua was dead, that he himself had been elected chief of the realm and that anyone who cared to accompany him back would be richly rewarded for their loyalty. The only ones who accepted this offer were Muspratt and Burkett, both of whom had anyway long since tired of the boat-building work. So Churchill returned to Taiarapu again, obviously in a savage mood because on the way back he shot down in cold blood a harmless native, without any apparent reason at all.

Scarcely a month later even more incredible news arrived

from Taiarapu. In the middle of April Brown appeared at Matavai and reported that both Chief Churchill and his prime minister, Thompson, were dead. Since no one had any confidence in Brown, however, Morrison despatched one of his own men to find out what really had happened. The messenger returned with the following account which was subsequently confirmed by the natives themselves.

Shortly after his arrival at Taiarapu in the middle of March, Churchill had fallen out with Thompson, who also seems to have had ambitions to become a chief. Thompson now left Teahuupoo on the south side of the peninsula where Churchill had settled, and paddled up to Tautira on the north side. Here Vehiatua's uncle Titorea and the conniving Teina received him with open arms. Churchill suspected, probably on good grounds, that Thompson would make trouble for him and thus, to be on the safe side, one dark night he sent agents up to Tautira with instructions to enter Thompson's residence and steal his muskets while he slept. The plan was completely successful, and Churchill even succeeded subsequently in assuring Thompson that he had had nothing whatsoever to do with the theft. Thompson, stupid and gullible, believed this and duly moved back again to Churchill's domains. Shortly afterwards, when Churchill had ill-treated one of his most willing servants, a man named Maititi, the latter took his revenge simply by revealing to Thompson who had really been responsible for the theft of his arsenal. Thompson did not make a fuss, he merely waited his opportunity and then carefully and conveniently shot Churchill in the back. Violence engenders violence, however; the vendetta is a common phenomenon on Tahiti. Some of Chief Churchill's subjects now felt it their duty to annihilate Thompson, and this they did at the first suitable opportunity by the simple method of beating his brains out with a number of large stones.

Shaken though they were by this bloody narrative, none of the *Bounty* men could bring himself to feel any genuine grief over the fate of the two men involved, and in his logbook Morrison solemnly declared that it was Providence herself in the form of the native assassins who had punished Thompson for his ghastly crime.

Free now from trouble and strife, the boat-builders were able to continue their work undisturbed, and in the beginning of

July, 1790 the schooner was ready for launching. They had every good reason to be proud of their work, since the completed vessel was thirty-six feet long, with a ten-foot beam and able to accommodate comfortably a dozen people.

The launching ceremony was carried out according to Tahitian traditions by Chief Poino, and Morrison described the proceedings in excellent detail in his logbook.

'All being ready on the 5th we applied to Poeno who told me that the priest must perform his prayers over her, and then he would have her carried to the sea, the priest being sent for and a young pig and a plantain given him when he began walking round and round the vessel, stopping at the stem and stern and muttering short sentences in an unknown dialect; and having a bundle of young plantain trees brought to him by Poenos order, he now and then tossed one in on her deck. He kept at this all day and night and was hardly finished by sunrise on the 6th. When Poeno and Tew, Matte's father, came with three or four hundred men, and having each made a long oration, their men were divided into two partys and the servants of Tew having received a hog and some cloth which was provided by Poeno for the occasion, one of the priests went on board and several plantain trees were tossed to him from both sides. He then ran fore and aft and exorted them to exert themselves, and on a signal being given they closed in, and those who could not reach by hand got long poles, a song being given they all joined in chorus and she soon began to move and in half an hour she reached the beach where she was launched and called the Resolution. Tho' several trees were cut down which stood in the way, yet she received no damage, except breaking the masts in a passage of about ¾ ths of a mile.'

Christian and his party had taken all the sail cloth with them when they left Tahiti for the last time, and thus the only alternative for the boat-builders was to rig the schooner with sections of leaf matting sewn together. But to their intense disappointment this proved anything but satisfactory, since time and time again the sewn seams tore and the sails collapsed. After having tackled this problem in various ways and with very little success, Morrison sensibly decided to postpone indefinitely his plans for crossing the Pacific. Nevertheless the ship proved perfectly adequate for pleasure cruising, and everyone keenly looked forward to the first excursion. Curiously enough, however, the maiden voyage of the *Resolution* was to be anything but a pleasure cruise, and to examine the circumstances surrounding this it is necessary to look back a few months.

When Christian and his men had tried to colonize Tupuai, they had made the grave mistake of taking the part of one of the three island chieftains, thus making enemies of the other two. Despite this obvious lesson, the party who remained on Tahiti made the same error only a few months later when they allied themselves with the Teina dynasty instead of remaining strictly neutral in the island's interior affairs.

Once they had more or less accepted the so-called protection of Teina, it was naturally not long before he began to make use of them. As early as April 1790 Teina had cautiously approached his English friends with the proposal that they should support his brother-in-law Metuaaro, a powerful and despotic chieftain on Moorea, who was quarrelling with his neighbours. Probably with the fate of Churchill fresh in their minds, the *Bounty* men had on this occasion contented themselves with repairing Teina's stock of muskets and lending him their experienced strategist Hitihiti, who, incidentally, quickly defeated all the neighbouring forces.

This was a very modest contribution on the part of the *Bounty* men, but the real danger lay in the fact that it could in itself easily lead to more significant assistance later on. Sure enough, a few months' later, on the 12th September, a new appeal arrived. This time it was Teina's younger brother Ariipaea who was concerned for the safety of himself and the young 'heir apparent', Tu. According to Ariipaea, the neighbouring kingdom of Tefana was preparing for an attack on Pare. Without investigating the charges or offering to act as mediator, Morrison now made all haste to Pare with his entire force plus the ever belligerent Brown. Ariipaea was awaiting them with a large company of spearmen, lancers and sling-throwers, and flanked by these bold warriors Morrison and his men marched upon the enemy. Before General Morrison even had time to give the order to open fire, the Pare warriors rushed into a desperate hand-to-hand battle with their opponents. This made it impossible for the musketry to open fire, since there was nothing to distinguish the natives from each other, and consequently the élite corps became no more than crestfallen spectators. But their very presence apparently gave the Pare company increased confidence, because in due course the enemy broke up in confusion and fled. This unjustified and pointless intervention incensed Chief Tepahu of Tefana, and since he knew that he would be unable to defeat the well-armed white men alone, he proceeded to recruit the assistance of two chieftains in the powerful kingdom of Atehuru on the west coast of Tahiti. He was able to convince them with the perfectly valid argument that their turn would be bound to come, once the ambitious Parenese had succeeded in subjugating Tefana. Thus, according to a rumour which Ariipaea was quick to convey to the *Bounty* men, the aim of the triple alliance which was forming was to slay the perfidious foreigners and destroy their schooner warship.

Faced with this ominous situation, the position of the *Bounty* men was clearly irrevocable. Their fate was now allied to that of the Pare dynasty, and the only way out was to crush the enemy as quickly and effectively as possible. In collaboration with Ariipaea, and even the peaceful Poino, who likewise felt himself threatened, Morrison decided to apply the classical pincer movement and attack the enemy from both north and south. In order to achieve this, they sought the alliance of Chief Temarii whose kingdom, Papara, adjoined that of Atehurui in the south—Atehurui being one of the rival trio. Temarii was a scheming, two-faced rascal who had watched Teina's tactics and had several months previously recruited Burkett and Sumner into his régime. As yet he felt that he was not powerful enough to take up arms against Pare itself, so for the time being he had nothing at all against helping to annihilate their common rivals. To be on the safe side, Temarii's modest little force was strengthened by Hitihiti and Brown.

On the 22nd September the action began. While Temarii advanced comfortably from the south, Morrison and his men encountered an unexpected hindrance in the form of a powerful fortress with a high rampart strategically erected on top of a hill in Tefana. The Parenese, who were now campaigning according to some sort of order and discipline, allowed the *Bounty* men to lead the attack, yet once the inhabitants of the fortress gave up the struggle and fled the Parenese broke order and pursued them with unprecedented fury. The most intelligent move at this juncture would have been to conclude a peace with generous terms, but the natives were insistent that the campaign should continue, and after a short conference the musketeers agreed to this.

Now, at last, the schooner was to plays its part in the sad story. The major part of the enemy forces had been reassembled and were more anxious than ever to go into action again. It was obvious that if the attackers were going to achieve a decisive victory a major effort would have to be made. Morrison thus decided to use the *Resolution* as a warship, and his plan was simple but effective. While the land forces advanced slowly around the lagoon, the schooner, manned by the best shots among the musketeers, would keep abreast of them just offshore and fire on the enemy's flank. The plan was duly put into action with the *Resolution* accompanied by a fleet of forty canoes with some two thousand warriors on board. Last but not least Temarii and his well-armed troops continued to press the enemy from the south.

The Atehuru warriors, although roughly equal in numbers to the enemy, were no match for such skilled strategy, and it was not long before they were forced to revert to the old Polynesian defence tactics of retreating to inaccessible positions in the hills. They collapsed completely, however, when the merciless enemy ran amok in their villages, burning their homes and destroying their breadfruit trees and their plantations. The victory was celebrated with a week of festivities back in Pare, though even then the real victor, Teina, seems not to have had the courage to come out from his hiding place on the Taiarapu peninsula.

Having scarcely had time to observe the sea-going qualities of *Resolution* during her brief maiden voyage, the victors now resolved to make a more peaceful run, this time to Moorea. As might be expected they were received with tremendous hospitality by Teina's brother-in-law Metuaaro, and also succeeded at the same time in modifying certain minor construction faults in their fast and surprisingly roomy craft. Thoroughly satisfied with *Resolution* they now returned to Matavai and hauled her up on shore to protect her against the inevitable seasonal gales.

One of the trophies which the victors had borne home with them from the campaign against the Atehuruese was a narrow belt of plaited pandanus leaves embellished with red feathers. This simple belt, known in Tahitian as a *maro ura*, has the same significance as a coronet since it was a symbol of the bearer's position and power. When such a valuable possession changed hands—usually through inheritance, although force was sometimes used to acquire it—the event was normally celebrated by a sort of investiture comparable with a European coronation. On such occasions all those chieftains who were regarded as vassals of the holder of the belt were required to attend the investiture. As a rule, however, the number of vassals was very limited, and so far no Tahitian chieftain had ever been so powerful as to be recognized by everyone as absolute monarch of Tahiti. After the successful campaign against Atehuru, however, Teina was seized with a sort of megalomania, and decided to send his son Tu, adorned with the belt, on a tour of the realm to be paid homage to by each and every chieftain in Tahiti. There was a certain amount of calculated confidence behind this gesture, moreover, because Teina was fairly certain that if the worst came to the worst the *Bounty* men would once again support him wholeheartedly.

Since Teina's influence had diminished considerably on the Taiarapu peninsula following the death of Vehiatau, he decided to begin his son's tour of triumph in Papara where Chief Temarii owed Teina a considerable debt of gratitude. The *Bounty* group were of course present to a man when this impressive ceremony took place at the end of January 1791. A newly created symbol of kingship, which was almost as sacred as the feathered belt and which was equally prominent in the procession, was a Union Jack lavishly decorated with feathers. Another contribution, which was likewise equally symbolic of the occasion, was a musketry salute bravely fired by the English guests of honour. It is quite evident from Morrison's notes that the *Bounty* men were fully aware of, and not a little flattered by, their political and military importance. He wrote that the Tahitians interpreted their presence as 'a declaration on our part to support our flag in circumventing the island, as it was composed of English colours, and they made no scruple to say that war would be instantly made on those who should attempt to stop it.'

In view of the white men's clear indication of their position, the chieftains made no attempt to prevent the curious procession from passing through their domains, and although their acceptance of it did not imply any degree of actual submission, it was nevertheless a good start for Teina, and he should have been satisfied for the time being. But he was anxious to make use of his powerful allies while they were in the right frame of mind, and he now conceived a cunning plan for provoking them into joining him in the final campaign which would lead to his becoming absolute monarch of all Tahiti. He simply made a proclamation to the effect that all the chiefs of the island were required to present themselves in Pare to acknowledge their prince—knowing at the same time that many would ignore such an humiliating order.

The great ceremony took place on February 13, 1791 at a newly consecrated place of sacrifice near the Toara harbour where the *Bounty* had lain at anchor under Bligh's command some two years previously. Morrison has described the repugnant and barbaric ceremony as follows:

'Toonoeaiteatooa the young king being placed on the morai, a priest making a long prayer put the sash around his waist and the hat or bonnet on his head and haild him king of Taheite. Moottooaroo then began by his orator making a long speech and acknowledging him his king, when three human victims were brought in and offered for Morea, the priest of Moottooaroo placing them with their head towards the young king and with a long speech over each, he offered three young plantain trees. He then took an eye out of each, with a piece of split bamboo, and placing them on a leaf took a young plantain tree in one hand, and the eyes in the other made a long speech holding them up to the young king, the bodys were removed and buried by his priests in the morai, and the eyes put up with the plantain trees on the altar.'

At this point, apparently, Morrison, who was just as interested in ethnology as Bligh, took the opportunity to ask one of the priests for an explanation of the ritual and was informed that, 'the eye being the most valuable part is the fittest to be offered, and the reason the king sits with his mouth open, is to let the soul of the sacrifice enter into his soul, that he may be strengthened thereby, or that he may receive more strength of disernment from it.' Numerous modern ethnologists have interpreted this very usual symbolic gesture of eating the eye as one of the last relics of Polynesian cannibalism, and it is very possible that this is true.

Morrison continued:

'The rest of the chiefs then brought in their sacrifices in the same manner, going through the like ceremony, some bringing one victim and some two according to the bigness or extent of their districts, after which large droves of hogs and an immense quantity of other provisions, such as bread, yams, tarro, plantains, cocoa nuts &ca. were brought and presented to the young king. Several large canoes were also hauld up near the morai on the sacred ground; these were dressed with several hundred fathoms of cloth, red feathers, breast plates &ca.—all which were secured by the priests and young kings attendants. . . .Several large hogs were placed upon the altar and the human sacrifices offered this day were 30, some of which had been killed near a month.'

More important than the number of gifts laid at the feet of Tu on this auspicious occasion were the actual donors. Just as Teina with Machiavellian cunning had reckoned, among the chieftains who had failed to turn up were all those whose territories were on the Taiarapu peninsula, and who through their more regular contact with Teina had seen through him and recognized his political ambitions. Tu's relations immediately declared that the absence of these chieftains was a deliberate insult to the young prince, and consequently the *Bounty* men (with four exceptions), as good as their word, began to make plans for the most effective means of defeating the unfortunate Taiarapu peoples who, of course, had done them no harm whatsoever. The four men who refused to have anything more to do with Teina's disgraceful schemes were the two midshipmen Stewart and Heywood, Cole the armourer and Skinner, an ordinary seaman. In contrast to these four, Brown was once again agog with excitement and anticipation, and was evidently determined to turn this latest campaign into a veritable bloodbath.

Temarii, who for egotistic and opportunist reasons was still a warm supporter of Teina's conquests, produced the best plan of attack. He pointed out that the Taiarupa people were just as numerous and well-drilled as themselves, and thus the only way to beat them would be through the element of surprise. Large troop movements would undoubtedly be reported well before a battle could be begun, which meant that cunning would have to be used. He therefore proposed that, on the pretext of holding a feast for his own friends, he should invite all their own forces to Papara, and that from there in the middle of the night they should make a swift attack on the peninsula and catch the inhabitants literally napping.

Having thus agreed on their plan of action, they now casually put it aside and concentrated upon the more immediate pleasure of eating up the vast piles of foodstuff which had been presented to Tu, a business which took several weeks to complete. The *Bounty* men took advantage of this welcome respite to relaunch *Resolution*, and once again equip the ship for service as flagship of His Tahitian Majesty Tu's canoe fleet. In order to keep up the white men's enthusiasm, Tu's advisers saw to it that he visited them regularly to ensure that they were contented. 'He made us presents, and appointed each to a portion of land, being very fond of the whole of us, and desired his subjects to treat us as his relations, calling us his uncles,' wrote Morrison happily. In view of such wholehearted friendship and generosity, argued the *Bounty* men, how could they refuse the young monarch a helping hand when he needed it, even though it might entail spilling a little blood!

It was not until the 22nd March that the fighting force was ready to embark for the false festivities in Papara. They landed on the 24th March and were made welcome with a tremendous banquet. But this was scarcely over when a perspiring messenger arrived with news which was to put a stop to the elaborate and treacherous plans for the subjugation of the Taiarapu peninsula. An English naval vessel, the *Pandora*, had anchored the same day in Matavai Bay, and when Coleman, Stewart, Heywood and Skinner had gone aboard they had immediately been put under close arrest. The remainder of the *Bounty* men were even more alarmed when they learned that two of *Pandora's* ship's boats were on their way to Papara with the ever helpful Hitihiti as pilot and guide. All at once the bold white conquerors had become a crowd of scared criminals who were at a loss to know what to do. After a panic-stricken conference they decided, loyalists and mutineers alike, to flee in their schooner, without any idea where they were going. The only sensible exception was Byrne the fiddler, who resolved to make his own way back to the *Pandora* and give himself up. When the two well-armed and well-manned ship's boats arrived at Papara the reception committee consisted of no more than Temarii and the for once exculpatory ruffian Brown. The schooner was still in sight, however, and the two ship's boats, one of which was commanded by Lieutenant Hayward, took up the chase. But it did not take the *Pandora* men long to realize that they had no chance of overtaking the fast sailing vessel, and after a short time they returned to their own ship, taking Brown with them.

Meanwhile the crew of the schooner, after having sailed aimlessly hither and thither for several days until their provisions and water ran out, returned apathetically to Papara. Temarii, who could not bear the thought of losing his valuable mercenaries just when he needed them most, now begged of them to flee to the mountains and hide, promising them both guides and supplies of provisions. All the panic-stricken sailors, except three, accepted Temarii's offer and fled to the mountains. The three who remained on the schooner were Morrison and Norman and, curiously enough, one of the original mutineers, Ellison. It was their intention apparently to sail round to Matavai and surrender, but when Temarii learned this, aghast at the thought of losing the fine sailing vessel as well, he promptly took them prisoner, presumably with the intention of ingratiatingly handing them over to the commander of the *Pandora*. A couple of nights later, however, Brown appeared and contrived their escape. By canoe and on foot they made their way along the west coast and right through the war-torn Atehuru district where, had they been discovered, they would undoubtedly have been killed in revenge for their contribution to the ravaged villages and plantations. Halfway to Matavai they came upon one of the *Pandora's* ship's boats, and immediately awoke the duty officer and told him whom they were. To the astonishment of the two loyalists Morrison and Norman, Lieutenant Hayward, who turned up shortly afterwards, ordered them to be bound hand and foot before bundling them off to the *Pandora*. Their reception on board was even more disconcerting since here Captain Edwards, without permitting them a word of explanation, had them put in irons and sent below to join Coleman, Stewart, Heywood, Skinner and Byrne.

Norman and Coleman at least, whom Bligh had quite definitely promised he would exonerate if he managed to reach England again, had good reason to complain over the treatment which they were receiving. As a matter of fact Bligh had kept his promise and assured the authorities in his report that four of Christian's companions on board the *Bounty* were completely innocent. But Captain Edwards had his orders, and these stated that no distinction should be made between any men who might be captured, since in the eyes of the law they were all guilty until found innocent by a court martial.

Edwards toyed with the idea of holding Temarii as a hostage until the remaining defectors were recovered. But he was by no means certain that this would produce the desired result, and instead he despatched Hayward and Brown to Papara at the head of a force of twenty-five marines, while another lieutenant and sixteen men were ordered to march right across the island to hunt the fugitives out of any eventual mountain hideout.

Teina, needless to say, was on board practically as soon as he learned of the presence of the English warship, and now, as terrified as ever for his own safety, he offered without any qualms whatsoever to help hunt down the men who had served him so well. To his intense annoyance, however, the wily Brown proved to be a more effective Judas, since in no time at all he had bribed a number of natives to reveal the simple mountain hideout of the hapless fugitives, and is said to have entered their cave at dead of night and checked their identity by the extraordinary method of feeling their toes; a European's toes, instead of being spread like a native's, are crumpled and deformed. The next day, finding their hideout surrounded by marines, the remaining men surrendered after brief and pathetic resistance, and were shepherded back to the *Pandora*. The smaller party, who had actually been sent up into the mountains to search systematically for the fugitives, found nothing of course, and finally returned to their ship half dead with exhaustion.

The capture of the last of the mutineers not only meant that Teina had to give up his dreams of conquest at the very moment when they were near to realization, it also placed him in a very dangerous situation. His first thought was to get out altogether, and he implored Captain Edwards to take him with him to

England. But Edwards was a hard and ruthless man, and now that he no longer had any use for the ingratiating chieftain he ordered him to leave the ship, which Teina did; now it was his turn to take to the hills.

Even though peace and order would seem to have returned to Tahiti at last, the truth of the matter is that the interference of the English sailors in the natives' political and military affairs had catastrophic results for forthcoming generations. Up to this time there had always been a satisfactory balance of power among the chieftains, and this had effectively protected the island as a whole against the perils of tyranny and dictatorship. But Teina's use of his well-armed mercenaries had definitely and permanently upset the *status quo*, and even though in his life-time he was never to get any closer to his dream of absolute monarchy, he had nevertheless proved that it was possible, and also shown which means were needed to achieve it. His son Tu was not slow in following his father's example, moreover, and by carefully cultivating the friendship and support of the English missionaries and ship's captains, and by building up a corps of mercenaries he finally succeeded after bloody conflicts and unspeakable atrocities in conquering the entire island.

Once his prisoners were all assembled on board the *Pandora*, Edwards ordered a special prison to be built for them. This grim construction which stood on the after part of the quarterdeck was a mere eighteen feet by eleven feet and little taller than a man. The details of 'Pandora's Box', as it was inevitably dubbed, were described by Morrison as follows:

'The entrance being a scuttle on the top of 18 or 20 inches square, secured by a bolt on the top through the coamings, two scuttles of 9 inches square in the bulkhead for air with iron grates and the stern ports bar'd inside and out with iron.'

Two guards were posted on top of the box by the entrance, while a midshipman patrolled the four walls. No one on board was permitted to talk to the prisoners except the master-at-arms, with whom the prisoners had the right to discuss their food rations.

Edwards claimed that this arrangement provided the best possible means of keeping a proper guard and control over the prisoners, that it was more healthy and gave the prisoners more fresh air than they would have got below decks, and finally that it ensured their complete isolation from the rest of the crew.

During the *Bounty* voyage Bligh had likewise recognized the danger of keeping prisoners below decks in the tropics, and had accordingly given orders for his various prisoners, (including Hayward, one imagines) to be kept above decks whenever the weather permitted. Edwards was now pursuing the same policy, and presumably it was his intention only to use the 'box' so long as they were in tropical waters. It should be remembered, furthermore, that Edwards had very little real idea how the mutiny had taken place, and was thus inclined to regard his prisoners as a gang of unscrupulous and violent scoundrels who would be ready to incite his own crew to mutiny at a moment's notice. In view of this he felt it essential to keep the offenders absolutely isolated, and the box seemed the most obvious solution.

The *Pandora's* surgeon, George Hamilton, who wrote an entertaining little volume on the voyage, described the 'box' as 'the most desirable place in the ship'. As a matter of fact it was anything but desirable when one considers the conditions under which the inmates existed. They were manacled hand and foot, and the irons were so tight on their limbs that they quickly led to swellings and abrasions. Each man had been provided with a hammock, but there were no facilities for hanging these; the only alternative was to spread them out and try to sleep on the hard deck. Morrison gave a brief and vivid description of their life on board the *Pandora*:

'The heat of the place when it was calm was so intense that the sweat frequently ran in streams to the scuppers, and produced maggots in a short time; the hammocks being dirty when we got them, we found stored with a vermin of another kind, which we had no method of eradicating but by lying on the plank; and though our friends would have supplied us with plenty of cloth they were not permitted to do it, and our only remedy was to lay naked,—these troublesome neighbours and the two necessary tubs which were constantly kept in the place helped to render our situation truly disagreeable.'

The *Bounty* men were confined here for the full two months

in which the *Pandora* remained in Matavai having her leaks stopped. Not once were they permitted to leave their prison. Their womenfolk and friends from the island were not permitted even to speak to them, and were turned away in despair every time they approached the vessel. Midshipman Stewart's woman, a chieftain's daughter whom he called Peggy, is said to have died of a broken heart a couple of months after the *Pandora* sailed. The *Bounty* men had fathered six children during their stay on the island, and several of the women were pregnant when the *Pandora* arrived. Hamilton wrote that the children were permitted to visit their imprisoned fathers and added, 'To see the poor captives in irons, weeping over their tender offsprings was too moving a scene for any feeling heart.'

Even though Captain Edwards might have meant well with the 'Pandora's Box' arrangement, there is nevertheless no denying that all in all his treatment of the prisoners was unnecessarily brutal, and he could have done a great deal to ease their suffering. At the same time, however, he was well aware the whole time in Tahiti that there was considerable risk of an attack by the natives, and in view of this he was obliged to maintain a constant guard and lookout system.

Meanwhile he fed his prisoners well. He could have adhered to the regulation 'two-thirds allowance', which was all they were entitled to, but he gave orders that they should receive exactly the same rations as everyone else on board, and he even went so far as to permit them a daily rum ration. Finally all coconuts and other foodstuffs which the natives brought aboard for the prisoners were handed to them.

On the 8th May the *Pandora* was shipshape, seaworthy and ready to sail and the *Resolution*, equipped and manned, was to go with her as a sort of tender. Brown had been recruited as an ordinary seaman for the voyage home, and Hitihiti was also allowed to go along; he was to be landed on his native Borabora, one of the northwest Society Islands. The reason why these two gentlemen were so anxious to leave Tahiti is, of course, obvious.

Edwards now began the search for the *Bounty* herself. It has often been claimed that he somewhat stupidly searched in all the places where she quite evidently would not be. But the fact remains that he was merely following Admiralty orders which stated quite clearly that he should comb the leeward side of the

Society Islands and then investigate the islands west of Tahiti, in particular the Aitutaki and Tonga groups.

Even had he not been hindered by these instructions, however, the task would have been more or less hopeless since there are thousands of islands in the Pacific, and a search for the *Bounty* among these might have gone on for years without result. The irony of the whole thing was that the *Pandora* had passed within a hundred miles of Pitcairn and the mutineers' settlement two weeks before her arrival at Tahiti. True, they had been too far away by forty miles to see the island, but even if they had done it is doubtful if it would have made any difference; the mutineers would have doused all their fires the moment they spotted the ship, and Edwards would hardly have been likely to try to approach the barren rock when his orders were to land at Tahiti. In fact the orders of the search vessel were exactly as the calculating Christian had anticipated —first a landing on Tahiti and then a systematic search of the islands farther west.

Captain Edwards now investigated the Society Islands on the leeward side according to his orders. Incidentally, the adventurous Hitihiti did not manage to reach home this time, apparently he got drunk on Huahine and was left behind there.

Next on the programme was Aitutaki, and the search there proved equally fruitless. Christian after all could scarcely have been expected to have been there; in the first place Bligh had discovered this island and recorded it just before the mutiny, and in the second place Christian had mentioned it in connection with the pirate fabrication with which he had deceived the Tahitians during his first return to Matavai after the mutiny.

Some days later the *Pandora* reached the Palmerston atoll where amidst great excitement they discovered a number of spars, one of which was marked 'Bounty's Driver Yard'. Edwards immediately organized a large-scale hunt throughout the island, at the same time giving orders for everyone to be on the watch for an attack by the mutineers. The two reconnaissance companies, led by lieutenants Hayward and Corner respectively, suffered considerable discomfort in investigating the barren coral island, and their general predicament was worsened by the constant fear of a desperate attack by the men they were hunting. There was an entertaining, if somewhat ludicrous, interlude during their night ashore there. After having made a meal of mussel soup and coconuts, the weary patrols settled down for the night to sleep. Someone, however, had inadvertently placed a coconut too near the fire, and in the middle of the night it exploded with a tremendous bang. The sleep-dazed patrolmen stumbled to their feet, waving muskets in all directions and practically blowing each others brains out before finally realizing that they were not being savagely ambushed by half-wild mutineers after all.

But there was no further sign of the *Bounty*, and Edwards was forced to conclude, quite correctly, that the pieces they had discovered must have drifted over from Tupuai where, according to one of the mutineers, a number of booms and spars had actually been lost on one occasion.

There was one unfortunate incident during the *Pandora's* halt at the Palmerston atoll. A ship's boat, commanded by a midshipman, disappeared and was never seen again. It was reluctantly assumed that the small craft had been seized and smashed to pieces by one of the tremendous breakers which lashed the outer reef, and that the five men on board had immediately perished.

When all hope of recovering the boat had been abandoned, Edwards set a northwesterly course for the Tokelau islands north of the Samoa group. It seems that one of the prisoners, Hillbrant, had been informed by Christian the night before he left Tahiti for the last time that he intended to make for the Tokelaus and settle there. The island in question was reputed to be uninhabited and had been discovered by Byron during his circumnavigation. So far as Edwards could make out, this was Duke of York's island, known today by its native name of Atafu.

He investigated the group thoroughly and fruitlessly, and then sailed on towards Samoa and Tonga. In the latter area another tragedy occurred. The schooner, which had proved an excellent vessel for reconnaissance work, suddenly disappeared with a midshipman, a master's mate, a quartermaster and a seaman on board. No trace of her could be found and the *Pandora* and the *Resolution* were destined never to encounter each other again. The worst aspect of the tragedy was that the schooner's provisions were practically finished at the time, and she was due to have them replenished before the ships continued on their way.

During the hunt for the *Bounty* and the *Resolution*, among other places that Edwards visited was Nomuka. Tofua is just visible from this island, and it was now the turn of the *Pandora's* crew to admire, as the crew of the *Bounty* had once done, the fiery, awe-inspiring peak of the volcano there. What they did not realize, however, was that as they gazed out towards the volcano the schooner was anchored in its shadow wondering what had happened to *Pandora*! The *Resolution's* crew had apparently confused Tofua with Nomuka. Needless to say in due course the Tofua natives turned up, ostensibly to trade with the white men, exchanging goods for provisions. But it was not long before they adopted the same tactics as they had used a year ago against Bligh and his men. After obstruction, insinuation and threats they finally reverted to violence to take the boat from the strangers. But the crew of the *Resolution* were well armed with muskets, and despite the fact that they were only half the number that Bligh and his men had been, they were able to beat the natives off without loss to themselves and get away unscathed.

The unwitting oceanic hide-and-seek continued to go on, however, since scarcely had the *Resolution* got well away from Tofua than the *Pandora* sailed into the same bay. The wily natives turned up again but now, faced with the huge warship, they were ingratiating and sycophantic. No, they had seen nothing of the schooner, and how deeply they regretted the unfortunate misunderstanding which had led to their conflict with the noble Captain Bligh and his men last year!

It must have been with very mixed feelings that Hayward viewed again the grim little bay where scarcely a year ago he and his companions had been almost massacred. He immediately recognized several of the natives, and among them the one who had attacked the ships boat and murdered John Norton, but Captain Edwards refused to consider any form of retribution, pointing out that the schooner might easily decide to put in there after the *Pandora* had left. Perhaps it might have been as well if he had known the truth, whereupon he could have given those treacherous natives a lesson that they would have taken a long time to forget, and which might have helped to save the lives of the many ship's crews who were to be murdered in subsequent years on the Tofua group.

In the beginning of August Edwards gave up the search for

both the *Bounty* and the *Resolution*, and set course for the Torres Straits which he had been ordered to survey in greater detail. En route he discovered a number of new islands, among others Rotuma. Passing the island of Vanikoro in the Santa Cruz group, they noticed smoke, but Edwards did not bother to investigate and continued on his way westwards. This was yet another example of the bad luck which accompanied Edwards on his Tahitian voyage, for had he gone ashore at Vanikoro he would undoubtedly have gone down in history as the man who solved the mystery of the La Perouse expedition. A French expedition under the command of Comte de la Perouse had disappeared without a trace in the South Seas in 1788. It was not until well into the nineteenth century that an Englishman named Dillon was able to reconstruct the course of events, when it emerged that both ships had foundered on the Vanikoro reef on a dark and stormy night three years before the *Pandora* sailed by in August 1791. The smoke seen from the *Pandora* was undoubtedly a distress signal from at least two survivors from the wreck, and thanks to Edwards' lack of interest no survivors of the ill-fated expedition were ever to return to civilization again.

The *Pandora* was now approaching the Great Barrier Reef, and was thus in some of the most dangerous waters in the world. Unfortunately, in his eagerness to get home, Captain Edwards had given up the practice of heaving to overnight, and this lack of caution was probably the chief reason for the catastrophe which was about to occur. On the 28th August the *Pandora* was sailing slowly southwards on the lookout for an opening in the reef where they could slip through. Lieutenant Corner was sent out in the evening with a party in one of the ship's boats to make a closer inspection, and after some time he was able to signal the *Pandora* that he had found what he was searching for. He was now ordered to return on board, but the swift tropical night had already fallen and Edwards decided to move in towards the ship's boat, since he was anxious not to lose a second one. The two vessels maintained contact with each other the whole time through musket fire and flares.

At the same time, however, the powerful currents were pushing the *Pandora* closer and closer to the great reef, and the roar of the breakers was becoming increasingly loud. But the sounding line continued to show a depth of around one hundred and ten fathoms, so that there seemed to be no direct danger. At about half-past seven, to everyone's relief, Corner and his men were back aboard and the ship's boat had been taken up on the davits.

But now the situation changed, suddenly and terrifyingly. All at once the sounding line registered only fifty fathoms, and the ship began to heave dreadfully over a different type of swell. Desperately the captain ordered all sails to be set in order to run out of the vicious surf. But it was too late, the *Pandora* bumped, ground, and then began to crash wildly against the terrible coral reef. In a matter of minutes she was leaking badly and pumps were manned and bucket chains formed in an effort to combat the rising water. But it was no good, the water rose steadily, and even the added efforts of the three non-mutineer prisoners who were released for the purpose failed to help matters.

And then, just as suddenly, everything was calm again. The *Pandora* had been driven right over the reef and was lying quietly in a small lagoon in some fifteen fathoms of water. Here, where the breakers could no longer get at her, she dropped anchor for an inspection of the damage. She was a sorry sight indeed. Listing heavily and with her rudder and part of the stern-post missing, it did not look as if she could last long. The captain's plan was to draw one of the topsails down under the hull and up again the other side, and thus stop her leaking to some extent so that she could be pumped dry. But this scheme proved completely unsuccessful, and all they could do was to keep pumping and bailing through the night and see what daylight might offer. The cannons were dumped overboard, though not before one of them had crushed a man to death. A spar came crashing down from the rigging and killed another man. Finally the pumps broke down and could not be repaired. Exhausted they sat around miserably drinking ale brewed on Nomuka and waited for the dawn.

Probably the night's experiences had been most terrifying of all for the occupants of 'Pandora's Box'. While the ship was being pounded on the reef, the manacled prisoners were thrown helplessly around in their restricted quarters, unavoidably bruising and injuring each other in the process. Fearing that they would be drowned like rats, they contrived somehow or other to shatter their irons, but no sooner did this come to the captain's notice than he ordered them to be manacled again. The panic-stricken prisoners shrieked desperately for mercy, or begged to be given a chance on the pumps, but Edwards turned a deaf ear to their entreaties. Thus, while the water rose higher every minute, the manacles of the mutineers were cold-bloodedly replaced and additional guards were posted over the entrance to the cell. Finally the captain made it known to the prisoners that if any one of them should break his irons a second time he would be shot or hanged.

By six-thirty in the morning it was evident to everybody on board that the *Pandora* was liable to sink at any moment, since she was almost full of water by this time. The ship's boats were now loaded with provisions and other requisites, and everything floatable above decks was cut loose so that there would be something to hold on to in the water.

By this time water was beginning to surge in through the upper gun port, and it was every man for himself. It was not until the order had been given to abandon ship, however, that the captain gave orders for the prisoners to be released. This done, he jumped over the side together with his officers. The task of releasing the prisoners' manacles fell to an armourer's mate, and this unfortunate man had to clamber up on to the roof of the 'box', open the hatchway, and scramble down to the petrified prisoners inside. Muspratt, Skinner and Byrne were the first to emerge and even so Skinner was so panic-stricken that he leapt into the water with his handcuffs still on and drowned almost at once. At this point the master-at-arms, apparently unaware that the captain had ordered the prisoners' release, noticed that the hatchway was open and clambered up and fastened it again. At the same moment, the stricken *Pandora* gave a great dying lurch and threw the master-at-arms into the water. Inside the cell there was total panic; the ship would undoubtedly sink within a matter of minutes or even seconds, they were locked in from outside and there was no one left on board to help them. The armourer's mate worked frenziedly to release as many men as possible, but the hull was very deep in the water now and only the after-deck abaft the main mast was above the surface. There seemed to be no hope at all left for the men in the cell when, at the last moment, a sailor named William Moulter clambered up on to the roof and shouted down to the prisoners that he would let them out or go down with them. As good as his word, he pulled the bolt-fastening out of its socket and flung it into the sea. As a result of his swift and resolute action, everyone in the cell, with the exception of poor Hillbrant, managed to escape. Hillbrant was still manacled hands and feet, and when the ship dived he in company with many other anonymous mariners went down with her.

The men in the water made their way by devious means to a sandbank some three miles away, and when they were all assembled and the captain had organized a rollcall, it was found that of the total of one hundred and thirty-four on board ninety-nine had survived, and thirty-five, including Stewart, Hillbrant, Skinner and Sumner, had perished.

The only alternative now was to do as Bligh had done and try to reach Timor. Captain Edwards, needless to say, was in a vile temper by this time, and it is very possible that it was this mood which led him to refuse the prisoners permission to use an unwanted sail which was lying on the sandbank to protect themselves from the baleful sun. These men, after all, had no clothes, and the sunburn which they had acquired on Tahiti and which would have stood them in good stead now had disappeared during their long term of confinement. They were therefore in grave danger of being roasted alive by the merciless sun, which was burning down from a cloudless sky only a few degrees south of the equator. Another serious problem, and one which involved everybody, was that of drinking water, since the supplies which they had rescued from the *Pandora* were no more than sufficient to allow each man a few spoonfuls a day.

There is no denying that Edwards had violated his instructions concerning the handling of his prisoners. It is fairly evident that it was his fault entirely that four of them drowned in the shipwreck, and that the others survived more by good fortune than design. His behaviour towards them on the sandbank, was likewise unnecessarily heartless, so much so that when he deliberately refused to permit them to make use of the sail they had no choice but to bury themselves up to the neck in sand in order to find protection. Edwards' first lieutenant John Larkin seems also to have been a cruel-natured individual who took every opportunity to make the life of the prisoners as miserable as possible, and after the shipwreck the two officers made it their business to blame the prisoners personally for every mishap that occurred. When the four ship's boats finally set off for Timor, Morrison had the misfortune to be assigned to the captain's boat, and from his reports of Edwards' treatment of the other three prisoners during the course of this journey, one is forced to conclude that the captain of the *Pandora* was a singularly cruel and ruthless individual.

The voyage to Kupang took almost two weeks. They succeeded in acquiring a certain amount of water and food along the north coast of Australia, but everyone seems to have suffered severely from thirst and starvation. The four boats were exceptionally heavily loaded, carrying not less than thirty, twenty-five, twenty-three and twenty-one men respectively, which was considerably more than the eighteen men aboard Bligh's launch. Nevertheless, nothing particular happened during the course of the voyage, and they reached the little Dutch colony on the 13th September. They were received here just as kindly as Bligh's party had been, a fact which Hayward, poor fellow, was able to substantiate since he had been here before as well. As a matter of fact the Dutch were beginning to get used to English mariners in distress, since between Bligh's and Edwards' visit another boat had arrived at Kupang, though this one had been manned by escaped convicts from the Penal settlement at Port Jackson. They had managed to persuade the Dutchmen that they were shipwreck survivors from an English vessel, and had consequently been welcomed and well cared for at Kupang. Now, however, when one of their Dutch friends hurried to them with the glad news that a shipwrecked captain, presumably theirs, had turned up, one of the convicts gave the game away by exclaiming involuntarily, 'What captain? Dam'me, we have no captain!' That was the end of their successful hoax, and the convicts, including a woman and two children, were locked up in company with the ten *Bounty* men for the remainder of their sojourn there. (The woman prisoner has gone down in history, since, after her return to England, she enjoyed the patronage of none less than James Boswell.)

When Edwards and his men had recovered in Kupang, they continued by the Dutch vessel, *Rembang*, to Batavia. En route they stopped in Samarang, and there to their great surprise and delight they encountered the *Resolution*, which after an adventurous voyage had made her way through the Torres Straits and finally reached this little Dutch outpost in the East Indies. On their arrival at Samarang, the Dutch examined their boat, noted that it was built of a South Seas timber and assumed that the crew were the *Bounty* mutineers. When no one had any papers to prove who they were, the Dutchmen to be on the safe side locked them all up until their identity could be established. Apparently, however, they were extremely well treated by their captors, since it was generally accepted in the Dutch East Indies that Bligh's violence and brutality had been the true cause of the mutiny. (Needless to say, during their stay in Kupang, Fryer and his friends on the launch had lost no opportunity informing their inquisitive Dutch friends as to the true facts of the *Bounty* mutiny.)

When Edwards reached Batavia he sold the *Resolution* and gave the proceeds to his men to buy clothes. The prisoners who had laboured and sweated to build her did not get a penny of course. His next move was to divide his men up into groups to take different boats home. He himself travelled with his precious prisoners whom he was determined not to let out of his sight. After a very rough trip across the Indian Ocean, they arrived at Cape Town in March 1792, and there embarked upon H.M.S. *Gorgon* which was on her way back to England after a visit to Port Jackson. Now for the first time the wretched prisoners were afforded a little better treatment, and the journey home continued without any outstanding incidents. On the 19th June *Gorgon* anchored at Spithead, and shortly afterwards the *Bounty* men were transferred to H.M.S. *Hector* in Portsmouth harbour, where they were confined until the court martial. It was now a full four and a half years since they had sailed away from England under Captain Bligh in the *Bounty*.

CHAPTER IX

THE COURT MARTIAL

IT was not until three months after the *Pandora* foundered that the ten surviving *Bounty* mutineers were finally brought to trial. The court martial was held in the main cabin of a ship-of-the-line called the *Duke* in Portsmouth harbour, and it continued from the 12th to the 18th September, 1792. The president of the court was Vice Admiral Lord Hood, the other members all being full naval captains. The charge was the same for all ten men and amounted to, 'Mutinously running away with the said armed vessel, the *Bounty* and deserting from His Majesty's Service'. According to the law the penalty for this crime was death for all those who had not made a definite attempt to leave the ship.

The chief witness here should, of course, have been Bligh himself, but he had left England the previous year on a second breadfruit expedition, and at this time he was still somewhere on the other side of the globe. Thus, in their eagerness to punish the offenders, the Admiralty contented themselves with Bligh's written report on the mutiny and the testimonies of the loyalists who had survived the voyage to the East Indies and to England, and who were still at home at this time. These were Fryer the master, Boatswain Cole, Gunner Peckover, ship's carpenter Purcell, Bligh's steward John Smith and the midshipmen, now lieutenants, Hayward and Hallet. Captain Edwards and lieutenants Corner and Larkin from the *Pandora* were also called as additional witnesses to describe the capture of the prisoners on Tahiti.

The proceedings began with a reading of Bligh's description of the mutiny, a report which was misleading in various respects. Here, as all along, Bligh persisted in maintaining that the mutiny had been carefully planned long in advance and that the principal reason for it was the mutineers' longing to return to Tahiti. He made no mention whatever of the extraordinary coconut incident the day before the mutiny actually broke out, nor did he mention the various other misunderstandings and his own wilful torrents of invective, all of which had contributed to the final insurrection. Admittedly he kept his promise to Norman, Coleman, McIntosh and Byrne, and exonerated them from all blame, inasmuch as they had been forced to remain on board the *Bounty* against their will, but on the other hand, to the utter dismay of Morrison and Heywood, he insisted that they were active members of the mutiny, and for some inexplicable reason he asserted that 'Morrison was the worst of the mutineers next to Christian and Churchill, if not their adviser'. Nevertheless, all things considered, there is little doubt that Bligh made these accusations in good faith believing what he wrote to be true, and that the real blame for the emergence of such injustice and misrepresentation lay with the Admiralty, who should have made a proper investigation and examination of the facts before the case opened.

As the case developed, it soon became perfectly evident that the four men whom Bligh had exculpated were completely innocent. In the same way, it was quite obvious that the quartet, Ellison, Burkett, Millward and Muspratt had seized arms and actively participated in the mutiny. Once these facts had been established, the court turned to the more complicated question of Morrison and Heywood's conduct.

The first witness to be called in this respect was Fryer. Fryer had a number of unpleasant things to say about Bligh, and pointed out that on numerous occasions Christian had said that he was 'living in Hell', whereupon the court asked Fryer what he thought Christian meant by this.

'The persistent ranting and insults that Bligh directed at him,' replied Fryer promptly.

Fryer now went on to describe how, the day before the mutiny, the captain had accused all the gentlemen, i.e. the petty officers, on board of having stolen coconuts. It was on this occasion, said Fryer, that it first became evident that a serious state of tension existed between Bligh and Christian. But the court was more anxious to get on to the actual mutiny, and pressed Fryer to tell what he could of Morrison's behaviour and attitude after it had broken out. Fryer stated that he had met Morrison in the after hatchway and had asked him if he had anything to do with the mutiny. Morrison's reply had been an emphatic no. Convinced now that Morrison was loyal, Fryer had whispered to him to be ready to help retake the ship. To Fryer's great surprise, however, Morrison had replied:

'Go down to your cabin, sir, it is too late.'

When the prisoners' turn came to cross-examine the first witness for the prosecution, Morrison questioned Fryer carefully on the above exchange. Fryer insisted that Morrison had advised him to go down to his cabin, pointing out that it was too late to do anything. Morrison now claimed that he himself had expressed the intention of getting a party together and retaking the ship, but Fryer denied having heard him say this. Morrison's next question was:

'Did you observe any part of my conduct particularly on that day, which leads you to think I was one of the mutineers?'

'I never saw him, only at that time, and his appearance gave me reason to speak to him to be on his guard; he appeared to be friendly and his answer rather surprised me; I did not expect it from him, or whether he spoke thro' fear of the others or not, I do not know,' was Fryer's reply.

The court now sought to find a more reasonable explanation.

'Might not Morrison's speaking to you, and telling you to keep below, be from a laudable motive, as supposing your resistance at that time might have prevented a more advantageous effort?'

'Probably it might,' admitted Fryer. 'Had I stayed in the ship he would have been one of the first that I should have opened my mind to, from his good behaviour in the former part of the voyage.'

'Did he speak to you in a threatening tone or address you as advice?'

'Addressed me as advice.'

'Did you see any person that appeared to be forcing Morrison the prisoner to hook the tackles upon the launch?'

'No.'

'Did you see the prisoner Morrison employed in any other way than that which you have related, from the time you were

first confined until the boat was cast loose from the ship?'
   'No.'
   'In hoisting out that boat did you consider it as assisting the
mutineers or as giving Captain Bligh a better chance of his life?'
   'Assisting Captain Bligh and giving him a better chance of
his life.'
   Thanks to the court's intervention, the unfavourable impression which had been created by Fryer's initial statements were
dispersed, but nevertheless there still remained an uneasy feeling that Morrison had something to hide.
   Concerning Heywood, Fryer had not seen him at all during
the course of the mutiny, nor had Cole, the next witness for
the prosecution, anything disparaging to say of his conduct. On
the contrary, in fact, Cole stated that at the beginning of the
mutiny he had seen Heywood in his bunk, which was a direct
contradiction of Bligh's claim that Heywood was one of the
principal instigators of the mutiny. Cole admitted that later on
he saw Heywood helping to lower one of the ship's boats into
the water, but this, he considered, was purely on account of the
midshipman's intention to go where his captain went. Cole
went on to point out that shortly afterwards Heywood had
gone below decks, and that Churchill had then ordered a couple
of the mutineers to 'keep them down there'. In Cole's opinion,
Churchill was at this point referring to the two midshipmen
Heywood and Stewart, which was correct. Altogether, then, it
is reasonable to assume that at the end of the first day's proceedings Heywood had more grounds than Morrison for being
satisfied with the way things had gone.
   The following day, the 13th September, Morrison asked Cole
if he remembered the conversation that they had had with each
other after the outbreak of the mutiny. According to Morrison,
he had asked Cole as his immediate superior what he should do,
whereupon Cole had replied: 'By God, James, I don't know,
but go and help with the cutter.' Morrison claimed that he had
acted properly when he did as he was told. He then asked Cole:
   'Do you recollect that I came to you when you were getting
your own things which were tied up in part of your bedding,
into the boat, and telling you that the boat was then overloaded,
and that Captain Bligh had begged that no more people should
go into her, and that in consequence of that I would take my
chance in the ship, and that you then shook me by the hand and

said, "God bless you my boy, I will do justice if ever I reach England"?'

Cole: 'I remember shaking hands with him and he telling me that he would take his chance in the ship. I had no other reason to believe but that he was intending to quit the ship; I do not remember the whole of our conversation; I may have said that I would do him justice when I got to England; I make no doubt but I did.'

Morrison: 'Was my conduct such during the voyage and particularly on that day, as to give you reason to suppose that I was concerned in the mutiny?'

Cole: 'I had no reason to suppose it.'

The court now interrupted:

'Did you hear Morrison, the prisoner, say that Captain Bligh had desired that no other man might come into the boat, as she was deeply laden already?'

Cole: 'I remember taking him by the hand but from the confusion I do not remember the conversation.'

Court: 'Did you at that time believe that the prisoner Morrison would have gone with you into the boat, if it had not been apprehended that the boat was too deeply laden?'

Cole: 'I had no reason else but to believe it; he was giving his attention, and whatever I told him to do he obeyed it.'

Court: 'You have said that Morrison assisted in getting out the boat. Do you consider that everyone who helped in this work was of the captain's party?'

Cole: 'No, some were under arms.'

Court: 'Do you consider those who were not under arms at that time to have been of the captain's party?'

Cole: 'I certainly did think that they had no hand in the mutiny.'

Court: 'Did you hear the prisoner Morrison express any desire to come into the boat, and was he prevented from doing so?'

Cole: 'He did not express a desire to me, nor was he prevented that I know.'

The next witness was Peckover, who had sat in his cabin astern during the greater part of the mutiny and had thus seen nothing whatever of either Morrison or Heywood. Nevertheless Morrison was quick-witted enough to get Peckover to admit that during the entire voyage his conduct had been irreproachable, and therefore that it would be unreasonable to assume that he had had anything in common with the mutineers.

Purcell was now called and, like Fryer, he too had a number of uncomplimentary comments to make concerning Bligh's treatment of his subordinates. Of Morrison he claimed that he could not remember his having been armed, and he considered that he could not possibly be accused of participating in the mutiny, even though he may have helped to lower the cutter into the water. The main part of Purcell's evidence concerned Heywood, and consequently the case against the latter began to look somewhat grave. Purcell went so far as to assert that he saw Heywood on deck with one hand on the hilt of his cutlass while the boat was being lowered into the water. He said that he then shouted to him: 'In God's name Peter, what are you doing with that?' Heywood had then removed his hand from his cutlass and began to help launch the cutter. Purcell had also heard Churchill's order to Thompson to keep a number of men below decks, and he confirmed that after this Heywood had not been seen topsides again.

Purcell's statement that Heywood had had his hand on the hilt of his cutlass was a very serious accusation, and the court subsequently went to great trouble to establish whether or not, under the circumstances, he could be said to have been armed. Purcell, who was generally favourably inclined towards Heywood, now began to realize how serious his charge had been for the accused, and hastened to explain, somewhat tardily, that he felt that Heywood had reached for his cutlass quite impulsively and thoughtlessly, and that this gesture could in no way be interpreted to mean that he had taken the side of the mutineers. Following this observation the unfortunate ship's carpenter was subjected to a veritable barrage of questions by the court, but he nevertheless adhered to what he had said, and insisted time and time again that in his opinion Heywood was innocent. But despite this, his testimony had already done the accused midshipman a great deal of harm.

On Friday, September 14, at nine in the morning the court assembled again. The remainder of the witnesses for the prosecution were due to be heard, and the first to be called were the two ex-midshipmen, now lieutenants, Hayward and Hallet. Neither of these officers, of course, mentioned that they had been guilty of gross neglect of duty on the morning of the mutiny. On the other hand, however, they had a good deal to say about the behaviour of Morrison and Heywood, and both made a number of statements which were to compromise further the positions of the two accused men. When the court asked Hayward if, in his opinion, Morrison had supported the mutineers or Captain Bligh when he helped lower the ship's boat, Hayward replied with deliberate malice:

'If I were to give it as my opinion I should say that he was assisting the mutineers, he perhaps might have wished to get the boats out to get quit of us as fast as possible.'

The court now asked Hayward, with a certain amount of justifiable surprise, if he also regarded McIntosh as guilty, since he too had helped with the cutter. Needless to say Hayward could not but deny this, but he then hastily added the following ludicrous explanation:

'The difference was in the countenance of the people, tho' opinion may be ill-grounded: the countenance of the one was rejoiced and the other depressed.'

Morrison now asked Hayward straight out:

'You say that you observed joy in my countenance and that you are rather inclined to give it as your opinion that I was one of the mutineers; can you declare before God and this court that such evidence is not the result of private pique?'

To which Hayward replied:

'No, it is not the result of any private pique, it is an opinion that I formed after quitting the ship, from the prisoner's not coming with us when he had as good an opportunity as the rest, there being more boats than one.'

This argument seemed even more contrived, and Morrison was not slow in taking advantage of it:

'Are you certain that we might have had the large cutter to have accompanied you?'

'Not being present at any conference between you, I cannot say, but perhaps you might,' replied Hayward lamely.

Morrison continued to press him:

'Can you deny that you were present when Captain Bligh begged that the long boat might not be overloaded and that he did say he would do justice to those who remained?'

Hayward countered:

'I was present at the time Lieutenant Bligh made such a

declaration but understood it as respecting clothes and other heavy articles with which the boat was already too full.'

Muspratt now asked permission to address a question to Hayward:

'In answer to a question just asked by Morrison, you allow Captain Bligh used these words—Don't let the boats be over-loaded, my lads, I'll do you justice—which you say alluded to the clothes and other heavy articles. Do you mean to understand the latter words—my lads, I'll do you justice—to apply to clothes or to men whom he apprehended might go into the boat?'

Hayward now tried to avoid admitting his deliberate perjury by an even more ridiculous and confusing explanation:

'If Captain Bligh made use of the words—my lads—it was to the people already in the boat and not to those in the ship.'

The president of the court now lost his patience with the witness and said irritably:

'To whom do you imagine Captain Bligh alluded when he said that he would do them justice, was it in your opinion to the men in the boat with him or to any persons then remaining in the ship?'

By this time Hayward realized that he had gone too far and he answered miserably:

'To persons remaining in the ship.'

The president continued mercilessly:

'Are you of the opinion that he meant he would do them justice on account of their remaining in the ship or that he would cause satisfaction to be given to them for any property they might lose?'

'I rather imagine that it was to those few whom Captain Bligh knew to be of his party that were detained contrary to their inclinations and that he would do them such justice which would throw aside all doubt of their being true to the service of their country,' conceded Hayward.

With these words Hayward's capitulation could hardly have been more complete, and yet when the court now asked him which members of the crew he considered as having been kept aboard against their will he named only Coleman and Byrne!

The next witness, Hallet, produced an even more serious charge. He claimed that Morrison was holding a musket when the launch pulled away from the ship, and that he went aft and shouted down to the loyalists, 'If my friends enquire after me, tell them I am somewhere in the South Seas.' Morrison asked Hallet if he were not mistaken in this claim, but the latter insisted that this was what had happened.

Both Hayward and Hallet also made grave accusations against Peter Heywood. The former stated that he had found Heywood sitting idly on his bunk and had urged him to hurry up and get aboard the launch. The court now asked:

'When Peter Heywood was in his berth and you admonished him to go into the boat, was he prevented by any force or restraint from going on deck?'

Hayward: 'No.'

Court: 'What was Mr Heywood employed about in his berth when you went below?'

Hayward: 'Nothing but sitting with his arms folded on his own chest, in the fore part of the berth.'

Court: 'Did you from his behaviour consider him as a person attached to his duty or to the party of the mutineers?'

Hayward: 'I should rather suppose after my having told him to go into the boat, and he not joining us, to be on the side of the mutineers, but that must be only understood as an opinion as he was not in the least employed during the active part of it.'

Court: 'Did you observe any marks of joy or sorrow on his countenance or behaviour?'

Hayward: 'Sorrow.'

It was obvious that Hayward had reverted again to malicious conjecture, and the court now turned on him with crushing logic:

'You have just said that you supposed McIntosh not to be attached to the mutineers because he had a depressed countenance; might not the sorrow that you perceived in the countenance of Peter Heywood arise from the same course?'

'It might so,' replied Lieutenant Hayward.

Hallet relieved his confused colleague and proceeded to put forward an entirely new accusation against the unfortunate Heywood. He stated that at one point Captain Bligh had addressed Heywood directly, and that the latter, instead of replying, had laughed impudently and turned his back on him.

One can well imagine the unfavourable impression that the

testimonies of these witnesses must have made upon the court. Meanwhile Heywood refrained from putting any questions to the witnesses, since from the beginning he had requested permission to save his cross-examination until such time as he held his speech of defence. It may be mentioned here, however, that after the court martial was over, Hallet became conscience-stricken and admitted that he may well have confused Heywood with someone else at the time of the mutiny.

The next witness to be called was Bligh's steward, John Smith. He had seen neither Heywood nor Morrison armed. After Smith, Edwards, Corner and Larkin from the *Pandora* described how the accused had been taken prisoner on Tahiti, and it was obvious from their evidence that both Morrison and Heywood had surrendered voluntarily.

There were no further witnesses for the prosecution, and now all that remained was for the accused to question the witnesses and to make their defence speeches. (It should be mentioned that of all the accused men the only ones who could afford to engage a defence counsel were Heywood and Muspratt.) Coleman's turn came first, on Saturday morning the 15th September. His comments were brief since he knew that he had nothing to fear.

On Monday, September 17th events took a more dramatic turn when all the remaining accused men presented their cases. Heywood's defence, prepared by his counsel, took longest since it was full of unnecessary repetition and rhetorical excesses. His first argument was Heywood's youth and lack of perception (he was less than seventeen years of age when the mutiny took place) and his fear of perishing in the overloaded open boat. His second argument was that when he had finally been persuaded by his friend Stewart to go with the launch, both Churchill and Thompson had prevented him from doing so.

While Heywood was being heard, Fryer, Cole, Peckover and Purcell all attested warmly to Heywood's good character and behaviour on the voyage. Cole confirmed that he had ordered Heywood to help him lower the ship's boat, and Heywood also managed to get the witnesses to admit how miserably both Hayward and Hallet had conducted themselves throughout the mutiny. All four of the above witnesses stated definitely that Heywood had not taken the side of the mutineers, and Purcell said that he was quite convinced Churchill was referring to Stewart and Heywood when he ordered Thompson to 'keep them down there'.

Morrison made a long, pathetic defence speech wherein he argued above all that there was absolutely no room for anyone else in the launch, and that Bligh had most urgently requested that more men should not come aboard. Hayward's stupid assertion that Morrison could have gone with his captain in another boat was easily disposed of since it was quite obvious that Christian would not have permitted the loyalists to take the cutter too, particularly in view of the fact that the jolly was practically useless.

When cross-questioned, Fryer proved very well disposed towards Morrison, and now claimed that when Morrison advised him to return to his cabin it was because the mutineers were listening to their conversation. Cole's evidence, on the other hand, was not so favourable for Morrison. Although he had nothing but praise for his general character and behaviour during the voyage, he nevertheless confirmed Hallet's assertion that Morrison had stood in the stern of the *Bounty* and taunted the mutineers. Cole's statement was as follows:

'I did not see him under arms. I heard him say that if anyone asked for him, to let them know that he was to the southward of the line, or something to that purport.'

The court now asked Cole:

'When you heard the prisoner Morrison say that if anybody enquired for him, you should answer, he was to the southward of the line, or words to that nature, were those words spoken in a jeering manner or did he seem to be in sorrow, at being left behind in the ship?'

'They sounded to me as tho' they were spoken jeeringly,' answered Cole.

At the same time Purcell could not remember having heard anything of the sort, and had only good to say of Morrison's behaviour. This was the end of the case against Morrison, and the remainder of the accused were quickly dealt with on the same day.

At 9 a.m. on Tuesday the 18th September the accused were led into the main cabin of the *Duke* for the last time. First the president of the court asked if anyone had anything to add to his defence. Heywood was the only one to reply to this, and he produced a baptismal certificate to prove that he was under seventeen years of age when the mutiny took place. Apparently this certificate made no impression whatever upon the members of the court, since the president now called for silence and began solemnly to read the court's decision.

First came the names of those who had been found guilty, and this list was headed by Peter Heywood and James Morrison, the other four being Ellison, Burkett, Millward and Muspratt. These six men were all sentenced 'to suffer death by being hanged by the neck, on board such of His Majesty's ship or ships of war, at such time or times and at such place or places, as the commissioners for executing the office or Lord High Admiral of Great Britain and Ireland, etc. or any three of them, for the time being, should in writing, under their hands direct.' Before Heywood and Morrison had recovered from the shock of this, however, the court's president continued, 'that in consideration of various circumstances the court did humbly and most earnestly recommend the said Peter Heywood and James Morrison to His Majesty's Mercy.' Norman, Coleman, McIntosh and Byrne were declared innocent of any participation or blame, and were ordered to be released immediately.

The sentence on Heywood and Morrison came as a shock to all concerned. The reason for their having been found guilty, of course, was that they had been unable to prove that they had made any real effort to go with the other loyalists in the launch. If Heywood had built his defence more carefully upon the claim that he had been held on board the *Bounty* against his will, and had worried less about stressing his immaturity, it is not unlikely that he would have got off altogether. However, the two men at least had the comfort of knowing that there was a good chance of their being given a royal pardon.

During the case, Muspratt had asked to be allowed to call Norman and Byrne as witnesses for his defence, but this had been refused because the latter were both standing trial themselves. Immediately after the case was over, Muspratt's counsel declared that Norman and Byrne should have been tried separately, and that it would then have been possible to call them as witnesses for Muspratt. He thus claimed that the sentence on Muspratt should be quashed on the grounds of a technical legal error. This proved to be an extremely astute argument since, after the finer points had been discussed at great length by numerous legal authorities, Muspratt was given a full pardon and allowed to go free.

The five remaining men had to wait a full six weeks, either for their execution or their pardon. Heywood and Morrison, who suffered most from this delay, nevertheless devoted themselves to writing in the meantime. Heywood maintained a regular correspondence with his family, and also compiled an extensive list of Tahitian dialect words. Morrison, too, seems to have become more and more preoccupied with the past happiness of the South Seas, since he wrote both a detailed description of the voyage and also a long account of the habits and behaviour of the natives on Tupuai and Tahiti. This excellent report has fortunately been preserved, and constitutes a most valuable source today for ethnologists, historians and other researchers interested in these islands.

Towards the end of October the long awaited pardon came for Heywood and Morrison, and a few days later the remaining three sailors, Burkett, Millward and Ellison were executed on the ship-of-the-line *Brunswick*. According to a witness who was present the condemned men spent their last hours as follows:

'The evening preceding the day of execution, the prisoners, under the charge of the provost-marshall, escorted by a guard, came onboard. I expected to have seen them emaciated, wan and half expiring with the keenness of their afflictions; but, to my astonishment, they tripped up and down the ladders with the most wonderful alacrity; and their countenances instead of being (as I expected) the index of woeful depression of mind, were perfectly calm, serene and cheerful. It really gave me a shock to see them, but a few hours before their solemn exit, in the full possession and vigour of their health and spirits, as in a seeming ignorance of their approaching fate. Herein I was mistaken as it was nothing less than a calm resignation, acquired by a length of confinement, and habit of study on religious subjects for some considerable time.

The gun-room was set apart for their reception; the ports securely barred-in. Skreen upon skreen enveloped the sad apartment. Not a ray of light was permitted to obtrude. All was silent, solemn and gloomy and put on the sad aspect of misery and affliction. In one corner of this wretched asylum was a small spot, again partitioned off as a cell, to which they were consigned. In this small space they employed their night occasionally in devotion, conversation and sleep. Through a small opening to their cell, I, unperceived, observed them very minutely, heard their conversation, which was cheerful, resigned and manly. Their faces were the cheerful indexes of serene and placid minds. I never saw them shed a tear. After ten they reposed themselves in beds spread for the purpose in the cell, when the provost-marshall retired beyond the hanging skreen.

At nine o'clock the next morning the fatal gun was fired and the yellow flag displayed the dreadful summons to claim the attention of all the fleet. Boats from every ship assembled, and in a short time the ship was crowded with officers and men without with boats manned and armed. All along the shore, and even afloat in wherries were men, women and children, to the amount of thousands, as if, instead of a solemn scene of sorrow, it had been a spectacle of joy. The officers and men were arranged along the deck in columns, the yard ropes stretched along in each man's hand. At eleven o'clock the prisoners were summoned up, and marched, preceded by four clergymen and Morrison through the ranks of men along the main deck upon the forecastle, when the eternal separation took place between the one who hung on the starboard and the two who hung on the larboard fore yard arms. On the cat-head Millward addressed the ship's company, confessed the errors they had been guilty of, acknowledged the *justice* of their sentence and warned them by his fate to shun similar paths of impropriety; his speech was nervous, strong and eloquent and delivered in an open and deliberative manner. After half an hour spent in devotion. during which time Morrison performed the last offices to his departing companions, the gun was fired, and their souls took their flight in a cloud, amid the observations of thousands.'

Thus ended the final act in the tragedy of the *Bounty* mutiny, a scene of vicarious suffering shared by but three of the eighteen men who had instigated the revolt.

Meanwhile the delicate question of to what extent the captain himself was responsible for the mutiny was left untouched. So far as their lordships were concerned, he had stood his trial, a trial for the loss of his ship, and been exonerated, and thus in their eyes his responsibilities ended. It must be admitted, moreover, that from the strictly legal point of view no blame could be attached to him for the mutiny. But what of the moral aspect of the question? Perhaps it was his relentless oppression and brutal treatment of his crew which finally drove them to mutiny. This is a question that has arisen many times, and which ought to be satisfactorily answered if we are to be just to William Bligh.

Despite the unflattering things which Fryer and Purcell had had to say of Bligh during the court martial, it is safe to say that during the years directly following the mutiny it was generally felt that Bligh's misfortunes were a result purely and simply of his having under his command during the voyage a remarkable collection of scoundrels. Yet by the time he had returned from the second, and completely successful, breadfruit expedition in August 1793, he had lost a certain amount of his popular prestige, as a result of what the relations of Heywood, Morrison and Fletcher Christian had had to say of him both in writing and by word of mouth. Although Morrison's description of the voyage was never published, he nevertheless lent it to a number of important and influential people, who in their turn by degrees influenced public opinion. Bligh, however, in his delight over receiving the promised gold medal and the reward of one thousand guineas, apparently did not notice that there had been any change of feeling for him.

Even more damaging to his reputation, however, was a sort of polemical pamphlet which Fletcher Christian's brother Edward, a Cambridge professor of law, published the following year. This contained many unflattering statements on Bligh by Fryer, Purcell, Morrison, Heywood, Muspratt, Coleman, McIntosh and others. The main theme of the paper was to the effect that Bligh himself, through his ruthless and uncompromising treatment of Christian, was chiefly responsible for the mutiny. Bligh tried to defend his reputation with a hastily devised reply, but it was too late; the damage was already done. His notoriety has increased with the years, and he is generally regarded today as having been a base little tyrant and the epitome of ruthless brutality. This general attitude has been summed up by the publicity department of Metro Goldwyn Mayer shortly before the latest film on the mutiny:

'His very name struck terror in the hearts of all his crew. A sea-going disaster, begotten in a galley, and born under a gun! His hair was rope, his teeth were Marlin spikes; and the seaman who dared to disobey his mad, ruthless orders seldom lived to do it twice.'

Certainly Bligh had many serious faults, the worst of which were his violent temper and lack of psychological insight. Neither can it be denied that when he grew angry he had a peculiar gift for selecting the most cutting and humiliating terms in which to express himself. But at the same time, there is no evidence whatever to support the general conception of him as an inhuman monster. In fact he was anything but this, and might even be described by the standards of his day as a mild and good-natured captain. Consider, for example, flogging. Books and films on the subject of the *Bounty* mutiny have generally depicted William Bligh as a sadist who had members of his crew flogged for the least offence, and sometimes for no reason at all except for the pleasure it gave him personally. But the truth of the matter is that, during the course of the entire *Bounty* voyage, right up to the time of the acutal mutiny, Bligh only ordered eleven floggings with a total of two hundred and twenty-nine lashes, which is an incredibly low figure compared with that of other ships at the end of the eighteenth century. The deserters on Tahiti, for instance, could think themselves lucky that they had Bligh as their commander, because there was many a captain in the British fleet at that time who would have flogged a man to death for desertion and theft in similar circumstances. Nor can Bligh be accused of having starved his men or neglected their general wellbeing, since the evidence related in previous chapters of this book proves that he went to great trouble to feed his men properly and keep them as contented and comfortable as possible.

Perhaps the only way to obtain a satisfactory picture of the real Bligh, stripped of all the prejudiced ideas arising from subsequent misconstruction, conjecture and hearsay, is to hear what those who knew him personally had to say of him. Fortunately the archives in England contain plenty of comments on him by his contemporaries, all of which are surprisingly unanimous. A certain Lieutenant Tobin has probably left us the best concise summary of William Bligh's faults and favours. Tobin served under Bligh in the *Providence* during the second breadfruit expedition to Tahiti, and some twenty-five years later, on the occasion of Bligh's death, he wrote as follows to a brother officer:

'So poor Bligh, for with all his infirmities, you and I cannot but think of him otherwise, has followed Portlock. He has had a busy and turbulent journey of it—no one more so, and since the unfortunate mutiny in the *Bounty* has been rather in the shade. Yet perhaps he was not altogether understood—I am sure my dear friend, that in the *Providence* there was no settled system of tyranny exercised by him likely to produce dissatisfaction. It was in those violent *tornados* of temper when he lost himself. Yet when all, in his opinion, *went right* when could a man be more placid and interesting? Once or twice I felt the *unbridled licence* of his *power of speech* yet never without receiving something like an emollient plaister to heal the wound. Let our old Captain's frailties be forgotten, and view him as a man of Science and an excellent practical seaman. He had suffered much, and even in difficulty, by labour and perseverence extricated himself. But his great quality was Foresight. In this I think, Bond, you will accord with me. I have seen many men in his profession with more resources, but never one with so much precaution—I mean chiefly as a Navigator.'

CHAPTER X

THE PITCAIRN SETTLERS

AMONG the many mariners in the 1790's who were greatly interested in the *Bounty* mutiny and the ultimate destiny of Christian and his men were two American sealing skippers, Amaza Delano and Mayhew Folger. On one occasion in 1800 these two men chanced to bring their respective ships to anchor at the island of Masafuera off the coast of Chile, and in due course they made each other's acquaintance. During the evenings of their stay there they were in the habit of visiting one another and yarning at random over their adventures on the high seas.

Among the subjects which they discussed by the light of a whale-oil lamp and accompanied by the aroma of rum and cigars was the infamous *Bounty* mutiny which had taken place eleven years before. It is doubtful if, during these years, any other event was the subject of such lively discussion in cabin and forecastle across the seven seas as the mysterious and total disappearance of Fletcher Christian and his ship in September 1789. The most fantastic rumours circulated, and there even appeared a set of fictitious memoirs purporting to have been written by Christian after the mutiny, and describing among other things his adventures in South America!

The more Folger and Delano discussed the mystery and Fletcher Christian, the more sympathy and understanding they felt for him. From the very outset Delano had been convinced that the *Bounty* revolt was no ordinary mutiny, that Christian was no common or garden agitator and that very special circumstances lay behind his regrettable and desperate action.

It was some ten years after their first encounter at Masafuera that these two men met again, this time in Boston, Massachusetts. One can well imagine Delano's amazement when Folger reminded him of their past conversation, and then went on to describe how in February 1808 by pure chance he had stumbled on the solution to the fate of Christian and the *Bounty*.

It appears that in April 1807 Captain Folger had left Boston for a world voyage in his ship the *Topaz* in search of new and undiscovered sealing grounds. This voyage was to be one of the most extensive and eventful ever made by any sealing skipper. Once he was well down into the 'roaring forties' in the south Atlantic he turned east and sailed down the westerly winds. The *Topaz* successfully weathered the fearsome winter gales in those godforsaken latitudes, but the seas ran so high and the snowstorms were so blinding that even the experienced and weather-wise Folger was forced to admit that he had never in his life seen anything like it. Week after week he sailed on without any sign of land of any sort, and it was a very weary crew and battered ship which during a brief lull in the weather at last approached Kerguelen Island in the extreme south of the Indian Ocean for fresh water. But even as the *Topaz* neared the island, the weather turned again, a violent and prolonged snowstorm driven by a tremendous gale set in and Folger had no choice but to continue east. Finally, a full month later, the *Topaz* anchored in Adventure Bay, Tasmania, where the *Bounty* had likewise anchored some twenty years previously, on her way to Tahiti.

By this time, however, a little colony had been established in Tasmania—at Hobart, the present capital—where Folger paid a brief visit. As a matter of fact the governor of New South Wales was none less than Bligh himself, and the English naval vessel which escorted Folger from Adventure Bay into Hobart was the same ship which the year before had conveyed Bligh to his new post in Australia.

But the *Topaz* was soon on her way again. She rounded the southernmost point of New Zealand, and in the Chatham Islands, west of New Zealand, Folger succeeded at last in making his first catch, some six hundred seal. Encouraged by his success, he continued southwards, and after an unyielding halt in the Antipodes he again entered the extreme southern latitudes. This time it was the Pacific, but these waters proved no more profitable than the equivalent latitudes of the Atlantic and the Indian Ocean, and by January 1808, when all he had sighted was an endless procession of icebergs, Folger decided to turn north again to warmer and more inviting climes.

The *Topaz* was a long way east by this time, and when Folger consulted the various charts on board it became fairly evident that the most suitable place for watering the ship would be Carteret's Pitcairn Island. Apparently no one had actually visited Pitcairn since Carteret had charted it, but from the description it promised to be a satisfactory watering place, provided one could get ashore, and furthermore there was a good chance that there would be seal there.

Folger now took his ship well east of the given position, took up the correct latitude and proceeded to steer a westerly course. This was the normal practice when seeking an island, the given longitudinal position of which was doubtful. At half-past one on the afternoon of the 5th February they sighted an island, and as they approached it Folger studied it closely; there could be no doubt whatever that this was Carteret's Pitcairn Island. Admittedly it had turned up earlier than expected, on a one hundred and thirty degrees longitude while Carteret had put it three degrees farther west, but there could be no doubting the general appearance, and Folger was convinced that he was the first white man to have set eyes on it since the *Swallow's* visit nearly forty years before.

At dawn on the 6th February two ship's boats, with Captain Folger at the helm of one of them, pulled in towards the steep cliffs of the island to see if there were any seals about. Sweeping the island with his glasses Folger suddenly stiffened in his seat. According to Carteret the island was uninhabited and yet he could clearly see smoke. Smoke must mean people, whether they were natives or shipwrecked mariners!

Folger had scarcely recovered from his astonishment when he saw a twin-hulled canoe steering out through the breakers in their direction. The craft was manned by three youths who, as soon as they were within hailing distance, shouted to the *Topaz* men, asking them whom they were—in English!

Folger was practically speechless with incredulity, since he had taken it for granted that these youngsters were Polynesian natives, and it was some time before he was able to recover himself sufficiently to shout back that he was an American from Boston, Massachusetts.

The canoe came a little nearer now, and one of the youths said in a puzzled tone:

'You are American; you come from America; where is America? Is it in Ireland?'

Folger was too excited to indulge in a geographical discussion at this point, however, and instead began to question the youths, whereupon the following extraordinary conversation ensued:

'Who are you?'

'We are Englishmen.'

'Where were you born?'

'On that island which you see.'

'How then are you Englishmen, if you were born on that island, which the English do not own, and never possessed?'

'We are English because our father was an Englishman.'

'Who is your father?'

'Alec.'

'Who is Alec?'

'Don't you know Alec?'

'How should I know Alec?'

'Well then, did you know Captain Bligh of the *Bounty*?'

This last remark must have come as a tremendous surprise to Folger, the truth struck him in a flash and he became speechless with excitement. He later told Delano that when the strange youngster in the canoe mentioned Bligh and the *Bounty* 'the whole story immediately burst upon my mind, and produced a shock of mingled feelings, surprise, wonder, and pleasure, not to be described.'

The youths now proceeded to reply to Folger's eager questions as best they could. They explained that 'Alec' was the only remaining member of the mutineers, all the others being dead. By this time Folger was desperately anxious to get ashore and learn the full details of the story, but on the other hand he was by no means sure that the mysterious Alec would appreciate his presence. Folger knew perfectly well that by the laws of his native country Alec was liable to death by hanging, and in view of this it was fairly certain that he would be on his guard against visiting strangers. Meanwhile the youngsters in the canoe were waiting to return to the settlement to spread the news of the visitors.

Folger himself, first as an American and secondly as a definite supporter of Fletcher Christian, had no desire at all to become involved with the legal aspects of the *Bounty* mutiny, and decided to make it perfectly clear to Alec that his motives were essentially neutral and friendly. He therefore asked the youths to convey his compliments to Alec and to inform him that the captain of the *Topaz* would be happy to make his acquaintance, and to supply him with any such necessities as he might have with him. The canoe rapidly disappeared, and when it finally returned Alec was not on board, but the youngsters extended his greetings to Captain Folger, saying that he was unfortunately prevented from accompanying them but that Folger was heartily welcome ashore.

Folger, however, was equally wary and cautious, and once again he sent the youths back with further assurances of his friendly intentions.

It is difficult to say which of the two men were most apprehensive; Alec of being seized by the unknown ship's captain and taken into custody, Folger of being made captive ashore, in case he should return to civilization and reveal the whereabouts of the fugitive mutineer and his colony.

Thus when the canoe returned for the third time Alec was still not in it, and this time Folger was frankly informed that the womenfolk ashore were so concerned for the safety of their leader that they would under no circumstances permit him to put out in the canoe. At the same time, the somewhat weary youngsters insisted that Folger was most welcome ashore, that no harm would befall him and that the islanders would do everything in their power to make him and his men comfortable.

Since not a single man aboard the *Topaz* had set foot on dry land for several months Folger decided to take the settlers at their word and accept the offer. In this way the hiding place of the *Bounty* mutineers was thus finally discovered a full eighteen years after the *Bounty* had been burned in the harbour below. On their arrival ashore, the crew of the *Topaz* were given a warm welcome by Alec and a crowd of women and children, and it now emerged that Alec himself was none other than Able Seaman Alexander Smith, now in his mid-forties and the leader of the colony. The population of Pitcairn consisted of thirty-five people at this time, of whom only Smith and eight Polynesian women remained from the older generation. The remaining twenty-six were all children or youths, the oldest being between eighteen and nineteen. One of the latter was a full-blooded Tahitian who had been a newly-born infant when the *Bounty* left Tahiti for the last time.

But what had happened to all the others who had originally landed on Pitcairn in January 1790? There had, after all, been nine mutineers, twelve Tahitian women and six male natives from Tahiti, Raiatea and Tupuai. Of this total of twenty-seven only nine were now alive, Smith and eight women!

Folger remained only some five or six hours on the island, and during this time he did his utmost to pump Smith as much as possible concerning the mutiny itself and the subsequent death of the mutineers on Pitcairn. But Smith was equally curious to know what had been going on in the outside world during the period of his exile since December 1787 when the *Bounty* had left England. Naturally enough Smith's first questions concerned Bligh and the occupants of the ship's launch, and consequently Folger had to go through the entire story of their miraculous voyage, of the fate of the *Pandora* and the outcome of the court martial. But during the past twenty years there had occurred many greater and more sensational events than the *Bounty* affair, and Alexander Smith must have listened spellbound to Folger's accounts of the French Revolution and the exploits of Napoleon and Nelson. It is difficult to say which of the two men had most questions to ask and most to tell, but one thing is evident, however, and that is that Folger did not manage to extract from Smith any of the facts concerning the deaths of the colony's first generation.

Folger and his men left Pitcairn again at about four in the afternoon, overwhelmed with kindness and generosity and loaded down with suckling pigs, coconuts and fruits, and also *Bounty's* old compass and her valuable Kendall chronometer (now in the Royal United Services Institution museum, Whitehall). In his turn Folger allowed the Pitcairners to help themselves to anything and everything they might want from the *Topaz*, particularly clothing. Folger was apparently greatly moved and impressed by the little colony. The moral and religious code of the settlers was in keeping with the strictest of nineteenth-century European codes and there was a delightful innocence and naive freshness about the youngsters. Concerning Smith, Folger wrote in his log: 'Whatever may have been the errors or the crimes of Smith the mutineer in times back, he is at present in my opinion a worthy man and may be useful to navigators who traverse this immense ocean.'

There is not much to tell concerning the remainder of Folger's voyage. The fine chronometer was taken from him by the Spanish governor at Juan Fernandez some weeks later. In Valparaiso Folger met an English naval officer and, rather imprudently one feels, told him about the Pitcairn colony. The latter immediately despatched a report to the English admiral in Rio de Janeiro, which was duly forwarded to the Admiralty where it was received on the 14th May 1809. But at this time England was deeply engaged in the war against France, and their lordships had other things to think about than a minute settlement in an exotic island on the other side of the world. The report was mentioned briefly in one or two newspapers, and then the whole affair seems once again to have been forgotten and the colony, the oldest in the South Seas with the exception of the penal colony on Norfolk Island, continued to flourish undisturbed.

It was not until 1814 that Pitcairn was rediscovered, again by pure chance, and this time by two English naval captains, Staines and Pipon of H.M.S. *Briton* and *Tagus* respectively. Fortunately these two senior officers were just as impressed by the idyllic little community as Folger had been, and consequently Alexander Smith (who now called himself John Adams) was permitted to retain his patriarchal position as head of the colony instead of being seized and taken home to England to stand trial.

Staines and Pipon also questioned Smith concerning the fate of the remainder of the first generation of settlers, and their descriptions subsequently appeared in various newspapers and magazines. Once the news spread, Pitcairn received more and more visitors, chiefly whaling ships, and in 1825 another English naval vessel, this time commanded by a Captain

Beechey, visited the island for the purpose of mapping it and making a detailed investigation of the colony and its conditions. Thus at last the real facts began to emerge, the pieces of the puzzle fell into place, and the true story of the terrible course of events which had taken place in the 1790's on Pitcairn became known. The final picture is built up upon the reports of the three naval captains, information provided by the Tahitian girl known as Jenny, and the accounts of the various members of the community who had been born during those early, terrible years and who had afterwards heard their parents talk of what happened.

To return to 1790 when the twenty-seven colonists landed on Pitcairn, the women were divided up among the men as follows:

Fletcher Christian	Mauatua (Isabella or Mainmast)
Edward Young	Teraura (Susannah)
John Mills	Vahineatua
William Brown	Teatuahitea
Isaac Martin	Teahuteatuaonoa (Jenny)
William Mickey	Teio (Mary)
Matthew Quintal	Tevarua (Sarah)
Alexander Smith	Puarai
John Williams	Pashotu (Fasto)
Tararo (from Raiatea)	Toofaiti (Nancy: from Huahine)

Manarii (from Tahiti) ⎫
Teimua (from Tahiti) ⎬ Mareva
Niau (from Tahiti) ⎭

Oha (from Tupuai) ⎫
Titahiti (from Tupuai) ⎬ Tinafanaea

The twenty-eighth member of the party was the little Tahitian girl whom Mickey's woman, Teio, had with her when they left Matavai. She was christened Sarah and later married Christian's second son Charles Christian. Sarah died in 1826.

As can be seen from the list, the natives did not have many women between them, and those that were available were divided up according to the island groups. Tararo, who was considered to be of exalted blood because he came from Raiatea, had a woman to himself, at least to begin with. The three Tahitians shared the unfortunate Mareva, while the two from Tupuai made do with Tinafanaea between them. One of these two latter women was called Prudence by the mutineers, though which one this was is not known. Finally it may be mentioned that the name Titahiti had nothing whatever to do with the island, but meant, curiously enough, 'the transplanted ti-plant'.

Once the group had landed and the ship had been burnt they set about clearing land and building places in which to live. Christian carefully ensured that none of the buildings were visible from the sea, and he selected a suitable site for the colony on the north side of the central plateau. The question next arose about which parts of the island should be cultivated, and in due course the available land was divided up into nine lots. Nine, needless to say, was the number of the mutineers, which implied that the Polynesians were without land in the new settlement. But this was more or less understood, since the natives, both male and female, had been brought along for the specific purpose of serving the white men—in their respective capacities.

Exactly what Fletcher Christian's attitude to the land allotment was is difficult to say; possibly he felt, as the others, that this was the right and proper way of doing it, or possibly in depriving the natives of all rights he was simply giving way to the will of the majority among his companions. Whatever his attitude may have been, however, he went ahead with his plans enthusiastically and optimistically, determined to make the most of the situation and to create a flourishing and successful community. At least he had no difficulty in retaining the respect of his companions, since they continued to address him dutifully as Mr Christian, just as they continued to call Young, Mr Young.

But no matter how optimistic he might have been, from the very beginning there existed two undeniable and practically unsurmountable problems in the colony: the reconciliation of two separate races with two distinctly different codes of living, and the pronounced shortage of women. The latter problem was delicate enough at the outset and was bound to become even more critical once any of the precious women died.

And sure enough this is exactly what happened. Before the year was out two of the Tahitian women had died, Williams' woman, Pashotu, from a disease of the throat and Smith's woman, Puarai, who fell from the steep cliffs into the sea while gathering eggs. Needless to say none of the other men was prepared to hand over his woman to the two bereaved mutineers, or even to share his woman with them. It was therefore inevitable that after a time these two should begin to cast hungry glances in the direction of the natives' women-folk, and in due course Tararo was forced to surrender his Nancy to Williams while Smith relieved the two Tupuai islanders of Tinafanaea.

One evening Mauatua and Teatuahitea heard Nancy mono-tonously singing an odd couplet, the words of which were more or less as follows:

> Why does black man sharpen axe?
> To kill white man.

The two women immediately grasped the significance of this macabre chant, and hurried off to inform Christian that the Polynesians were apparently planning to kill the white men. It subsequently emerged that Tararo, Oha and Titahiti had grown tired of living alone and were planning to get their women back again. Tararo was the leader of the conspiracy.

Christian now set off resolutely for the house where these three men lived. His intention was to reveal to them that he knew all about the conspiracy and that he did not intend to put up with any nonsense from them. This, he felt, would be sufficient to make them give up all such plans. To be on the safe side, however, he decided to take a musket with him, being none too sure of how desperate the three men might get when they saw him coming.

But their immediate reaction was apparently fear, since no sooner did they catch sight of the determined looking Christian and his musket than they fled to the mountains and hid.

Nothing happened for a few days now, and then suddenly Nancy left Williams and went to the mountains to return to Tararo. Williams immediately made it known that unless he got his woman back he would leave the island, and the remainder of the mutineers, anxious not to lose the services of their excellent smithy, agreed to help him.

First they sent Manarii to spy out the land. He returned shortly and reported that Tararo, Nancy and Titahiti were on the west side of the island beyond the great hog's back which divided Pitcairn in a north-south direction. Having established the whereabouts of the deserters the mutineers, like the natives had done a few days earlier, drew up a murder plot.

The plot itself was naive enough. Three puddings were made, one of which was poisoned. Manarii was then sent off with the puddings as a sort of peace offering and it was up to him to ensure that Tararo was given the poisoned pudding. But when the puddings were handed over Tararo suddenly became suspicious, refused his own pudding and helped himself to half of Nancy's instead.

But Manarii's orders were not to return to the village until Tararo was dead, and he now evolved a new plan. He mentioned that his wife was in the vicinity and wondered if the three fugitives would care to come and visit her. They agreed to this and the four of them set off along a narrow path with Manarii bringing up the rear behind Tararo. At a suitable moment he drew his pistol, aimed it at Tararo's back and pulled the trigger; the pistol, however, did not go off. but Tararo heard the click of the hammer, realized what was going on and promptly fled into the woods. Manarii set off after him and in a few moments had overtaken him and thrown him to the ground. Titahiti seems to have made no effort whatsoever to intervene. A desperate fight now ensued between the two natives, and as soon as Tararo could get his breath he called to Nancy to help him. Nancy entered the fray without a moment's hesitation, but for some inexplicable reason it was Manarii and not Tararo she helped, and a few moments later Tararo was dead, slain by the joint efforts of Manarii and Nancy.

Manarii, Nancy and the terrified Titahiti now returned to the village where Titahiti was at once put in irons and locked up. Meanwhile the third deserter, Oha the other Tupuaian, was still at large. Manarii said that he believed Oha to be on the south side of the island, and shortly afterwards he left in company with Teimua, on the orders of the mutineers, to kill Oha. This mission was equally successful. They located Oha, assured him of their good intentions, and subsequently commenced the Polynesian ritual of combing his hair as a sign that they shared his sorrow and bitterness. In the middle of this excess of hypocritical weeping and wailing on his behalf they cut his throat!

After these bloody proceedings some measure of peace returned to the island. Nancy went back to Williams, Tinafanaea lived with Smith, and the lonely Titahiti was in due course released from prison and worked as a slave for Martin and Jenny. Already now there was probably a certain circulation of the womenfolk among the men, since it seems that Tinafanaea occasionally lived with Titahiti and Martin while Jenny sometimes moved over to Smith, with whom she had lived both in Tahiti and Tupuai.

Several children had been born by this time. Christian had two sons, Quintal and Mickey had a son each and Mills had a daughter. None of the Polynesians had fathered any children, however. There were four of them left now, the three Tahitians Manarii, Teimua and Niau and the Tupuaian, Titahiti. The existence of these four natives was becoming increasingly miserable, since their white masters drove them cruelly and relentlessly and ill-treated them brutally whenever they failed to do what was required of them. Added to all this was the tension between the natives and the white men over the latter's women, and thus it was inevitable that sooner or later violence would break out again.

In September 1793 Teimua and Niau deserted their masters and retreated to the mountains, taking with them two muskets and a supply of ammunition. At the same time they kept in contact with Manarii and Titahiti and also with Young, who seems to have been in league with them, possibly on account of his designs on Williams' girl, Nancy.

And then came the most terrible day in the history of the Pitcairn colony. The nine mutineers were spread out across the island working on their plantations when Titahiti, on the pretence of going pig shooting, borrowed a musket and promptly set off to join Teimua and Niau. Manarii, the fourth member of the native quartet, remained behind to lead the white men into the trap should this prove necessary.

The first to fall to the native assassins was Williams; he was shot in his kitchen garden by the trio Titahiti, Teimua and Niau, who afterwards made for Mills' and Mickey's plantation where Manarii also worked. Mills and Mickey had both heard the shots which had killed Williams, so in order to allay their suspicions Titahiti went out to where they were working and asked them if Manarii could help him carry a pig which he had shot. The two mutineers agreed to this. and once in among the trees the four Polynesians joined forces and set off for Christian's plantation which was nearby.

They shot Fletcher Christian without any discussion, and as he fell dying to the ground he is reputed to have cried 'Oh dear'. Mills and Mickey apparently heard this desperate exclamation, whereupon Mickey said in horror 'That was surely some person dying!' to which Mills replied impatiently, 'Nonsense, it was only Christian's wife calling him to dinner.'

The next step was to separate Mills and Mickey from each other. Teimua and Niau entered Mickey's house, and Titahiti then rushed out and informed him excitedly that the two fugitives had come down from the mountains and were at that very moment stealing various valuable objects from his home. Mickey immediately dropped what he was doing and hurried off towards his home, determined to give the 'niggers' a lesson they would never forget. He charged into the house and the two natives fired at pointblank range, and both missed! Mickey backed out before they had time to reload, but was now attacked from behind by Manarii who was lurking outside. Mickey was a powerful man, however, and succeeded in throwing Manarii into the pigsty before sprinting back to the plantation to warn Mills. Curiously enough, Mills refused to believe that his faithful slave Manarii would do him any harm, and he made no effort to leave the plantation. Mickey for his part had already seen too much to stop and argue, and he ran on again to warn Christian. Just as he came across Christian's dead body lying in the field he heard more musket shots and realized that Mills had been murdered too.

Every minute counted now, and Mickey dashed first up to Christian's house to inform the horrified Mauatua that her man was dead before carrying on to warn Quintal. Quintal in his turn ordered Tevarua to go round and warn the other mutineers, and then fled with Mickey to the mountains.

When Mauatua rushed past Smith's plantation she saw him quietly at work there and screamed at him, 'How can you go on working at such a terrible time as this?' Smith immediately grasped that something serious was amiss and hurried after the panic-stricken native woman.

While this was going on, the four Polynesians were pursuing their bloody plan. Having disposed of Mills they carried on to Martin's house and found him working peacefully in the garden. 'Do you know what we have done this day?' they asked him with a certain savage elation. 'No,' replied the slightly puzzled American, 'What have you done this day?' whereupon they stuck their muskets into his stomach and said, 'We have been doing the same as shooting hogs.'

Martin laughed uneasily but the laugh was transformed into a horrible gurgle as the musket balls tore into his stomach. Terribly injured, yet still alive Martin dragged himself into his cottage, but the bloodthirsty natives followed him inside and finished off their ghastly work by beating his brains out.

A few minutes later Brown met the same fate. Here it must be admitted one of the natives actually tried to save his life by loading his musket without balls, but Brown did not play dead for long enough and one of the others turned and shot him again.

After having remained hidden for several hours Smith emerged again to gather a few yams from his plantation. But the natives spotted him at once and let fly with their muskets. One of the balls hit him in the right shoulder and passed out through his throat. He fell and in an instant his assassins were upon him, beating at him with their gun butts and making further frenzied attempts to reload and shoot him. But by some miracle Smith managed to survive this savage treatment, and just at the crucial moment one of the natives remembered that Young, who seems to have been the brain behind the entire plot, had ordered them not to take Smith's life if they could possibly avoid it. Therefore, after a brief conference, they conveyed the badly injured mutineer to Young's house where the native women took charge of him and bathed and bound his wounds. Young was in the best of health and had nothing to fear from the natives, but Quintal and Mickey were still up in the mountains, and their ex-slaves were determined to finish off their two worst taskmasters at the earliest possible moment.

After this massacre there was no longer any question of a

shortage of women on the island, and yet the men who were left still continued to fight over them like dogs over bitches, and consequently a few weeks later there was another act of violence. Teraura was sitting one evening singing to the accompaniment of Teimua's flute. Teraura was really Young's girl, but just now Young was chiefly interested in Mauatua and Nancy, while Manarii and Teimua were rivals for the favours of Teraura. Manarii now decided to put a stop to the flirtation between Teimua and Teraura by firing four shots at his rival, whom he succeeded in wounding but not killing. Teimua shouted to Teraura to fetch his musket and shoot Manarii, but while she was away Manarii reloaded and finished Teimua off. When Titahiti and Niau heard of this murder they both swore to get Manarii and the latter had no choice but to flee to the mountains. Up there he managed to contact Quintal, Mickey and Tevarua and immediately offered to join forces with them, but the two white men, naturally enough, were not inclined to trust him and insisted that he first hand over his musket.

During the following weeks a series of complicated intrigues developed between the quartet in the mountains and the settlers down in the village. Everyone was apparently prepared to betray everyone else, and each individual was regarded by the next as a potential traitor. The quartet, incidentally, was soon reduced to a trio again, since one day, after some deliberation, the two mutineers decided to rid themselves of their Polynesian accomplice, and shot him in the back with the same musket that he had so trustingly handed to them on his arrival.

Down in the village, however, the inmates continued to murder each other to their heart's content. The widows of the dead mutineers resolved to take their revenge on their husband's assassins, and Young and Teraura agreed to help them in this. According to the plan, Titahiti was to have his head lopped off while he lay sleeping alongside one of his girls (the girl in question, who was part of the conspiracy, was carefully instructed that on the night she was to make sure that the Tupuaian's head was not resting on her arm when he fell asleep). On the same night as the decapitation of Titahiti Young was to shoot Niau. It is unnecessary here to go into the horrible details of the night in question; all we need to know is that the bloody plot went according to plan, and that when the next day dawned there was an even greater sufficiency of females in the colony than there had been previously.

There were now four mutineers left: Young, Smith, Quintal and Mickey. All the male Polynesians were dead, but there remained ten females and a number of children.

Quintal and Mickey refused to come down from the mountains until Smith produced the severed hands of Titahiti and Niau as evidence of their death. The hands were conveyed to them on the 3rd October 1793.

The four surviving white men now proceeded to live in unrestrained promiscuity with their miniature harem of Polynesian females and were apparently thoroughly satisfied with life, but not so the women. They were so dissatisfied with their lot, and particularly with the bestial behaviour of Quintal and Mickey, that they tried on one occasion to flee the island en masse with their children. This attempt seems to have been foiled by the men, but the women then began to plan among themselves to murder their white oppressors; they had, after all, muskets and ammunition and a numerical superiority of two and a half to one.

On the 27th December a ship was seen approaching the island, and the entire colony promptly forgot their differences and went into hiding. Fortunately, however, there was such a heavy sea running that a landing was out of the question and in due course the unknown vessel disappeared over the horizon again.

Gradually now the general state of affairs in the colony began to improve. The men, apprehensive of the schemes of their womenfolk, decided it would be easier and safer to compromise, and consequently their behaviour became more reasonable. The routine of the settlement became ordered and neighbourly, and a spirit of contented harmony seems to have prevailed.

But then a new catastrophe occurred. Mickey, who had once worked in a whisky distillery in Scotland, discovered that alcohol could be extracted from the local Ti-root. With the aid of a piece of copper tubing and a boiling pan he contrived to fix up a fairly satisfactory still, whereupon production—and consumption—began.

The first Ti spirit was produced on the 20th April 1798,

many years after the last of the *Bounty's* stocks of wine and rum had been finished, and the subsequent course of events makes a grim and deplorable story. Within a year Mickey, the distiller, was dead. In a fit of delirium he had tied a heavy stone around his neck and thrown himself from a cliff into the sea.

Quintal, a violent, vicious man at the best of times, continued to brew and drink heavily, and the more he drank the more brutal he became. By this time he was the scourge of the entire colony, and his bestial treatment of the unfortunate Tevarua was unprecedented. On one occasion he is reputed to have bitten off one of her ears because she was unable to produce sufficient fish for his evening meal. Altogether then, it is not surprising that scarcely a year after the advent of the still, the weary and miserable woman fell, or threw herself, from the cliffs while out gathering birds' eggs with the other womenfolk.

This, of course, meant that Quintal was without a woman, since his other concubine Teahuteatuaonoa, Jenny for short, had left him shortly after he had taken her over following the death of Martin. He now began to pursue the other women in the colony, and the upshot of the whole affair was that Young and Smith, disgusted by this Caliban who had once been their shipmate, and frightened for the safety of their womenfolk and children, and probably themselves too, decided there was nothing for it but to get rid of Quintal.

One day, not long after the death of Tevarua, Quintal was inveigled into participating in a sort of drunken revel in Smith's house. In the course of the evening he went berserk, and Smith seized his opportunity, approached the raving drunkard from behind and split his skull in two with an axe. Mills' little daughter, Elizabeth, was present during this terrible slaughter and for the rest of her life (she lived to be ninety-three) she never forgot the horror of this bloody scene.

To all intents and purposes this was the end of the long period of bloodshed and violence on Pitcairn Island. Young and Smith, the last male survivors, were at last shaken into a sense of reality and responsibility, moral and Christian order was restored, the distilling of spirits was forbidden, a proper basic schooling system for the twenty children was introduced under the tutorship of ex-midshipman Young (Smith was

226

apparently completely illiterate), and regular morning and evening prayers were held. Finally the shattered and feud-worn little settlement, after more than ten years, was moving in the direction of the contented and idyllic society which Fletcher Christian had dreamed of from the beginning.

In 1800 Young died of a chronic disease of the lungs (the only man on the island who had died a natural death), and Smith was left alone with his huge family of women and children. But he now proved to be a man of character and resource, and he continued to lead the little community with prudence and benevolent consideration. As time passed, he became increasingly religious and, thanks to Young's past instruction in the art of reading, he devoted more and more time to studying the *Bounty's* old ship's bible; a book which is still one of the community's most valued possessions.

Smith died in 1829, and the last of the original Tahitians in 1850. Today Pitcairn is still inhabited by descendants of the *Bounty* mutineers, some of whom, incidentally, moved over and settled Norfolk Island between Australia and New Zealand in 1836. None of the original Polynesian males left any children behind them, and neither did Williams, Brown or Martin. But the surnames Christian, Young, Mills, McKay (Mickey), Quintal and Adams (Smith) are still in circulation on both Pitcairn and Norfolk Island, and these people, two or three hundred of them of mixed Tahitian-English blood, are very proud of their descent. Pitcairn's chief source of income today is the wide selection of extremely beautiful stamps issued there. Meanwhile the tiny colony continues to thrive, after what is surely one of the most violent, original and colourful histories in the world.

EPILOGUE

FINALLY, what happened to the remaining *Bounty* men?

Bligh's entire career, as might be expected, continued to be stormy and eventful. In 1797 he took part in the Battle of Camperdown, and was personally responsible for the destruction of the Dutch flagship. Four years later in 1801 he commanded a ship-of-the-line under Nelson in the Copenhagen action, and conducted himself so well that Nelson later thanked him publicly for his contribution. In 1804 Bligh faced a court martial on a charge of 'tyranny, unofficer-like conduct and ungentlemanly behaviour.' The case as a whole must have been one of the most comical in naval legal history, and the protocol from the witnesses' testimonies is splendid evidence of the scope and bizarre ingenuity of Captain Bligh's vocabulary when provoked. The pattern of behaviour as reported by the witnesses is familiar from the *Bounty* days, but the inventiveness of the choleric commander seems to have ripened with age so that in the evidence of the court martial in question we encounter, besides such terms as scoundrels, rascals and villains, expressions like 'a damn'd long pelt of a bitch' and numerous other phrases as colourful as they are unprintable.

The members of the court martial, who had probably never taken part in such entertaining proceedings, finally found Bligh guilty to a certain extent of the charges, 'judged him to be reprimanded' and exhorted him in future to be a little more considerate when addressing or rebuking his subordinates.

In 1806 he was appointed governor of New South Wales, and in due course he was faced with a new mutiny there. On the 26th January 1808 (only a few days before Folger discovered the mutineers' settlement on Pitcairn), he was seized by a hostile group in the colony and kept prisoner in the governor's residence for more than two years. This was the end of Bligh's active career. Unfortunately there is no record of what he said when he heard the news of the Pitcairn colony, though it is doubtful if his comments on the subject could be included here anyway. He returned to England in 1810, and was subsequently promoted vice-admiral and made a Fellow of the Royal Academy, the president of which, until his death in 1820, was Bligh's old patron Sir Joseph Banks. Bligh died in London in 1817.

Fryer and Tinkler also took part in the Copenhagen action, though not on the same ship as their previous commander. Fryer's conduct was exemplary throughout the rest of his naval career, and he too died in 1817.

Despite all his setbacks, Peter Heywood also successfully continued his career as a naval officer, and when he died in 1831 he held the rank of post-captain. Heywood claimed to have seen Fletcher Christian in Portsmouth in 1808, and there were also rumours in circulation that Christian had returned in secret to his childhood home district in Cumberland. Generally speaking, there has been a great deal of speculation as to whether or not Christian succeeded in getting home again in later years, but on the other hand there is not a shred of evidence in support of his return, and we are thus forced to conclude that he did in fact die in the manner reported in the previous chapter.

James Morrison, who acquired a certain degree of fame for his descriptions of Tahiti, served as a gunner on various English naval vessels, and died in a shipwreck off Madagascar in 1807. The last survivor from the *Bounty* seems to have been ship's carpenter Purcell, who died in England in 1834—in an asylum.

One of the principal themes of this book from the very beginning has been the breadfruit, and it is therefore only right and proper that we should conclude by mentioning what happened to the thousand odd shoots which Bligh brought back successfully from the second expedition. These shoots were transplanted on various islands in the West Indies where they thrived and were extremely fruitful. But this was as far as the ambitious plans of the planters got, since, ironically enough, the Negro slaves did not like their new, economical diet, and refused absolutely to eat breadfruit. In other words

Bounty's ill-fated voyage to the South Seas had been pointless from the outset.

THE END

GEORGE ALLEN & UNWIN LTD
London: 40 Museum Street, W.C.1

Bombay: 15 Graham Road, Ballard Estate, Bombay 1
Buenos Aires: Escritorio 454-459, Florida 165
Calcutta: 17 Chittaranjan Avenue, Calcutta 13
Cape Town: 109 Long Street
Hong Kong: F1/12 Mirador Mansions, Kowloon
Ibadan: P.O. Box 62
Karachi: Karachi Chambers, McLeod Road
Madras: Mohan Mansions, 38c Mount Road, Madras 6
Mexico: Villalongin 32-10, Piso, Mexico 5, D.F.
Nairobi: P.O. Box 12446
New Delhi: 13-14 Asaf Ali Road, New Delhi 1
São Paulo: Avenida 9 De Julho 1138-Ap. 51
Singapore: 36c Prinsep Street, Singapore 7
Sydney, N.S.W.: Bradbury House, 55 York Street
Toronto: 91 Wellington Street West

THOR HEYERDAHL

AKU-AKU

'. . . . this is a most remarkable book. . . .Few will be able to read without mounting excitement Mr Heyerdahl's story of the discoveries he made above and below the ground of Easter Island. . . .and even those who may find parts of the prose narrative abstruse and over technical must be enchanted by the forty pages of superb colour photographs. . . .Seldom can so sumptuous a book have been published at so reasonable a price. . . . there has been nothing to equal this book since the voyage of the Kon-Tiki was described.'   GEOFFREY GORER in *The Observer*

'. . . .Aku Aku is as exciting a book as Kon Tiki. . . .He is an adventurer, an archaeological buccaneer; but it emerges from every page of his books that he is also a restless inquirer, a great leader and an immensely likeable man.'

NIGEL NICHOLSON in *The New Statesman*

'. . . .he has, once more, written a book which lays on its readers a magic spell of excitement and charm.'

Evening Standard (London)
Demy 8vo.   Illustrated.   21s. net.

ARCHAEOLOGY OF EASTER ISLAND
With EDWIN N. FERDON JR.

In his world best-seller, *Aku-Aku*, Thor Heyerdahl gave us a popular account of his adventurous expedition to Easter Island to solve the mystery of the giant statues that stand or lie all over the hills and plains of that tiny speck of land in the midst of the Pacific Ocean. In the interval since then he and his colleagues have sorted and sifted all the scientific information gathered during many months on the island and here present the first volume of the official report, entitled the *Archaeology of Easter Island*. It is a monument of scientific industry, filled with facts and figures, illustrations and maps, and although primarily addressed to professional archaeologists, no one with the least interest in this enigmatic island can afford to miss it. This was the first systematic expedition and its discoveries are as fascinating as they are numerous.

11½" x 9¼".   *Illustrated.   £11 11s. net.*

GEORGE ALLEN & UNWIN LTD